ADEQUACY, ACCOUNTABILITY, AND THE FUTURE OF PUBLIC EDUCATION FUNDING

ADEQUACY, ACCOUNTABILITY, AND THE FUTURE OF PUBLIC EDUCATION FUNDING

By

DENNIS PATRICK LEYDEN
The University of North Carolina at Greensboro

 Springer

Library of Congress Cataloging-in-Publication Data

A C.I.P. Catalogue record for this book is available
from the Library of Congress.

ISBN 0-387-23360-1   e-ISBN 0-387-23361-X   Printed on acid-free paper.

Cover designed by Marc Palmer, Sigil Design.

Printed in the United States of America.

9 8 7 6 5 4 3 2 1   SPIN 11052715

springeronline.com

Dedication

*To the memory of my beloved father –
Dennis Roger Leyden (1933-2000)*

Contents

Preface

    This book is about public education reform and the future of public education funding. Given the many articles, books, and conferences that have focused on the issue of public education reform, it is reasonable to ask whether the world needs still another volume on this subject. In my defense, I would argue that, although there is a large literature on public education reform, there is precious little that tries to sketch the big picture. Too often, both in research and in practice, it is easy to lose sight of the forest, for all the focus on the individual trees. While such detailed analysis is of critical value, that value derives both from its specificity and from its ability to fit into a larger, coherent whole. Unfortunately, our understanding of the public education process is still incomplete and disconnected, particularly with regard to the connections between research, policy, and practice. This book is an attempt to step back for a moment to get one's bearings before jumping headlong back into the forest.

    It is my hope that this book will be of value to a wide variety of readers – researchers in departments of economics and schools of education, policy makers at all levels, and, of course, the practitioners slogging away in the trenches. Unfortunately, the various readers often speak quite different languages, and, as a graduate student friend of mine once observed many years ago, a proof is in the eye of the beholder. As a result, I have attempted to use a variety of approaches so that I might have the chance of reaching this wide range of readers. For those readers who prefer a more verbal and historical approach, I encourage them not to avoid *Chapters 2, 3,* and *4* because of the mathematics. While the mathematics may be a bit thick at times, I have tried to provide diagrams and additional verbal arguments to help make sense of the underlying arguments. And certainly, the introductions and conclusions to those chapters provide verbal distillations of that material which provide the foundation for the verbal and historical analysis found in *Chapters 6* and *7*. Likewise, for those readers who delight in more formal, mathematical approaches, I encourage them to not stop after *Chapter 4*. The issue of public education reform and its connection to public education funding is a complicated one and there are limits to the ability to reduce it to (relatively simple) mathematical and econometric analysis. *Chapters 6* and *7* contain the core of the points I wish to make, and much would be lost if they were ignored.

Finally, I should note that while this book is about the future, the reader will quickly discover that much of this book focuses on the past. As George Santayana observed in his book *Reason in Common Sense*, progress is not simply change, but rather change based on memory and reflection. Public education reform has a long history, much of it seemingly forgotten, and as a result many ideas currently being paraded as new are, in fact, rather old. It is my hope that by better understanding the history of public education reform, we can avoid repeating previous failures. By better knowing the past, we can better chart a better future.

Chapter 1

INTRODUCTION

When we take account of social and cultural objectives, the question of finance looms even larger: it is precisely in the area of finance that so many of the nobler aims of educators are defeated.
— Mark Blaug, *An Introduction to the Economics of Education*[1]

This book is about recent efforts to reform public education[2] and the likely effects of such efforts on the future of public education funding. Despite its size, public education funding is traditionally seen by those interested in public education reform as a necessary, but subsidiary, issue that is addressed only after more substantive issues associated directly with educating students are addressed.[3] Over the past few decades, however, efforts to remedy inequities and improve quality in public education have been stymied – sometimes by the courts, sometimes by state legislatures. Such frustrations, in conjunction with the rise of interest in public education reform among those interested in more efficient government and those concerned with the nation's international competitiveness, have given rise to an increasing recognition by individuals in both the private and public sector that proposals for public education reform can only work if they are adopted and if sufficient resources are provided to assure their success. In short, effective public education reform must be both economically and politically feasible.

That these issues of public education reform and public education funding should be so closely connected should not be surprising. As

---

[1] Blaug (1972; p. 286).

[2] By "public education" I mean public elementary and secondary education, most commonly grades K-12. While public higher (or tertiary) education is an important issue as well, it is a separate issue and is not treated here.

[3] Such a view, perhaps inadvertently, is often reinforced by the structure of economics of education textbooks, which typically places the topic of public education funding toward the back of the book after such more interesting topics as human capital, enrollment choice, and the education production function are dealt with. Only then, it is argued, can public education funding be treated in an effective way. See, for examples, Blaug (1972), Sheehan (1973), Cohn (1979), and Belfield (2000).

Frederick Wirt and Michael Kirst note in their text on the role of politics in public education (Wirt and Kirst (1997; page 272)):

> School finances engage three of the four major education values – equity, quality, and efficiency. And if public school critics got their way with school vouchers, there would also be a choice value. Finance is also the issue that most engages legislators every year because it is the largest single expenditure in the state budget. The finance issue is always current, controversial, and relevant to almost everything that schools do.

Public education reform is thus a complex process in which pedagogical issues and funding issues both play an integral part. In broad terms, the direction of reform seems clear enough, for there is now a general consensus among public education advocates that all children should be given an adequate education, and that public schools should be held accountable for their performance. However, as the National Research Council's Committee on Education Finance notes in its recent study (Ladd and Hansen (1999)), there is no consensus on how this adequacy should be defined or measured, and if the notion of adequacy is unclear, then even more so is the issue of accountability. Moreover, while the Committee suggests a number of reforms, it notes that there is a decided lack of knowledge about what works and what does not work, and hence a need for further research. What is clear, however, is that whatever reforms are found to be productive and are put into place, the result will be an increased need for resources. Moreover, given the highly decentralized nature of the US education system, the pressure to provide those resources will lie primarily with state governments which have provided the lion's share of resources in the past and can be expected to continue to provide most of the resources in the future.

Whether states will provide the necessary support for the public schools to achieve the goals of adequacy and accountability is an open question. The purpose of this book is to provide a model for understanding the process by which states fund public education and to use that model to assess the political and economic implications of adopting adequacy and accountability goals for the future funding of public education. While much research has been done on the normative and legal rationales for the shift to adequacy and accountability standards and on how school districts respond to changes in state funding methods, there has been little work that focuses on state government behavior, their willingness to fund public education, and their reaction to public and court pressures. Clearly, however, given the critical role that state governments play in the provision and funding of public education and the fact that state governments have significant discretion in the policies that they adopt, it is important to have a thorough understanding of state funding behavior, lest proposed policies fall on legislative deaf ears.

Table 1-1. Public Education Revenues (2002 dollars), 1959-1960 to 1999-2000

School year	Public Education Revenues (millions), by source				Total Education Revenues as percent of ...		
	Total	Annual growth rate	Federal	State & local	Real GDP	Federal budget	State & local budgets
1959-60	74,582	4.4%	3,296	71,287	2.9%	0.8%	36.2%
1969-70	161,506	3.2%	12,913	148,59	4.1%	1.7%	36.8%
1979-80	205,223	3.0%	20,131	185,09	3.8%	2.0%	30.0%
1989-90	277,145	3.6%	16,878	260,26	3.8%	1.3%	31.6%
1999-00	394,127		28,643	365,48	4.0%	1.5%	30.2%

Note: GDP figures are for the calendar years in which the school year begins. Real values are calculated from nominal values using a GDP chain-type price deflator.

Sources: US Department of Commerce, Bureau of Economic Analysis (2003), Tables 1.1, 3.2, 3.3, and 7.1; and US Department of Education, National Center for Education Statistics (2003), Tables 156 and 160.

1. A BRIEF HISTORY OF PUBLIC EDUCATION

The size and importance of the public education sector in the US is sometimes underestimated because of its disaggregated nature. Unlike programs like Social Security or national defense, the national public education budget is comprised of more than 50 separate budgets (if we include the District of Columbia and other school systems not within the standard state structure), none of which typically grabs the national spotlight. Yet in the aggregate, public education is enormous. As *Table 1-1* reveals, public education revenues in real terms have grown steadily for nearly half a century and now receives approximately $400 billion every year.[4] Its share in terms of the nation's output (as measured by the GDP, the gross domestic product) is now 4%. While that share has varied over the past half century, it has been remarkably steady since the late 1960s.

Remarkably steady as well is public education's share of state and local governmental budgets. Though initially higher (approximately 36%) in the 1960s and early 1970s, by the end of the 1970s, that share had fallen to 30% and has remained in that range ever since. This fall seems not to have been the result of state and local governments spending less on public education (which grew in real terms throughout the past half century), but rather seems to have been the result of a conjunction of two forces – a rise in state

---

[4] The problem of how to properly adjust for price changes when dealing with education figures is not trivial. For an overview of the issues involved and a presentation of alternative methods, see Fowler and Monk (2001).

Table 1-2. Public Education Structure and Enrollments, 1959-1960 to 2009-2010

School Year	Public school districts	Public schools	Public Enrollments				
			Total (thousands)	Annual growth rate	As percent of ...		
					total population	public and private enrollments
1959-60	40,520	120,777	35,182	2.6%	19.9%	86.1%
1969-70	19,333	95,511	45,550	-0.9%	22.6%	89.2%
1979-80	15,929	87,004	41,651	-0.3%	18.5%	89.3%
1989-90	15,367	83,425	40,543	1.5%	16.4%	88.6%
1999-00	14,928	92,012	46,857	0.2%	16.8%	88.6%
2009-10	na	na	*47,607*		*16.0%*	*88.9%*

Note: Public school figures for 1959-60 and 1969-70 are based on an average of adjoining years. The public school-district number for 1969-70 is based on a weighted average of 1967 and 1970 figures. 2009-10 figures are projections.

Sources: US Department of Commerce, Census Bureau (1973), Table 157; US Department of Commerce, Census Bureau (1996), Table 2; US Department of Commerce, Census Bureau (2003), Tables 2 and 3 (middle series projection); and US Department of Education, National Center for Education Statistics (2003), Tables 3 and 87.

supported welfare and the passing of the baby boom through the public schools.

Federal government participation in public education, by contrast has been significantly smaller (never rising to more than 10% of all public education revenues) and has, relative to its base, fluctuated more. Interestingly, though the federal government has gotten more involved in public education in recent years, it has done so, from a budgetary perspective, judiciously, and there are no expectations for federal spending on public education to rise significantly in the future.

The number of students enrolled in public education has fluctuated more than the pattern of revenue figures might imply. As *Table 1-2* reveals, enrollments initially peaked in the late 1960s coincident with the peak in the baby boom coming of school age. With the 1970s and the exiting of the baby boom from the public schools, enrollment fell somewhat. However, with the 1990s enrollments began to rise again and have now surpassed the numbers seen at the peak of the baby boom era. While some of this recent growth is due to a new, though smaller, baby boom caused by baby boomers having children, it is mostly the result of a generally larger US population. As a result, public schools today, at least in terms of enrollment, no longer dominate the scene the way they did in the late 1960s when the proportion of the general population in public schools was more than 23%. While enrollments in absolute numbers are projected to continue to rise over the next several years, the general population is expected to rise faster, so that by the 2009-10 school year, public education students will only comprise

Table 1-3. Public School System Employment, 1959-1960 to 1999-2000

School Year	Total Staff			Instructional Staff	
	number (thousands)	annual growth rate	as percent of labor force	number (thousands)	as percent of total staff
1959-60	2,089	4.4%	3.1%	1,457	69.7%
1969-70	3,361	2.4%	4.2%	2,286	68.0%
1979-80	4,168	0.6%	3.9%	2,406	57.7%
1989-90	4,431	2.4%	3.6%	2,986	67.4%
1999-00	5,632		4.0%	3,819	67.8%

Sources: US Department of Education, National Center for Education Statistics (2003), Tables 36 and 80; and US Department of Labor, Bureau of Labor Statistics (2003), Table A-1.

16% of the population. This contrast between a rising number of students in public schools and a falling proportion of the population in the public schools suggests that the days of public support for quickly growing budgets as occurred in the 1960s when real public education revenues grew at a rate of 4.4% a year, are unlikely to return within the foreseeable future.

Interesting, too, is the change in the organization of public education over the past half century. While there has been a dramatic fall in the number of school districts and the number of schools since the late 1950s (in the 1960s alone the number of school districts fell by more than half), that process of consolidation appears to be coming to a close with the number of schools actually rising in the past decade. However, while the number of schools and school districts has fallen for most of the past half century, the same is not true of the number of people who work in public education. Throughout the past half century, employment by public school systems has steadily grown (the slowest period being the 1980s) so that today more than 5½ million people, or roughly one out of every 25 individuals in the US labor force, work for a public school system. When combined with the number of individuals in the private sector whose businesses interact with public education (from textbook and supply companies to companies that manufacture buses and sell food), the public education sector is clearly of significant interest to the economy.

In part because of its size and its claim on tax revenues, recent decades have seen increasing criticism of public education. One criticism is that public education has had an increasing tendency toward a bloated, top-heavy management structure. But an examination of the proportion of workers engaged directly in instruction (see *Table 1-3*) suggests that management is no top heavier today than it was in the late 1950s and the 1960s. To be sure, the proportion of instructional staff did fall in the 1960s and 70s (reaching a low of just under 58% in 1979-80 compared to a current proportion of just under 68%), but the fall seems to have been temporary. Given the dramatic

Table 1-4. Per-Pupil Education Expenditures (2002 dollars), 1959-1960 to 1999-2000

School Year	Total Expenditures		Current Expenditures	
	Amount	Annual growth rate	Amount	Annual growth rate
1959-60	2,382		1,897	
1969-70	3,830	4.9%	3,273	5.6%
1979-80	5,277	3.3%	4,813	3.9%
1989-90	7,376	3.4%	6,618	3.2%
1999-00	9,081	2.1%	7,814	1.7%

Notes: Pupil counts based on average daily attendance (ADA) numbers.   Current expenditures excludes capital outlays, interest payments, summer school, adult education, and other community services.

Sources: Department of Commerce, Bureau of Economic Analysis (2003), Table 7.1; and US Department of Education, National Center for Education Statistics (2003), Table 36.

fall in the number of schools and the number of school districts, this may have been the result of a learning process by which school districts learned to manage school districts with larger numbers of larger schools.

Another criticism is that public education has been a poor steward of its money and that as a result costs are out of control, resulting in an ever rising cost of educating students. This issue is a more complicated one, and an initial look at per-pupil expenditures over the past half century suggests that something is going on. As *Table 1-4* shows, since 1959 per-pupil expenditures, whether measured in the aggregate or only in terms of current expenditures, have risen consistently in real terms and in every decade. Whether this represents an increase in inefficiency, however, is less clear.

William Baumol argues in his analysis of urban fiscal crises (Baumol (1967)) that what distinguishes the technology for producing education from the production of, say, a car, is that with a car labor is incidental to its production while with education, labor is itself the point. With a car, no one cares how much labor was used to produce it, while with education a reduction in the amount of time that a student spends with a teacher is critical – reduce the time spent together, and the amount of education suffers. Hence, unlike with a car, there are limits to the ability to increase productivity in education through the use of greater and more sophisticated technology. To the extent that this argument is true, a problem arises in an economy that is growing because of technological improvements that increase productive efficiency in some, but not all, sectors. Such growth will result in an increase in real wage rates in those sectors in which there are improvements. However, in the education sector, no productivity takes place. As a result, while one might think that real wages would not rise, the fact is that they must. If teachers' wages do not rise, fewer and fewer individuals will be willing to take a job in education when they can get a

Table 1-5. Public Education v. Private-sector Service Sectors 1985 to 2000

Year	Public education workers		Private-sector service workers	
	Employment Cost Index (1985=100)	Annual growth rate	Employment Cost Index (1985=100)	Annual growth rate
1985	100.0		100.0	
1990	134.1	6.0%	130.0	5.4%
1995	155.6	3.0%	153.9	3.4%
2000	177.2	2.6%	183.2	3.6%
1985-2000 period		3.9%		4.1%

Source: US Department of Commerce, Census Bureau (2003), Table 615.

better paying job elsewhere in the economy. Thus, government is forced to raise the wages it pays its teachers at roughly the same rate as the wages elsewhere in the economy. And with that comes a rise in the real cost of educating a student.

Table 1-5 reveals that such a pattern does seem to have taken place in recent decades. Between 1985 and 2000, the cost of employing a service worker in the private sector rose on average 4.1% a year, while over the same period, the cost of employing a worker in the public education sector rose by 3.9% a year. While there is less match up when the period is divided into five-year increments, the correspondence is close enough to suggest that at least some of the rise in real per-pupil expenditures in public education is an unpleasant but unavoidable side effect of having a prosperous general economy that has become more productive over time.

Other factors, not associated with public education becoming less efficient, have also contributed to the rise in the real cost of public education per-pupil. In particular, as *Table 1-6* reveals, there has been a dramatic fall in the average class size since the late 1950s. This result seems to be in direct contradiction with the experience of parents whose perceptions are that classes are as large as they have ever been. In fact, both observations are correct. Public schools today provide a much larger array of public services (breakfasts for low income students, after-school programs, speech therapy, counseling services, etc.) than they did in the late 1950s, but many of these services are provided outside the regular classroom. This increased responsibility has resulted in an increase in staff in school districts' central offices, an increase in non-teaching staff at individual schools, and an increase in teaching staff at individual schools. As Hamilton Lankford and James Wyckoff observe in their study of New York spending patterns (Lankford and Wyckoff (1999)), these increases result in a statistical fall in class sizes but do not reduce the size of an "average" student's class. Some evidence of this increase in responsibilities can be seen in *Table 1-7* where the number of disabled children served by public schools through federally

Table 1-6. Alternative Measures of Average Class Size, 1959-1960 to 1999-2000

School Year	Total Staff		Instructional Staff		Teachers		
	Number (thousands)	ADA/Total	Number (thousands)	ADA/Instructional Staff	Number (thousands)	As percent of total staff	ADA/Teacher
1959-60	2,089	15.5	1,457	22.3	1,353	64.8%	24.0
1969-70	3,361	12.5	2,286	18.3	2,016	60.0%	20.8
1979-80	4,168	9.2	2,406	15.9	2,185	52.4%	17.5
1989-90	4,431	8.5	2,986	12.7	2,357	53.2%	16.0
1999-00	5,632	7.8	3,819	11.5	2,911	51.7%	15.0

Notes: ADA is average daily attendance. The 1979-80 measure of the number of total staff is for 1980-81.

Sources: US Department of Education, National Center for Education Statistics (2003), Tables 36, 65, and 80.

supported programs is displayed. Between 1976-77 and 1999-00, the number of such children increased in both absolute numbers (by 67%) and as a proportion of total public enrollments (by 59%). Interestingly, more than 80% of this growth can be accounted for by the growth in specific learning disabilities, which grew by more than 250% over the same time period and which now comprise almost half of all disabilities.

Whether Baumol's public service disease, the fall in class size, and the rise in the array of services provided by public schools is sufficient to completely explain the rise in real per-pupil costs over the past half century is not clear. However, it certainly suggests that the concern for *increasing* inefficiency in public education may be misplaced. Helen Ladd (Ladd (1996)), in fact, argues more strongly in the introduction to her volume on performance-based education reform that accounting for the faster rise in the cost of educational inputs would explain approximately two-fifths of the cost rise, and that much of the rest is most likely explained by the broader mission of public education today. Thus, what evidence there is suggests that the resources available to the average student have not increased much, if at all, despite the rise in per-pupil expenditures over the past half century.

If there is little evidence to support the conclusion that US public education has become increasingly inefficient over the past half century, international comparisons provide evidence that the US public education system is far from the best. While such evidence is useful in its own right for evaluating the status of US public education, it is also a critically important issue for those concerned with the nation's ability to grow economically over time and to compete internationally. By some accounts

Table 1-7. Children Aged 3-21 Served in Federally Supported Programs for the Disabled, 1976-1977 to 1999-2000

School Year	All Disabilities		Specific Learning Disabilities	
	Total (thousands)	As percent of total public enrollment	Number (thousands)	As percent of all disabilities
1976-77	3,694	8.3%	796	21.5%
1980-81	4,144	10.1%	1,462	35.3%
1998-99	4,631	11.4%	2,047	44.2%
1999-00	6,190	13.2%	2,830	45.7%

Source: US Department of Education, National Center for Education Statistics (2003), Table 52.

(Jorgenson (1996), Griliches (2000)), investments in human capital, and especially formal education, have accounted for about a third of all economic growth since World War II in the US, and there is now a general consensus that the long-term economic prosperity of an economically developed country depends critically on having a well-educated work force, among the most well known advocates in the public arena being Michael Porter at the Harvard Business School (Porter (1990)) and Robert Reich, former US Labor Secretary and currently at Brandeis University (Reich (1992)).[5] Moreover, there is a clear record of evidence that points to the value of education in generating higher earnings, increased participation in the political process, fewer health problems, reduced need for public support, and lower levels of crime (Behrman and Stacey (1997), Hanushek (1996)).

Unfortunately, a number of studies suggest that US public education is not as productive as it might be, perhaps the best known study being the federal government's report *A Nation at Risk* (US Department of Education, National Commission on Excellence in Education (1983)). An examination of international data of student test scores only reinforces that view, at least to the degree that education quality can be measured by standardized evaluations. *Table 1-8*, for example, reports the relative ranking of 27 countries belonging to the Organization for Economic Cooperation and Development (OECD) in terms of the performance of 15 year olds on competency tests of reading literacy, mathematical literacy, and

---

[5] There is some counter evidence that while more education may be beneficial for the individual, it may not be for a country as a whole. See Chapter 3 of Blaug (1972) and Chapter 9 of Belfield (2000) for an overview of the issue. However, recent work (Krueger and Lindahl (2001)) suggests that this counter evidence is the result of measurement errors, and that when such errors are corrected, the rate of return for a nation as a whole is at least as great as the return to individuals.

Table 1-8. International Comparison of 15-year-olds, 2000

Rank	Reading Literacy	Mathematical Literacy	Scientific Literacy
1	Finland	Japan	Korea
2	Canada	Korea	Japan
3	New Zealand	New Zealand	Finland
4	Australia	Finland	United Kingdom
5	Ireland	Australia	Canada
6	Korea	Canada	New Zealand
7	United Kingdom	Switzerland	Australia
8	Japan	United Kingdom	Austria
9	Sweden	Belgium	Ireland
10	Austria	France	Sweden
11	Belgium	Austria	Czech Republic
12	Iceland	Denmark	France
13	Norway	Iceland	Norway
14	France	Sweden	**United States**
15	**United States**	Ireland	Hungary
16	Denmark	Norway	Iceland
17	Switzerland	Czech Republic	Belgium
18	Spain	**United States**	Switzerland
19	Czech Republic	Germany	Spain
20	Italy	Hungary	Germany
21	Germany	Spain	Poland
22	Hungary	Poland	Denmark
23	Poland	Italy	Italy
24	Greece	Portugal	Greece
25	Portugal	Greece	Portugal
26	Luxembourg	Luxembourg	Luxembourg
27	Mexico	Mexico	Mexico

Note: Because specific scores are ordinal, not cardinal, in nature, they are not reported.
Sources: Organization for Economic Cooperation and Development (2003), Tables A5.2, A6.1, and A6.2.

scientific literacy. In none of the tests does the US rank in the top half of the nations for which data is available, and the best ranking the US achieves is in scientific literacy where it is only at the median among the 27 countries. Additional evidence suggesting that the US public education system is not the most effective comes from an international comparison of the amount of money spent per pupil (see *Table 1-9*). In particular (and despite the relatively low scores on the reading, mathematical, and scientific literacy tests), US spending per student is quite high (ranking in the top three for both primary and secondary education). Interestingly, however, spending per student as a proportion of GDP is not particularly high in the US compared to other countries, suggesting that the US sacrifice for public education is not particularly high. While one might suspect that poorer countries spend more on public education as a proportion of their GDP, the data suggest otherwise as witnessed by the presence of such nations as

Table 1-9. International Comparison of Per-Student Education Expenditures, 1999

Rank	Primary Education Per-Student Expenditures		Secondary Education Per-Student Expenditures	
	Absolute Amount	Relative to GDP	Absolute Amount	Relative to GDP
1	Denmark	Austria	Switzerland	Switzerland
2	Switzerland	Sweden	Austria	Austria
3	**United States**	Denmark	**United States**	France
4	Austria	Switzerland	Norway	Portugal
5	Norway	Italy	Denmark	Denmark
6	Sweden	Japan	France	Italy
7	Italy	Poland	Australia	Germany
8	Japan	Korea	Germany	Australia
9	Australia	Portugal	Italy	Belgium
10	Netherlands	**United States**	Belgium	Norway
11	France	Norway	Japan	Spain
12	Finland	Spain	Canada	Czech Republic
13	Belgium	Australia	Sweden	Sweden
14	Germany	Hungary	Finland	Korea
15	Spain	France	Netherlands	Finland
16	United Kingdom	Finland	United Kingdom	Japan
17	Portugal	Belgium	Portugal	**United States**
18	Ireland	United Kingdom	Spain	United Kingdom
19	Korea	Netherlands	Ireland	Canada
20	Hungary	Germany	Czech Republic	Netherlands
21	Greece	Greece	Korea	Hungary
22	Poland	Mexico	Greece	Slovak Republic
23	Czech Republic	Czech Republic	Hungary	Greece
24	Mexico	Ireland	Slovak Republic	Mexico
25			Poland	Poland
26			Mexico	Ireland

Note: List lengths vary because of unavailable data. Spending amounts converted to equivalent US dollars using purchasing power parity values.

Sources: Organization for Economic Cooperation and Development (2003), Tables B1.1 and B1.2.

Switzerland and Austria in the top of both lists. While some argue that the comparison may be a bit unfair because of the presence of much more diverse population of students in the US compared to the relatively homogenous societies of such countries as Switzerland and Austria, the impression remains that US public education is not as effective as it might be.

For all these reasons, the past decade has seen a significant push by individuals in both the private and the public sectors, and most notably by many in business,[6] for education reform in order to improve government efficiency and the international competitiveness of the US economy. However, the biggest push for education reform comes from a much older interest in remedying inequities in the provision of public education. The beginnings of that effort can be traced back to the push to desegregate US public schools that resulted in the 1954 US Supreme Court ruling in *Brown v. Board of Education*. By the late 1960s, though desegregation was neither complete nor perfectly achieved, the ability to achieve further gains following the logic of *Brown* seemed to have run its course. Recognizing that there were significant differences in the amount of resources that school districts had per pupil, and recognizing that many white children also suffered from such inequities, advocates for more equitable public education system began arguing that the US Constitution required that all school districts should be funded equally on a per-student basis. In 1971 they achieved their first success when the California Supreme Court ruled in *Serrano v. Priest* that all school districts regardless of their local property wealth should be funded equally. While the US Supreme Court later ruled in 1973 in *San Antonio Independent School District v. Rodriguez* that there was no such obligation under the US Constitution, many state supreme courts found that there was such an obligation under state constitutional law. But not all state supreme courts and state legislatures agreed, and by the 1980s interest for further reform seemed to have waned. The current interest in remedying public education inequities, which many trace to the 1989 Kentucky Supreme Court case *Rose v. Council for Better Education* and which continues to involve the courts, focuses on the notion of adequacy and accountability, and stems from dissatisfactions with the outcome of the older reform efforts, and from new concerns about the dramatic increase in immigrant populations and the poor state of public education in urban areas. Combined with the effort to reform public education by those interested in government efficiency and international competitiveness, public education reform is now, and is likely to continue to be, an issue of significant interest for the nation.

2.   PLAN OF THE BOOK

The issue, of course, is what will happen in the future to this current effort to ensure an adequate education for all students. While hopes are high

---

[6] See, for example, the forward in Denis Doyle, Bruce Cooper, and Roberta Trachman's book on education reform in the 1980s by David Kearns, then chair of the Xerox Corporation (Kearns (1991)).

and much initial work has been made on putting accountability structures in place, the history of public education reform is sufficiently full of failed attempts at reform to suggest that a more sober outlook may be more appropriate. It is generally recognized that one cannot know whether students are receiving an adequate education without some form of assessment. However, it is not clear whether the set of assessment structures that have already been put into place are useful to that end, and it is even less clear whether the nation's various legislatures, state and federal, will provide the resources if (when?) it is found that some students are not receiving an adequate education. On those questions will hinge the success or failure of the current reform movement and the education of the next generation. The purpose of this book is to make sense of the legislative process, as much an economic one as it is a political one, to better understand which strategies are mostly likely to bear fruit. If more resources will be needed, how much more are legislatures likely to provide? Will the courts be a useful tool for achieving objectives? Will reform entail redistributing existing resources away from more successful districts to less successful districts, and if so what are the economic and political limits on such redistribution?

The analysis of these questions begins in *Chapter 2* with the presentation of a general theory of intergovernmental grants. The majority of the funding of public education is provided by state legislatures to local school districts through grants based on various funding formulae. While there is some understanding of how the recipients of such intergovernmental grants react to changes in grant formulae, there is little understanding of why legislatures provide such intergovernmental grants and why they take the forms that they do. In large part, this failure is the result of a lack of a simple language to describe the structure of intergovernmental grant programs and a failure to recognize that individual intergovernmental grant programs are part of a comprehensive intergovernmental grants structure designed by legislators whose interests are not always the same as those who receive the grants. Chapter 2 provides a theory that redresses that failure and allows one to understand why intergovernmental grants exist and why they take the forms that they do.

Building on the general theory of intergovernmental grants, *Chapter 3* develops a specific theory of public education funding that is used in *Chapter 5* to trace the history of public education funding in the light of reform efforts over the past half century. The role of the courts in this funding process is examined, with particular emphasis on the shift in the courts' emphasis away from equalization standards and toward adequacy and accountability standards, and the reaction of state legislatures to that shift. While the courts ostensibly have a number of options available with regard to public education funding (ranging from no action to declaring a state's entire public education system unconstitutional), in fact, there are serious constraints that arise from the political process and that impinge on the courts' ability to effect change. *Chapters 3* and *5* examine the motivations and constraints that face the courts to better understand the value and limits to using the courts to achieve reform objectives. Finally, while issues of equality and adequacy are for the most part concerned with the *distribution* of resources among school districts, policies that effect the distribution of resources often have implications for the overall *level* of support for public education provided by state legislatures. As a result, the question of whether a legislature will level up or level down in response to pressures to equalize per-pupil school district expenditures or provide an adequate education for all students is also examined.

Chapter 4, which lies between the theoretical and the historical examination of US public education funding, provides an empirical case study to demonstrate the consistency of the theoretical model in *Chapter 3* with actual behavior so that the reader may have some confidence in the use of that model to explain and predict behavior in *Chapter 5*. In particular, *Chapter 4* examines Connecticut's 1980 experience with a court order to reform its public education funding structure. The order, based on the 1977 Connecticut Supreme Court case *Horton v. Meskill*, required that the legislature choose from among alternative grant structures. The resulting choice provides empirical support for the theoretical arguments in *Chapter 3*, and reveals, in addition, the extent to which legislative behavior, to the extent it is influenced by court orders, will depend on the specific legal reasoning of the court.

The fact that state legislative behavior will depend on the legal reasoning of the courts suggests that the shift from equality standards and to adequacy and accountability standards can be expected to have a significant effect on state legislative behavior. *Chapter 6*, in fact, finds that this is potentially the case, but only if legislatures and reformers come to terms with three problems – the general unwillingness of legislature's to increase the total level of support for public education, the current lack of a consensus about what adequacy means in practical terms and how to measure progress toward that functional notion of adequacy, and the current lack of sufficient knowledge to know how to make progress toward adequacy, however it is defined. The chapter then closes with an examination of possible structural reforms, such as decentralization and the use of markets, that are an increasing part of the public education reform debate and that are often seen as either the salvation for public education or its downfall.

Finally, Chapter 7 concludes with a brief recapitulation of the book and some final thoughts on the public education's future.

Chapter 2

A GENERAL THEORY OF INTERGOVERNMENTAL GRANTS

Having rejected the organic conception of the State and also the idea of class domination, we are left with a purely individualist conception of the collectivity. Collective action is viewed as the action of individuals when they choose to accomplish purposes collectively rather than individually, and the government is seen as nothing more than the set of processes, the machine, which allows such collective action to take place.

— James M. Buchanan & Gordon Tullock, *The Calculus of Consent*[7]

In order to understand the process by which public education is funded, it is important to begin by exploring the general nature of intergovernmental grants. Most money for public education is provided by state legislatures to local school districts in the form of intergovernmental grants and based upon some sort of funding formula. Such funding formulae are, in turn, the result of a complicated process in which legislators weigh alternative interests, some directly connected to education, others not connected at all but which compete for the money nonetheless.[8]

An extensive intergovernmental grants literature exists in economics.[9] However, this literature for the most part focuses only on individual grant programs and then only in terms of the effect that intergovernmental grants have on recipient behavior. While this is of value, it falls short of what is needed if we are to understand why legislatures provide intergovernmental grants and why they do so in the way that they do. In particular, it ignores the fact that intergovernmental grants policy is often formulated as an integrated package of grant programs rather than as isolated individual grant

---

[7] Buchanan and Tullock (1962).

[8] Witness, for example, the fall in the proportion of state budgets devoted to public education during the 1970s that was the result of a rise in state welfare programs (see *Table 1-1* in *Chapter 1*).

[9] Chapter 9 of Ronald Fisher's textbook on state and local public finance (Fisher (1996)) provides a nice overview of this material.

programs,[10] and it ignores the grantor legislator's motivation and behavior in the process, thus implicitly assuming that the grants are exogenous.[11] In part, this lack of attention to the donor side of intergovernmental grants can be attributed to difficulties in developing a simple language for describing the sometimes byzantine structures of individual grant programs.[12] Beyond that, however, this lack of attention to the donor side stems from limitations inherent in the typical model of intergovernmental grants. Decisions in these models are generally demand driven (see, for example, Fisher (1979)), and, where the grant structure is made endogenous, decisions continue to be made by the same pivotal recipient (see, for example, Slack (1980)). As a result, the endogeneity of the grant structure is limited and fails to account for the fact that intergovernmental grant systems are chosen by legislators whose actions are driven by a separate (though connected) sets of preferences (Wiseman (1989)).

The purpose of this chapter is to provide a general structure for understanding how a government's overall grants system, composed of numerous individual grant programs, is determined. Two tasks are required to fulfill this purpose. First, the salient details of individual grant programs must be distilled from the myriad of details which characterize actual programs and fit into a comprehensive whole. This task is accomplished below by noting the parallels between the structure of an individual tax and the structure of an individual grant program. Hence, a government's intergovernmental grants system can be described by a set of individual grant programs each of which is characterized by a rate structure, a base structure, and an intended purpose. Second, the choice of a particular structure for an intergovernmental grants system must be based on legislative preferences. While there is, of course, connections between the preferences of legislators and the preferences of their constituents, much potential explanatory power is lost if it is assumed that the preferences of

---

[10] For examples of the comprehensive nature of intergovernmental grants policy, see Timothy Conlan's (1988) description of the 1980s controversy over the transformation of the Federal government's grants system and Robert Peter's (1996) examination of New Jersey's struggle with reform of the state educational funding system and the impact of such changes on the funding of other programs.

[11] A partial exception to this observation can be found in Schwallie (1987, 1989a, 1989b) where the effects of grants from the US federal government on the overall size of the public sector is examined. Though not focused on the determinants of grants structure, the underlying theoretical model does include an independent, utility maximizing grantor government in which aggregate federal spending (net of grants), recipient expenditures, and personal per-capita disposable income enter as arguments.

[12] The wealth of detail that must be sifted through can be daunting. Vincent Munley (1990) provides a successful example of efforts to provide a comprehensive description of the workings of state grants for public education.

legislatures are identical with the preferences of their constituents. I therefore assume that legislative preferences are distinct from those who receive the grants. This assumption is actualized by characterizing a legislative decision-making process in which individual legislators seek to maximize the political support each receives from constituents. The notion of political support is left deliberately general so that it can capture a variety of political circumstances to explain how legislative preferences and the preferences of constituents are connected. Such connections may range from those in which political support is manifest only through the casting of votes, to more complex circumstances in which political support takes a variety of forms all of which eventually impact the probability of being reelected. The result of these modeling efforts is a decision-making process which in retrospect appears rather simple. The individual components of the optimal intergovernmental grants system are chosen by the donor government's legislature in a way that that assures that no additional net political benefit can be derived from increasing or decreasing the overall level of grant activities, from redistributing grant monies away from one grant program and into another, or from redistributing grant monies away from some constituents and toward others.[13]

This resulting model, used to understand how a government's overall intergovernmental grants system is determined, is presented in the next section, and that presentation is done in three steps. First, the salient details of individual intergovernmental grant programs are described and used to construct a relatively simple description of an overall intergovernmental grants system. Second, the political benefits that accrue to the donor government's legislature as a result of providing intergovernmental grants are described. And finally, the legislature's fundamental problem and the characteristics of an optimal solution to that problem are described. Because the resulting solution implies unrealistically that intergovernmental grants will take the form of general revenue sharing grants and not be provided to jurisdictions whose representatives are not part of the controlling political coalition in the legislature, the chapter concludes with an examination of why we see, in practice, intergovernmental grants often being provided to all lower-level jurisdictions whether their representatives are part of the ruling political coalition and why many (if not most) intergovernmental grants are categorical in nature. The answer, in brief, is the presence of spillovers (that is, what happens when individuals in one jurisdiction get benefits from grants provided to a different jurisdiction), fiscal illusion (that is, what

---

[13] Readers familiar with microeconomics will recognize this as the standard marginal analysis used to determine the conditions associated with the maximization of some objective under various resource constraints.

happens when individuals overestimate the benefits of intergovernmental grants or underestimate the cost of providing those grants), and political asymmetry (that is, what happens when political power is skewed in favor of some and away from others).

1.   THE DETERMINATION OF A SYSTEM OF INTERGOVERNMENTAL GRANTS

The essential components involved in the process of creating an intergovernmental grants system is a donor government, a number of lower-level recipient governments, and decision makers for each government who seeks to achieve an (as of yet unspecified) objective. The model below incorporates these components through the use of a two-tiered federal governmental structure composed of a donor government with decisions made by that donor government's legislature, and a number of lower-level recipient governments in which decisions are made by a plebiscite of its citizens. The analytical foundations for this model are derived from Walter Hettich and Stanley Winer's (1988) model of the determination of the overall structure of taxes employed by a government, and Robert Inman's (1988) empirical analysis of US intergovernmental grant spending levels.[14] Although neither article focuses on the structure of intergovernmental grants, Hettich and Winer's use of a systemic approach to fiscal decision making and Inman's explicit treatment of the political decision-making process are well put and are consequently adopted here.

1.1   Characteristics of a System of Intergovernmental Grant Programs

Although specifics vary considerably in practice, individual intergovernmental grant programs have three basic characteristics that define their structure. First, every intergovernmental grant program has a purpose for which it is intended. This purpose may be general, as in the case of revenue-sharing grants, or it may be quite specific, as, for example, an intergovernmental grant program designed to help towns with a population less than 20,000 purchase computer systems for traffic control in their central business districts. Second, every individual intergovernmental grant program allocates money on the basis of one or more criteria that we can

---

[14] Hettich and Winer's (1988) work on the overall structure of taxes has provided a foundation for other work as well. See, for example, Kiesling (1990) which argues that tax structures may be dependent on the pattern of governmental expenditures.

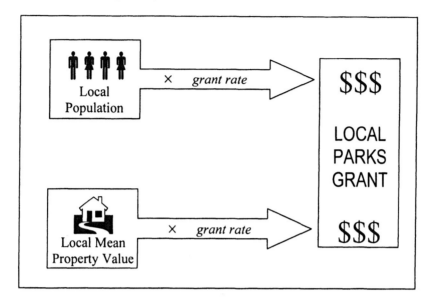

Figure 2-1. Structure of an Individual Intergovernmental Grant Program

call, in analogy with the analysis of tax structures, a grant base. Such grant bases may be simple, as in the case of an intergovernmental grant based solely on the number of people residing within the recipient government's jurisdiction. However, such grant bases can also be quite complicated so that, for example, one can imagine a particular intergovernmental grant based on a recipient jurisdiction's aggregate assessed property value times its poverty rate divided by its per-capita income. Finally, an individual intergovernmental grant program is characterized by one or more parameters that we can call, again in analogy with the analysis of tax structures, grant rates. Grant rates determine how much money a recipient government receives based on the values of its grant bases. The values of these grant rates will, of course, depend on how the various grant bases are measured and what the values of the various grant bases are.

Figure 2-1 illustrates this structure for some hypothetical state government interested in providing its local governments with an intergovernmental grant in order to stimulate the building of local public parks by those same local governments. Suppose that the state legislature wishes to give grants to all its local governments, but that it wishes to give more money to local governments with a larger population or with a larger number of poor people. Given that supposition, a simple grant structure that achieves those ends can be designed by having the grant calculated using two bases – local population and local mean property value. Then, by choosing the appropriate grant rate for each base (a positive grant rate associated with the local population grant base and a negative grant rate associated with the local mean property value grant base), every locality will receive a grant with the larger and the poorer localities receiving more than those localities that are smaller or more wealthy.

Mathematically, this structure can be represented using matrix notation. Let the vector Γ_j represent the set of activities that some grant j is intended to support, and let the levels of such activities for the ith recipient government be noted by the vector γ_j^i. Such activity may be measured in a variety of ways, and thus may include such diverse items as levels of local governmental spending on particular activities, physical measures of local tangible assets, or measures of student performance on skills tests. Define the set of grant bases used to allocate the grant by the $K_j \times 1$ vector $\mathbf{X}_j$, and let the values of these grant bases for the ith recipient government be noted by the vector $\mathbf{x}_j^i$. Finally, define the set of grant rates for the ith recipient government to be some $K_j \times 1$ vector $\mathbf{r}_j$. The set of grant rates $\mathbf{r}_j$, in turn, translate the set of grant bases into a total level of funding G_j^i. Thus, a typical intergovernmental grant to jurisdiction i used to stimulate the activities Γ_j can be represented by a sum of terms each of which represents the degree to which the various local grant bases $\mathbf{x}_j^i$ contribute to the overall size of the grant:

$$G_j^i = \mathbf{r}_j' \mathbf{x}_j^i. \qquad (2\text{-}1)$$

Given this structure for an individual intergovernmental grant program, the overall structure of a donor government's intergovernmental grants system can be defined as the aggregation of all such individual structures. Letting J be the total number of individual intergovernmental grant programs, the set of grants going to the ith recipient government can be described by the $J \times 1$ vector $\mathbf{G}^i$ composed of J individual grants G_j^i:

$$\mathbf{G}^i = [G_1^i \, G_2^i \ldots G_J^i]. \qquad (2\text{-}2)$$

Because each grant is a function of K_j bases, the total number of rates which the donor government must set is $K = K_1 + K_2 + \ldots + K_J$. A donor government's intergovernmental grants structure is therefore characterized by the number of grant programs, J, the set of activities for which each program is designed, $\{\Gamma_j\}_{j=1}^{J}$, the number and types of bases to be used for each program, $\{\mathbf{X}_j\}_{j=1}^{J}$, and the set of grant rates for each program, $\{\mathbf{r}_j\}_{j=1}^{J}$, that is, by the set Ω:

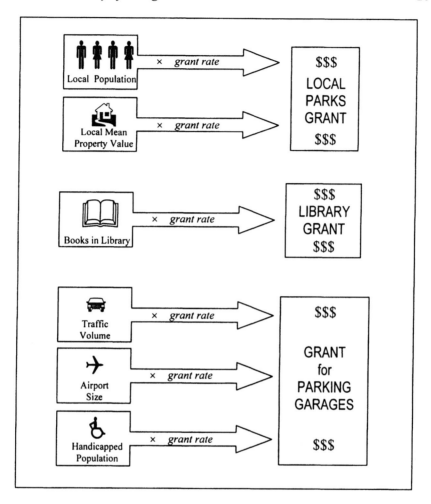

Figure 2-2. A Complete System of Intergovernmental Grants

$$\Omega = \left\{ J, \{\mathbf{\Gamma}_j\}_{j=1}^J, \{K_j\}_{j=1}^J, \{\mathbf{X}_j\}_{j=1}^J, \{\mathbf{r}_j\}_{j=1}^J \right\}. \qquad (2\text{-}3)$$

Schematically, this can be represented by *Figure 2-2* where our hypothetical state government provides an intergovernmental grant for local public parks based on the local population and local mean property value (as noted in *Figure 2-1*), an intergovernmental grant for local public libraries with larger libraries receiving greater aid, and an intergovernmental grant for local public parking garages based on local traffic volume, local airport volume, and the number of handicapped. The result is a complex intergovernmental grant system composed of three individual intergovernmental grant programs each with its own set of bases and grant rates.

1.2   The Political Decision-Making Structure and the Preferences of Individual Legislators

The decision-making structure within which this intergovernmental grants system Ω is determined is typically complex, involving at a minimum both an executive and a bicameral legislature, and additionally often including various governmental agencies as well as lobbyists representing recipient governments and private-sector interests who potentially may benefit or be hurt by the provision of intergovernmental grants and the imposition of taxes needed to fund those intergovernmental grants. A full model of such a structure is beyond the scope of this book. However, because different decision-making arrangements can sometimes result in different outcomes,[15] it is important to be explicit about the structure employed.

I assume that decisions of the donor government are made by a unicameral legislature and that each member of the legislature represents a single recipient jurisdiction. I further assume that each representative seeks to maximize the probability of reelection, and for simplicity assume that the donor government funds its intergovernmental grants system with a proportional tax levied on its constituents at some rate s on an exogenous tax base B^i in each jurisdiction i. Finally, I assume that the donor government must balance its budget.

The probability of reelection for each representative is assumed to be a positive (monotonic) function of the political support ψ^i that is provided by the representative's constituents. Hence, each representative seeks to maximize ψ^i. Political support may manifest itself in a variety of ways. Examples include active campaigning, volunteer work, cash contributions, and favorable voting. The value of a constituent's political support will generally depend on the form of the political support as well as who

---

[15] Chapter 11 of James Buchanan and Marilyn Flowers's (1987) textbook provides a relatively simple introduction to the importance of decision-making structures by contrasting the choices made by three individuals under different majority-rule voting arrangements. For an in-depth introduction to the approach used by Buchanan and Flowers and an examination of the effect that a variety of institutional structures have on decisions made in the political arena, see James Enelow and Melvin Hinich's (1984) textbook on spatial voting theory or Kenneth Shepsle and Mark Bonchek's (1997) textbook on rational political choice theory.

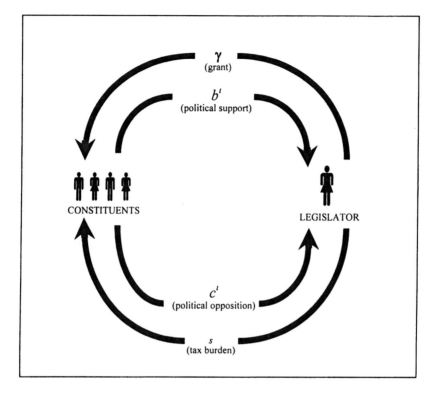

Figure 2-3. Net Political Benefit to an Individual Legislator

provides it. Thus, for example, an hour of volunteer work by a local politician or interest-group leader may result in greater political support than a similar effort by an ordinary constituent.

The level of political support which each representative receives is determined by two conflicting forces. On the one hand, intergovernmental grants increase the level of activities provided by recipient governments,[16] and thus increase the utilities of individual constituents. As a result, as *Figure 2-3* illustrates schematically, these individuals are willing (holding all other things constant) to provide a greater level of political support when the levels of intergovernmental grants are higher. On the other hand, individual constituents are made worse off by the taxes they pay to the donor government because of its effect on the amount of disposable income that these individuals will have available to purchase goods and services in the

---

[16] The degree to which the jth grant program affects recipient-government behavior will depend on both the grant program's rate structure r_j as well as the program's grant base X_j. See Fisher (1988).

private sector. As a result, holding all other things constant, they will provide a lower level of political support. Thus, given a particular grants structure Ω_1 and assuming that individual constituents do not perceive a connection between the level of activities that their recipient government engages in and the taxes they pay to the donor government,[17] the net political support which some individual α residing in the ith jurisdiction is willing to provide can be written as the (additively separable) function:

$$\psi_\alpha^i = b_\alpha^i(\gamma) - c_\alpha^i(s) \qquad (2\text{-}4)$$

where γ is the $(J \cdot N) \times 1$ vector of activity levels across all N jurisdictions, where $b_\alpha^i(\cdot)$ is assumed to be a positive, concave function of γ, and where $c_\alpha^i(\cdot)$ is assumed to be a positive, convex function of s.[18] Note that $b_\alpha^i(\cdot)$ is a function of the vector γ and not just γ_α^i, thus allowing for the possibility of spillover effects across recipient jurisdictions. These spillover effects may be due to either direct consumption by the individual (for example, a suburbanite using roads in the central city) or more indirectly as might occur if an individual receives utility from knowing that the residents of another jurisdiction have government supported health-care programs.

Thus the net political support that the legislator representing jurisdiction i will receive in total from her constituents can be defined as the sum ψ^i of all the net political supports ψ_α^i across all individuals α in jurisdiction i:

$$\psi^i = b^i(\gamma) - c^i(t) = \sum_\alpha b_\alpha^i(\gamma) - \sum_\alpha c_\alpha^i(s). \qquad (2\text{-}5)$$

A simplified schematic representation of the link between the choices of the legislator and the level of aggregate net political support ψ^i is provided

---

[17] Hettich and Winer (1988) argue that although these decisions are formally connected through the imposition of the donor government's budget constraint, "the separation of taxes and expenditures is an important characteristic of modern fiscal systems." Jack Citrin (1979) in his examination of the motivations for the passage of California's Proposition 13, which imposed state constitutional restrictions on the ability of local governments to level property taxes above certain levels, provides empirical evidence of this dichotomy in the minds of voters.

[18] The assumption of a positive, concave political benefit function $b_\alpha^i(\cdot)$ is intended to reflect the observation that political benefits to the legislator typically rise with increases in intergovernmental grants but that they do so at a gradually decreasing rate. Likewise, the assumption of a positive, convex political cost function $c_\alpha^i(\cdot)$ is intended to reflect the observation that the political costs to the legislator associated with higher taxes typically rise at an ever increasing rate as tax rates increase. Such assumptions, which are common in economic models of behavior, turn out to be important to assuring the existence of an equilibrium, that is, to assuring that decision makers can make determinate choices.

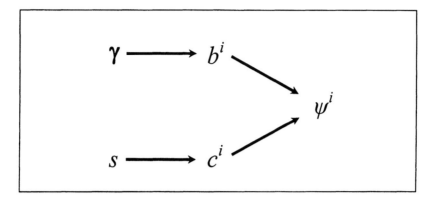

Figure 2-4. Determination of Net Aggregate Political Support for an Individual Legislator

in *Figure 3-4*. Through the choice of the various intergovernmental grant system parameters represented by the set Ω (see *Equation 2-3*), the representative essentially has control over the amounts and distribution of intergovernmental grants γ provided to all jurisdictions as well as the tax rate s that is used to fund the entire intergovernmental grants system. The amounts and distribution of the intergovernmental grants γ across all jurisdiction generates some level of aggregate positive political support b^i, while the level of the tax rate s generates some level of aggregate political opposition c^i. Together, b^i and c^i sum to yield the net aggregate political support ψ^i.

Note finally that net aggregate political support ψ^i is defined given a *particular* intergovernmental grants system. The ability to target those grants and thus generate political support is limited by the number of individual intergovernmental grant programs as well as by the number of criteria used to allocate those grants. Increases in either the number of individual grant programs or the number of allocation criteria (that is, the grant bases) will, in general, increase the ability to target grants to particular constituencies. Hence, a more complex intergovernmental grants system can be expected to result in a greater level of political support b^i, although, as discussed in the next section, such increased complexity will also result in increased costs. Thus, *Equation 2-5* can be restated as:

$$\psi^i = b^i(\gamma, J, K_1, K_2, \ldots, K_J) - c^i(s) \tag{2-6}$$

where b^i is a positive, strictly concave function of its arguments.

1.3   Characterization and Solution to the Legislature's Problem

An individual member of the legislature is, of course, unable to put into place a system of intergovernmental grant programs unilaterally. As a result, the ability of an individual legislator to maximize net aggregate political support ψ^i requires the cooperation of a majority of legislators. How the legislator achieves that majority, is, however, a rather complicated process. As Inman (1988) points out, the outcome of legislative choice problems is in large part determined by the particular legislative decision-making structure in place.[19] A legislature dominated by a single political leader who represents a coalition of the whole (what Inman calls a "cooperative legislature")[20] will behave quite differently from either a legislature that is dominated by a majority coalition (Inman's "majority-controlled legislature") or a legislature that approves any proposal put forth by any of its members (Inman's "fully decentralized regime").

Let the legislative decision-making structure be characterized by a dominant political coalition which has sufficient power to design and adopt an entire system of intergovernmental grant programs. Hence, only the preferences of those legislators who are members of the dominant political coalition will be considered in the design of the grants structure. If we let $\mathcal{C}$ represent the set of representatives in the dominant political coalition, the objective of the coalition will be to maximize the coalition's aggregate net political support Ψ defined as the sum of the individual legislators' aggregate net political ψ^i across all members of the coalition:

$$\Psi = \sum_{i \in \mathcal{C}} [b^i(\gamma, J, K_1, K_2, \ldots, K_J) - c^i(s)]. \tag{2-7}$$

Schematically, this process is represented in *Figure 2-5* with the legislature assumed, for simplicity, to be composed of three representatives, the first two of which belong to the dominant political coalition. Note that the political benefits and costs that accrue to the third representative are of no relevance to the dominant political coalition's decision making because

---

[19] In the context of game theory (see Rasmussen (1989; pp. 26-7), a legislative decision-making structure can be thought of as an equilibrium (or solution) concept employed by the legislature and which maps member strategies and payoff functions into an equilibrium.

[20] For an interesting example of empirical work implicitly based on the assumption of a cooperative legislature see Gavin Wright's (1974) analysis of the New Deal where he argues that the distribution of federal spending across states in the 1930s was determined by a desire to maximize the electoral votes for Franklin Roosevelt.

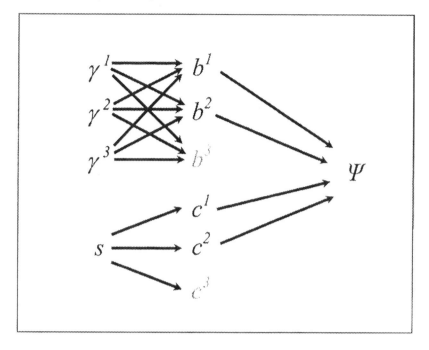

Figure 2-5. Determination of Aggregate Net Political Support for the Dominant Political Coalition

that representative is not a member of the dominant political coalition. Despite that, however, the grants that are provided to that third representative's jurisdiction are in general of importance to the dominant political coalition because all intergovernmental grants may have spillover effects, that is, individuals in the first two jurisdictions may get benefits from grants provided to jurisdictions even though they do not live in those jurisdictions.

As noted earlier, the legislature, and therefore the dominant political coalition, is constrained by the requirement that it balance the donor government's budget. Revenues are derived from the proportional tax already mentioned. Expenditures, however, while including the sum of all intergovernmental grants disbursed, also include costs associated with the enacting and administering of the entire intergovernmental grants system. Administrative costs A reduce the ability of the grantor government to distribute all of each tax dollar to recipient governments in the form of intergovernmental grants. These administrative costs include the cost of the legislative debate over the appropriate structure for each intergovernmental grant program that makes up the entire grants system,[21] the cost of gathering information on the political preferences of individual constituents and fellow legislators, the cost of measuring the various grant bases, the cost of processing grants, and the cost of enforcing restrictions on such grants to assure that recipients are using the grants in ways intended by the legislature. While the determination of these costs is a complex process, they will in general rise with the complexity of the grants structure. We can, therefore, think of these administrative costs as a positive, strictly convex function of the number of grant programs J as well as the number of criteria K_j used to disburse each grant:

$$A = A(J, K_1, K_2, \ldots, K_J). \tag{2-8}$$

Mathematically, then, the grantor's budget constraint can be written as an equation that requires that the sum of all grants G_j^i disbursed to individual recipient jurisdictions plus the amount of administrative costs A must equal the total amount of tax revenues tB collected:

$$\sum_{i=1}^{N} \sum_{j=1}^{J} G_j^i + A(J, K_1, K_2, \ldots, K_J) - sB = 0 \tag{2-9}$$

where B represents the aggregate tax base across all constituents and across all jurisdictions:

$$B = \sum_{i=1}^{N} B^i. \tag{2-10}$$

The general problem for the dominant political coalition, then, is to figure out (subject, of course, to the balanced budget constraint noted in *Equation 2-9*) what set of intergovernmental grant system characteristics and what associated state tax rate (which is needed to fund the intergovernmental grants) will maximize the dominant political coalition's net aggregate political benefit Ψ. More specifically, it entails determining:
- the optimal set of grant programs to have,
- the optimal set of grant bases K_j to employ for each individual grant program,
- the optimal set of grant rates r_j to employ for each individual grant program, and
- the optimal state tax rate s.

---

[21] Robert Gordon (1975) emphasizes these costs in his study of the determinants of inflation.

Although these choices must be made in a way that makes sense when taken together, we can think of them as four independent decisions.

The determination of the set of grant programs involves both choosing the number of grant programs, J, and assigning activities to the particular programs, that is, choosing the Γ_j. Assuming that the latter problem is solved for any given number of categories,[22] the choice of the number of individual grant programs can be made by balancing the political benefits and costs associated with increasing the number of grant programs. The addition of one more intergovernmental grant program generates political benefits (noted by the b^i in *Equation 2-7*). However, putting into place an additional intergovernmental grant program requires that additional revenues be raised to cover the additional administrative costs associated with this additional grant program (recall *Equation 2-8*). As a result, the addition of another intergovernmental grant program will require a higher tax rate s and that higher tax rate will result in additional political costs (noted by the c^i in *Equation 2-7*). Hence, the dominant political coalition will find it advantageous to increase the number of individual grant programs only as long as the additional political benefits are not exceeded by the additional political costs. As the number of individual grant programs increases, the political benefit of still another grant program will fall as more and more constituents become satisfied by the set of grant programs already in place. Likewise, as the number of individual grant programs increases, the political cost of still another grant program will rise as constituents become increasingly irritated by the ever higher tax rate needed to fund all the intergovernmental grant programs. Thus, the dominant political coalition will reach a point where the political benefit of adding another individual grant program will be exceeded by the political cost of doing so. It is at that point that it will stop.

The determination of the set of grant bases for each individual grant program involves a similar logic. Choosing the set of grant bases for each individual grant program involves choosing the number of grant bases for each grant program, K_j, as well as deciding what each grant base should be, that is, choosing the $\mathbf{X}_j$. Assuming that the latter problem is solved for any given number of categories,[23] increasing the number of grant bases allows

---

[22] The assignment problem can be thought of as being guided by the desire to minimize the loss of political support which comes from not having the ideal number of grants associated with zero administrative costs. Hettich and Winer (1988) discuss this problem in the context of tax rate brackets in their appendix. In brief, a solution can be found by minimizing the loss-of-support variance within each category.

[23] The assignment problem here takes on a more mechanical flavor. Given a grant program, the problem is one of choosing some minimum set of bases that will allow the state legislature to discriminate among recipient governments in a politically optimal manner.

the dominant political coalition to more finely target the grant to the constituents from whom it wishes to get political support. Thus, an increase in the number of grant bases K_j generates additional political benefits b^i as before. However, the increase in the number of grant bases K_j also increases the additional administrative costs A associated with that grant program. As a result, the addition of another grant base will also require a somewhat higher tax rate s and that higher tax rate will result in additional political costs c^i. Because the political benefit of using still another grant base falls as the total number of grant bases rises, and because the political cost of using still another grant base rises as the total number of grant bases employed rises, the dominant political coalition will increase the number of grant bases employed for any particular grant program only up to the point where the additional political benefits are not exceeded by the additional political costs.

The choice of the optimal set of K grant rates r_j (one for each grant base chosen) is made in a somewhat more subtle manner. On the one hand, one can think of the choice much like the choice of the optimal number of grant programs. An increase in the value of a particular grant rate increases the political benefits b^i that the dominant political coalition receives because some constituents (those associated with higher values of the particular grant rate's associated base) receive a larger grant. However, because this requires a higher tax rate s, the dominant political coalition will find there are limits to the advantage of raising a particular grant rate, and will set the value of the grant rate at that point where the political benefit of increasing the grant rate is just offset by the associated increase in political costs c^i. On the other hand, one can think of the choice of the optimal set of grant rates r_j as an issue of finding the right distribution of grants across recipient jurisdictions. Given a fixed pool of funds available to distribute in the form of intergovernmental grants (that is, given a fixed s), an increase in the value of one grant rate requires that some other grant rate be reduced. Hence, the optimal set of grant rates will be the one for which the political benefit of increasing any particular grant rate by some small amount (and thus increasing the grant for some jurisdictions) is the same regardless of the grant rate chosen. If this political payoff were not the same across all grant rates, then the dominant political coalition could increase its aggregate net political benefit Ψ by raising some grant rate for which the political payoff is relatively high and lowering the grant rate for some grant for which the political payoff is relatively small.

Note also that if stimulating an activity is desired in order to correct for spillover effects, the bases should be correlated with the level of desired stimulation.

Finally, the choice of the tax rate s, and hence the choice of the total amount of money to be distributed through the intergovernmental grants system, is embodied in the obverse of the above conditions. The ideal tax rate for the dominant political coalition is one at which the political cost of raising the rate by some small amount is just equal to the political benefit of distributing some additional small amount of money optimally.

Mathematically, these conditions can be expressed by a set of $K + J + 2$ first-order conditions plus the balanced budget constraint described by *Equation 2-9* that are associated with solving the implied Lagrangian problem:[24]

$$\sum_{i \in \gamma} \frac{\partial b^i}{\partial J} - \lambda \frac{\partial A}{\partial J} = 0 \qquad\qquad (2\text{-}11)$$

$$\sum_{i \in \gamma} \frac{\partial b^i}{\partial K_j} - \lambda \frac{\partial A}{\partial K_j} = 0 \qquad\qquad j = 1, 2, \ldots, J \qquad\qquad (2\text{-}12)$$

$$\sum_{i \in \gamma} \sum_{n=1}^{N} \frac{\partial b^i}{\partial \gamma_j^n} \cdot \frac{\partial \gamma_j^n}{\partial r_{jk}} - \lambda \sum_{n=1}^{N} x_{jk}^i = 0 \qquad \begin{matrix} j = 1, 2, \ldots, J \\ k = 1, 2, \ldots, K_j \end{matrix} \qquad (2\text{-}13)$$

$$\sum_{i \in \gamma} \frac{\partial c^i}{\partial s} - \lambda B = 0. \qquad\qquad (2\text{-}14)$$

The connection between these first-order conditions and the problems of choosing the optimal number of grant programs, the optimal number of grant bases, and the optimal values for the grant rates can be more easily seen by manipulating the above equations.

Consider first the issue of choosing the optimal number J of grant programs. A rewriting of *Equations 2-11* and *2-14* and defining T to be total tax revenue, sB, reveals the conditions associated with the optimal

---

[24] The Lagrangian approach allows one to convert a constrained maximization problem (in this case maximizing the dominant political coalition's aggregate net political benefit function Ψ) in an equivalent unconstrained form. The first-order conditions represent the first derivatives of this unconstrained problem with respect to λ, the Lagrangian multiplier associated with the constraint, and the decision variables.

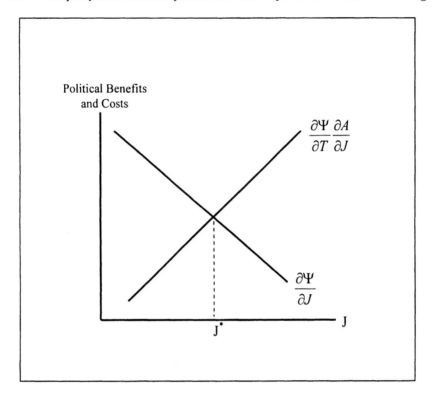

Figure 2-6. Optimal number of intergovernmental grant programs

number of individual grant programs J to be:

$$\frac{\partial \Psi}{\partial J} = \frac{\partial \Psi}{\partial T} \cdot \frac{\partial A}{\partial J} \qquad (2\text{-}15)$$

that is, as was discussed verbally before, the optimal number of grant programs J is one in which the marginal political benefit that the dominant political coalition gets from increasing the number of grant programs is equal to the marginal political cost of raising taxes sufficiently to fund the added administrative costs that result from the increased number of grant programs. See *Figure 2-6* for a visual representation of these conditions.

Likewise, the choice of the optimal number of grant bases can be illuminated by rewriting *Equations 2-12* and *2-14* to reveal the conditions associated with the optimal number K_j of grant bases for each intergovernmental grant program to be:

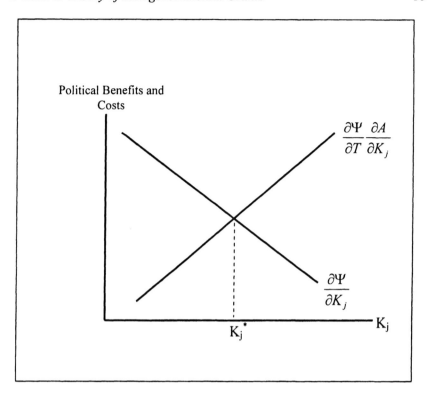

Figure 2-7. Optimal number of bases

$$\frac{\partial \Psi}{\partial K_j} = \frac{\partial \Psi}{\partial T} \cdot \frac{\partial A}{\partial K_j} \qquad\qquad (2\text{-}16)$$

that is, the optimal number of grant bases K_j for any individual grant program is one in which the marginal political benefit that the dominant political coalition gets from increasing the number of grant bases for any individual grant program is equal to the marginal political cost of raising taxes sufficiently to fund the additional administrative costs that result from the increased number of grant bases. *Figure 2-7* provides a visual representation of these conditions.

Finally, the choice of the optimal values for the grant rates can be illuminated by manipulating *Equations 2-13* and *2-14.* Given a fixed number J of intergovernmental grant programs and a fixed number K of grant bases, the marginal political benefit to the dominant political coalition of increasing grant spending by one dollar through an increase in the rate r_{jk} should be equated across all bases and all programs.

$$\frac{\sum_{i \in \gamma} \sum_{n=1}^{N} \frac{\partial b^i}{\partial \gamma_j^n} \cdot \frac{\partial \gamma_j^n}{\partial r_{jk}}}{\sum_{n=1}^{N} x_{jk}^i} = \frac{\sum_{i \in \gamma} \sum_{n=1}^{N} \frac{\partial b^i}{\partial \gamma_l^n} \cdot \frac{\partial \gamma_l^n}{\partial r_{lm}}}{\sum_{n=1}^{N} x_{lm}^i} \qquad for\ all\ i,j,l,m. \qquad (2\text{-}17)$$

Moreover, such marginal benefits should also be equated to the marginal political cost of raising a dollar through taxes.

$$\frac{\sum_{i \in \gamma} \sum_{n=1}^{N} \frac{\partial b^i}{\partial \gamma_j^n} \cdot \frac{\partial \gamma_j^n}{\partial r_{jk}}}{\sum_{n=1}^{N} x_{jk}^i} = \frac{\sum_{i \in \gamma} \frac{\partial c^i}{\partial s}}{B} \qquad k = 1,2,...,K_j. \qquad (2\text{-}18)$$

Note that the double sum in *Equation 2-13* reflects the existence of spillover effects. An increase in r_{jk} has two effects on members of the dominant coalition – directly through its effect on the grants going to the member's district and indirectly through spillover effects due to grants going to other districts. In the absence of spillovers, *Equation 2-13* would reduce to:

$$\sum_{i \in \gamma} \frac{\partial b^i}{\partial \gamma_j^i} \cdot \frac{\partial \gamma_j^i}{\partial r_{jk}} - \lambda \sum_{n=1}^{N} x_{jk}^i = 0 \qquad \begin{matrix} j = 1,2,...,J \\ k = 1,2,...,K_j \end{matrix} \qquad (2\text{-}19)$$

The first sum in *Equation 2-19* is less than the first sum in *Equation 2-13*. Thus, there will be less marginal benefit to raising any r_{jk} if there are no spillovers. Given *Equation 2-14*, this suggests that, in the absence of spillovers, grant rates will generally be lower as will the overall level of grant funding where there are no spillovers.

This, then, characterizes the optimal system of intergovernmental grant programs for the dominant political coalition. As can be seen, the optimal intergovernmental grant system is rather complex. However, that complexity is the result of two simple forces – a desire for more complexity and a desire for less complexity. The diversity of economic and political circumstances across districts and across constituents argues for greater complexity so that as much net political benefit can be extracted from constituencies as possible. And indeed, in the absence of administrative costs, the conditions associated with the optimal number of individual grant programs and the optimal number of grant bases for each individual grant program (*Equations 2-11* and *2-12*) reveal that the complexity of the intergovernmental grants system would only be limited by the condition that complexity not be pushed to the point where marginal political support becomes negative. It is only the presence of administrative costs that keeps the system of intergovernmental grant programs from being even more complex than it is. This has the interesting implication that to the degree technology improves and to the degree that such improvements result in a reduction in the costs associated with running and monitoring intergovernmental grant programs, we should expect to see an increase in both the number of intergovernmental grant programs and an increase in the complexity of each of those programs.

2. THE ROLE OF SPILLOVERS, FISCAL ILLUSION, AND POLITICAL ASYMMETRIES

Intergovernmental grants come in a variety of forms. Interestingly, however, the vast majority of such programs are categorical, that is, their use is prescribed by the donor government. At the state level, the bulk of intergovernmental grants are clearly categorical as witnessed, for example, by the dominance of state grants for local public education. At the Federal level, evidence is more difficult to come by since Congress shut down the Advisory Commission on Intergovernmental Relations (ACIR) in the mid-1990s. However, as *Table 2-1* reveals, data generated in 1994 by the ACIR reveals that even at the Federal level categorical grants have dominated total grant activity for the past several decades, regardless of whether one measures such dominance in terms of the number of programs or the number of dollars distributed. Indeed, though there was a small but seemingly permanent fall in percentage of categorical grant programs that began in the early 1980s, the percentage of dollars (as well as absolute number of dollars) distributed through categorical grants has steadily risen since the mid-1980s. Thus, it would appear that restricted grant giving is virtually ubiquitous in the world of intergovernmental grants. From the model developed in the previous section, it is clear that these restrictions must exist because they allow the dominant political coalition in the donor government's legislature to maximize political support. Yet what makes such restrictions beneficial to the dominant political coalition?

Three possible explanations suggest themselves – spillovers, fiscal illusion, and political asymmetry. Spillovers deal with the perception of benefits and costs across recipient jurisdiction lines and occur when the

Table 2-1. Federal Government Grant Programs (2002 dollars), 1975 to 1993

	1975	1978	1981	1984	1987	1989	1991	1993
Number	427	497	539	404	435	492	557	593
- % categorical	98.8%	99.0%	99.1%	97.0%	97.0%	97.2%	97.5%	97.5%
Amount (billions)	137.7	178.8	168.0	151.2	154.6	162.1	187.6	242.9
- % categorical	76.7%	73.0%	82.2%	79.7%	86.0%	87.6%	87.8%	88.3%

Note: Real values calculated from nominal values using a GDP chain-type price deflator. 1993 dollar values are estimates.

Sources: US Department of Commerce, Bureau of Economic Analysis (2003), Table 7.1; and Advisory Commission on Intergovernmental Relations (1994), Tables 1 and 2.

activity levels of one recipient government affect the constituents of another recipient government. Special interest groups, for example, often come into existence because of the existence of spillover effects and the desire by those who perceive those spillovers to coordinate their advocacy across local jurisdictions. Thus, for example, environmentalists from throughout the country derive benefits from knowing that the Alaska wilderness is protected, regardless of whether they ever visit that state.

Fiscal illusion, by contrast, deals with the *mis*perception of benefits and costs and can be defined as the overestimation of benefits received from intergovernmental grants by constituents in the recipient jurisdiction or the underestimation of the burden of donor-government taxes paid by those same constituents.[25]

Finally, political asymmetry deals not with an imbalance in perceptions but an imbalance in political influence. Essentially, political asymmetry exists if those who dominate lower levels of government have preferences that are different from those who dominate the higher-level government, which in the context of intergovernmental grants means that the preferences of those who make the decisions for the recipient governments are different from the legislators who control the donor government. For the donor-government, in particular, the political preferences of each representative are directly connected to the political support ψ^i that each representative receives. Hence, political asymmetry implies that the recipient government has a ψ^i function that is different from that defined for the donor government representative. Political asymmetry might occur if, for example, most constituents only participate in elections to choose representatives in the donor government's legislature, leaving local decisions to a small minority of the set of total voters. As a result, the local government would

---

[25] There is no single definition of fiscal illusion. See Fisher (1982), Logan (1986), and Mueller (1989) for critiques of the various characterizations. For examples of empirical studies which investigate the existence of fiscal illusion, see Winer (1983) and Grossman (1990).

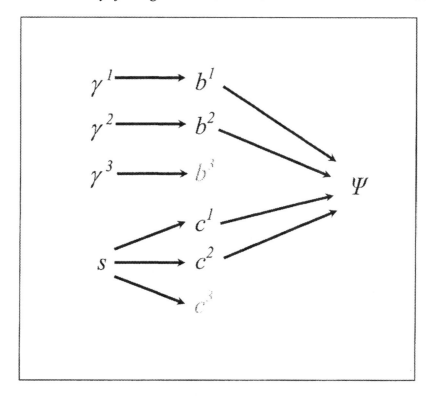

Figure 2-8. Political support for the dominant political coalition without spillovers

be dominated by an essentially different population than that which elects the donor-government representative.

When there are no spillovers, intergovernmental grants to jurisdictions whose representatives are not members of the dominant political coalition (see jurisdiction 3 in *Figure 2-8*) do not contribute to the dominant political coalition's net aggregate political support Ψ. As a result, there is no incentive for the dominant political coalition to provide grants to these non-member jurisdictions. However, when spillovers are present (contrast *Figure 2-5* to *Figure 2-8*), the dominant political coalition receives political benefits from providing intergovernmental grants to every jurisdiction.

When there is no fiscal illusion or political asymmetry, there is no particular advantage in having categorical grants. Categorical grants are valuable because they allow the donor government to target the benefits associated with an intergovernmental grant program to a particular set of constituents who would get benefits from the targeted activity. However, as *Figure 2-9* illustrates, without fiscal illusion or political asymmetry, a single, unconstrained grant will result in the same output effects at the recipient

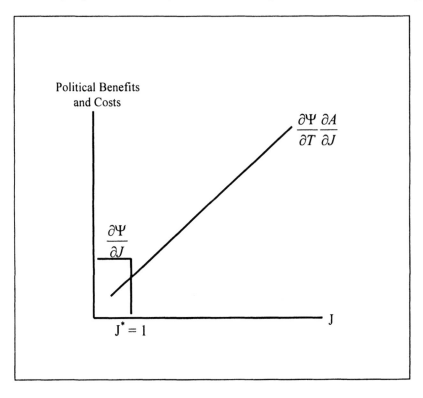

Figure 2-9. Optimal number of intergovernmental grant programs with no fiscal illusion or political asymmetry

level (that is, changes in the levels of γ_j^i) as an optimal categorical grants structure of the same total value, that is, $\partial\Psi/\partial J$ equals zero for J greater than 1 (see *Equation 2-15*).   Hence, because added grants-structure complexity increases administrative costs (that is, $\partial A/\partial J > 0$) and thereby reduces the pool of funds available, the donor government will prefer a single, unrestricted grant, that is, a system of intergovernmental grants composed of one grant program (that is, $J = 1$) and the set of target activities, Γ, equal to the set of all activities.

Thus, in the absence of spillovers, fiscal illusion, and political asymmetry, we would expect to see a very simple intergovernmental grants system in which a single, general revenue-sharing grant would be provided only to jurisdictions whose representatives belong to the dominant political coalition.   In fact, we can observe still further that even this system of a single intergovernmental grant will only exist if administrative costs A are less than the tax revenues $B^{-\gamma}$ taken from non-member districts, that is, not even a single intergovernmental grant will exist in the absence of spillovers, fiscal illusion, and political asymmetry if:

$$A > B^{\neg \gamma} \qquad (2\text{-}20)$$

where:

$$B^{\neg \gamma} = \sum_{i \notin \gamma} B^i \qquad (2\text{-}21)$$

Thus, for a world with no spillovers, fiscal illusion, and political asymmetry, intergovernmental grants serve simply as a mechanism for redistributing resources from jurisdictions that are not members of the dominant political coalition and to jurisdictions that are members of the dominant political coalition. As the number of jurisdictions in the dominant coalition increases, the likelihood that administrative costs will be less than the tax revenue taken from non-member districts will decrease, and certainly if the legislature is dominated by a coalition of the whole and there are no spillovers, fiscal illusion, and political asymmetries, the legislature would choose to eliminate the intergovernmental grants structure.

But of course, spillovers, fiscal illusion, and political asymmetry do exist, and these forces have effects on the optimal intergovernmental grants structure.

With spillovers, constituents in each jurisdiction whose representative is a member of the dominant political coalition receives benefits from the activities of other jurisdictions including those that are not members of the dominant political coalition. As a result, the general revenue sharing grant structure described above will no longer be optimal for the donor government's dominant political coalition. As a result, the structure of the intergovernmental grants system will need to be modified in two ways. First, because spillovers will typically include both jurisdictions that are members of the dominant political coalition and jurisdictions that are not, the optimal structure of an intergovernmental grants system will now include grants to non-member districts.[26] Second, although there is no political asymmetry, local decisions will not take into account the benefits that spillover to other districts. (Thus, for example, localities in Alaska deciding

---

[26] This is essentially a multi-person prisoners' dilemma game in which the categorical grants allow the players to coordinate their actions. Take, for example, a three-person prisoners dilemma in which two of the prisoners are friends and the third a stranger. If the two friends wish to form a conspiracy to beat the game, it may pay for them to include the stranger out of self interest.

on how much to protect the Alaska wilderness will not take into account the desires of environmentalists elsewhere in the nation who get benefits from the protection of that wilderness.) Hence there is a need for categorical grants to provide the proper stimulation of those local activities that result in spillovers. Thus, the expected intergovernmental grants structure will be a mixture of intergovernmental grants designed to compensate for spillovers and intergovernmental grants designed to redistribute wealth from jurisdictions that are not members of the dominant political coalition and toward jurisdictions that are members of that political coalition. If the donor-government's legislature is dominated by a coalition of the whole, the intergovernmental grants designed to compensate for spillovers will continue to exist. However, as before, the intergovernmental grants designed to redistribute wealth will not.

Much the same will occur when fiscal illusion is present. If constituents underestimate the cost of the taxes that they pay to the higher-level, donor government, or overestimate the benefits that they receive as a result of intergovernmental grants, the effect is likely to be limited to an increase in size of the system of intergovernmental grant programs, that is, taxes paid to the donor government will be higher than they would be otherwise and the total amount of money distributed through intergovernmental grants programs will be larger. However, because there are no spillover effects or political asymmetry, there would be no other change in the single, general-revenue sharing nature of the intergovernmental grants structure. However, it is possible that this fiscal illusion is not general but varies among government activities. In that case, a single, general revenue sharing grants structure will no longer be optimal. Consider, for example, a case in which constituents accurately perceive the benefits they get from fire protection services but overestimate the benefits associated with police services. In that case, the dominant political coalition can increase its net aggregate political benefits Ψ by increasing the funding of police services. Hence, the donor government can benefit by creating a categorical grant for police services. As with spillovers, a donor government whose dominant political coalition is a coalition of the whole will continue to enact intergovernmental grants that come about as a result of fiscal illusion. If that illusion is general, the result will be a general-revenue sharing structure funded at a higher level than would be the case if there were no fiscal illusion. If that fiscal illusion differs from activity to activity, the dominant political coalition, even if composed of a coalition of the whole, will find it advantageous to create a system of categorical intergovernmental grants that increase funding for those activities whose benefits are overestimated.

Finally, the presence of political asymmetry provides another rationale for the existence of categorical intergovernmental grants. The argument is much the same as for the case of differential fiscal illusion. If there is political asymmetry, the group that dominates the lower-level, recipient government's decision-making process will be different from the group that provides support to the representative in the higher-level, donor government. The latter group will not be satisfied with the decisions of their lower-level recipient government and will therefore provide political support for their representative in the higher-level donor government to create an intergovernmental grants structure that changes the mix of recipient-government activities to something more to their liking. But such differential manipulation requires the use of categorical grants so that the lower-level, recipient governments have less discretion. This structure will continue to exist if the donor government's legislature is dominated by a coalition of the whole.[27]

3.   CONCLUSIONS

This chapter has provided a conceptual framework for understanding what motivates higher-level, donor governments to provide intergovernmental grants and why intergovernmental grants systems take the forms that they do. Key to this understanding is:

- an ability to reduce individual grant program structures to a simple structure of rates, bases, and purposes;
- the underlying assumption that individual grant programs must not be analyzed separately but rather as components of a comprehensive, overall system of grant programs;
- that the donor government's choice of a structure for its system of intergovernmental grant programs is made by a group of individual legislators who belong to a dominant political coalition, that the preferences of these individual legislators are based on a desire for reelection, and that (as a result) the preferences of those who make decisions for the donor government are distinct from the preferences of the individuals who reside in the various recipient jurisdictions, and

---

[27] Daniel Schwallie's (1987, 1989a, 1989b) argument that higher-level, donor governments tend to discount the value of lower-level recipient-government expenditures not funded out of intergovernmental grants provided by the donor government is similar to the notion of political asymmetry developed here. For Schwallie, intergovernmental grants exist whenever the donor government is dissatisfied with either the amount or the mix of recipient-government expenditures. Though not concerned with the form of these grants, his parametric treatment allows him to quantify the degree of discounting and its effect on public sector size.

- a recognition that administrative costs are an important factor in explaining why we do not see even more complicated systems of intergovernmental grants programs.

The traditional motivation/justification for the existence of intergovernmental grants lies in correcting for spillovers and inequities (Fisher (1996)). In contrast, more recent work in the field of public choice has generally emphasized the importance of political self-interest and rent seeking, that is, the pursuit of private benefits not associated with an increase in benefits for society as a whole. The model in this chapter shows how those two rather different traditions can be reconciled. Spillovers, which often include equity concerns, are felt by constituents in the various recipient jurisdictions. Politicians as self-serving agents place no intrinsic value on spillovers per se. However, to the extent that their constituents provide political support to their higher-level donor government representatives and to the extent that these representatives have an effect on decisions made by the donor government's legislature, spillovers will be embodied in the structure of the donor government's system of intergovernmental grant programs. A legislature dominated by a particular political coalition will incorporate spillover effects only to the extent that such spillovers affect the constituents residing in jurisdictions that belong to that dominant political coalition. The preferences of constituents represented by members of the legislature who are not members of the dominant political coalition are not taken into account. Only if the legislature is dominated by a coalition of the whole will all constituent preferences be taken into account. Categorical grants exist in order to increase the levels of lower-level recipient-government activities to levels that they otherwise would not attain under more general, unrestricted intergovernmental grants. Political support for bringing about this distortion may be due to the presence of spillovers, fiscal illusion, and/or political asymmetry.

Chapter 3

THEORY OF PUBLIC EDUCATION FUNDING WITH COURT INTERVENTION

We must never forget that the only real source of power that we as judges can tap is the respect of the people.
— Thurgood Marshall in a speech before the Second Judicial Conference, May 8, 1981[28]

There is an extensive economics literature on the funding of public education. Unfortunately, like the more general literature on intergovernmental grants, this literature for the most part has focused on the reaction of local school districts to alternative public education funding mechanisms and does not focus on the funding decisions made by donor state legislatures. Clearly, however, such a focus is necessary if we are to understand the dynamics of the public education funding process and begin making predictions about its likely course in the future. For almost four decades, state legislative funding of local school districts in the United States has been surrounded by controversy involving the courts. In all but five states, courts have been asked to examine the constitutionality of state funding plans.[29] Though not unconstitutional under Federal law, state supreme courts have ruled that their state's method of funding public education is unconstitutional under state law. State legislatures have often responded only after considerable lag and further legal wrangling, and, while results vary, have generally ended up redesigning their public education grant structures so that total funding for such public education increases. The effect of such changes on reducing inequality in per-pupil spending or achieving some minimum level of per-pupil expenditure across rich and poor school districts is less clear. While some analysts (Wyckoff (1991), Evans, Murray, and Schwab (1997), Murray, Evans, and Schwab (1998), DeBoer et al. (2000), Moser and Rubenstein (2002)) have argued that such changes have had significant effects, others are more pessimistic that significant

---

[28] Williams (2004).

[29] For details concerning the legal history of the controversy over state funding of public schools, see *Chapter 5*.

reductions in spending disparities or improvements in minimum expenditure levels can ever be achieved through court-mandated changes in grant structure. Ronald Fisher (1996, pages 512-3) and Richard Murnane (1985), for example, argue that most increases in educational grants do not go to increasing expenditures and therefore are unlikely to result in significant reductions in spending disparities. Unfortunately, while these conclusions are based on the implicit assumption that reductions in spending disparities or increases in minimum expenditure levels can only be achieved by increasing total spending on education and that such increases in spending are politically infeasible, we have no theory of state legislative response to such court orders to support or refute such conclusions.

While there is some debate about the connection between the political process (and especially elections at the state and federal level) and the choices made with regard to public education funding and policy (Fusarelli (2002), Opfer (2002)), the dominant view finds the connection to be a significant one (Wirt and Kirst (1997), Meier (2002)). Using the model of intergovernmental grants developed in *Chapter 2* as a foundation, this chapter provides a theoretical model of the decision making process used by state legislatures to fund public education, and how that process is affected by judicial interventions intended to remedy inequities in public education funding. While issues of equity and adequacy are for the most part concerned with the *distribution* of resources among school districts, policies that effect the distribution of resources also often have implications for the overall *level* of support for public education provided by state legislatures. As a result, the theoretical model in this chapter also includes an examination of the conditions under which a state legislature will level up or level down per-pupil expenditures in response to pressures to equalize per-pupil school district expenditures or provide an adequate education for all students.

In developing the model, two issues need to be confronted. First, the decision making process of both the local school districts and the state legislature needs to be characterized. In the model below, local school districts are assumed to make their decisions by plebiscite, while the state legislature is assumed to makes its decisions through a more complex legislative process in which individual legislators seek to maximize political support from constituents.[30] Second, in recognition of the tensions that often

---

[30] An alternative approach, not employed in this book, would be to model the decision-making process as a bureaucratic one based on the seminal work by William Niskanen (1971). While it is clear that school systems have many of the characteristics of bureaucracies, whether the funding decisions are more in keeping with the local-plebiscite/state-legislature model adopted here or the inefficient bureaucracy that Steven Barnett (1994) and Allen Odden and William Clune (1995) argue for is an open question.

exist between a state legislature and its courts, the limits to a state legislature's willingness to obey court orders to reduce spending differences or impose adequacy standards across local school districts need to be characterized. In the absence of limitations on the willingness of a legislature to comply with a court order, the response of the state legislature to a court-mandated change in grant structure will often depend on whether the legislature is dominated by high-spending (usually property-rich) school districts or by low-spending (usually property-poor) school districts. For example, a state legislature that is dominated by high-spending school districts will reduce spending disparities by increasing aggregate spending on education, while a state legislature dominated by low-spending districts will reduce spending disparities by lowering aggregate spending on public education. However, when there are limits on the ability or the willingness of the state legislature to obey court orders, the process becomes more complicated, and, in the end, the legislature may simply refuse to fully comply with the court's order.

The value of the theoretical model presented in this chapter is that it provides a mechanism for disentangling the complicated relationship between state legislatures and the courts, allows us to assess the relative value of using the courts as a mechanism for effecting changes in the funding of public education, and gives us an ability to anticipate the future of public education funding. The future of public education funding is the subject of *Chapter 6*. However, it can be observed here that there are inherent limitations to pursuing governmental policy through third parties,[31] and the courts, in particular, are faced with significant constraints on their ability to affect changes in state legislative funding behavior despite the desire to follow the law. Thus, for a court (or for public education advocates who would use the courts) that is intent on reducing spending disparities or instituting minimum expenditure standards in public education, a number of fundamental issues concerning the appropriate scope of action for that court would need to be confronted. If the state is dominated by higher-spending districts, the required increase in aggregate spending may be so large that, as

---

However, the model in this chapter is robust to the introduction of such bureaucratic forces as long as they exist within the context of a local-plebiscite/state-legislature structure. Thus, the presence of a bureaucracy at the local or the state level can be thought of as simply shifting the political center of gravity toward the preferences of the bureaucracy. For an example of an analysis of the interactions between legislatures and bureaucracies in a non-education setting that highlights the influence legislatures have on the behavior of bureaucracies, see Leyden and Link (1993).

[31] Donald Kettl (1988) provides an overview and a number of case studies that document the limitations associated with pursuing governmental policies through third parties.

Fisher and Murnane have suggested, the state legislature may refuse to fully comply with the court's order. Hence, the court will have to choose whether to mandate specific expenditure levels, allow greater variation in local school district spending, or take a more radical approach intent on changing the entire structure by which education is provided. For states dominated by lower-spending districts, the overall fiscal burden will not be an issue. However, the court will still have to address issues of redistribution and maintenance of education quality. In either case, the process is likely to require more hands on involvement than might be foreseen at the outset, and perhaps more than the courts would prefer to have.

The theoretical model is presented in three parts. In the first part, a model of the state funding process in the absence of court intervention is developed. Next comes an examination of how that funding process is affected when a court seeks to eliminate disparities in per-pupil spending across local school districts and how that outcome is affected by a legislature's inability or unwillingness to accede to the court's wishes. Finally, the chapter concludes with an examination of how the funding process is affected by a court that seeks to increase minimum per-pupil spending levels and the degree to which legislative inability or unwillingness affects that outcome.

1.   STATE FUNDING OF PUBLIC EDUCATION IN THE ABSENCE OF COURT INTERVENTION

State funding of public education takes place within a two-tiered federal governmental structure in which the state government's legislature chooses a particular educational grant structure and provides grants based on that grant structure to local school districts, and local school districts receive those grants and choose the level of educational expenditures for their district. In the model below, the state legislature is assumed to correctly anticipate the effect of its choice of educational grant structure and level of funding on the spending decisions of its local school districts. Of course, it is always possible that a state legislature will make mistakes in anticipating the effects of its educational funding structure on the spending decisions of its local school districts.   However, experience suggests that state legislatures through informal networking and the floating of trial balloons are generally adept at learning how local school districts will react before the educational funding structure is formally adopted.[32]

---

[32] The assumption that the state legislature makes its decisions first but correctly anticipates the reaction of its local school districts that make their decisions afterward is a type of

1.1   Local School-District Behavior

In the United States, the type of government used to provide education at the local level ranges from the town-meeting form of government common in the New England states to more representative forms such as school boards chosen in non-partisan elections.[33] While not perfect, these forms of local decision-making come closer to a plebiscite form of government than other parts of the US political system.   Assume, therefore, that the expenditure and taxation decisions of local school districts are made by simple majority rule.[34]

Each local school district receives revenues from a locally chosen property tax and a grant from the state government's legislature. Assuming that school districts must balance their budgets, district *i*'s budget constraint will be:

$$\gamma^i = t^i \overline{V}^i + G^i \tag{3-1}$$

where γ^i is district *i*'s per-pupil expenditures on public education,[35] t^i is district *i*'s property-tax rate, $\overline{V}^i$ is district *i*'s per-pupil property value, and G^i is district *i*'s per-pupil grant from the state.

Educational grant structures vary considerably from state to state.[36] Despite that complexity, however, we can use the approach developed in *Chapter 2* to represent the typical educational grant as a combination of a

---

Nash equilibrium known as a Stackelberg equilibrium, and is commonly assumed when there is a large number of decisions makers who wait on a single decision maker before making their decisions.   See Rasmussen (1989; pp. 79-82) for a more formal characterization of this notion.

[33] Kenneth Meier (2002) provides a more detailed description of the give-and-take in the political process that suggests that school boards are susceptible to influence by local political forces.

[34] The assumption of simple majority rule results in decisions that can be identified with the the median set of individual voter preferences. For arguments for and against the use of a median-voter specification, see, for example, Fort (1988), Holcombe (1989), and Romer and Rosenthal (1979). From the perspective of this chapter and the conclusions that are drawn, the median-voter specification is not critical, though it does make exposition of the local school district's decision making process easier. What is important is that there is a large number of school districts (so that local school districts either individually or in groups cannot manipulate the state's decision-making process) and that local decision making is sufficiently consistent to allow the state legislature to correctly anticipate the decisions that are made.

[35] The use of per-pupil expenditures as a measure of government consumption is common in and out of economics. See, for example, Romer and Rosenthal (1978) and Rubinfeld (1979).

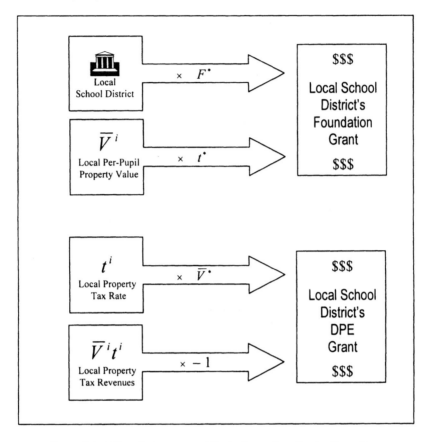

Figure 3-1. A Foundation versus a District Power Equalization Grant Structure

particular set of grant bases **X** used to allocate the grant (for example, a district's average income or property wealth) and a particular set of grant rates **r** that translate those grant bases into a level of funding. Thus, a typical education grant can be represented as:

$$G^i = \mathbf{r}'\mathbf{x}^i \qquad\qquad (3\text{-}2)$$

where **r** is a $K \times 1$ vector of grant rates and $\mathbf{x}^i$ is a $K \times 1$ vector representing the values of the $K \times 1$ set of grant bases **X** for district i. Common forms of educational grant structures include a foundation grant:

---

[36] Vincent Munley (1990) provides a valuable and comprehensive description of the variety of state educational grants and how they affect school-district decision making.

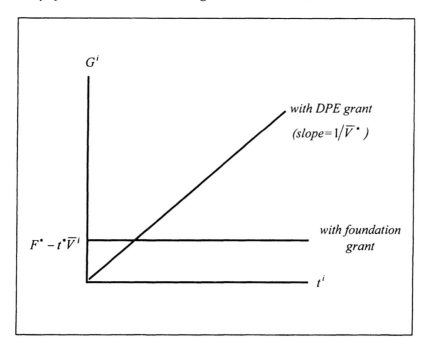

Figure 3-2. Local Ability to Control Grants with a Foundation versus a Power Equalization Grant Structure

$$G^i = F^* - t^* \overline{V}^i \qquad (3\text{-}3)$$

where the foundation level of per-pupil expenditures F^* and the tax rate t^* are chosen by the state, and a district power equalization (DPE) grant:[37]

$$G^i = (\overline{V}^* - \overline{V}^i)t^i \qquad (3\text{-}4)$$

where the guaranteed per-pupil tax base $\overline{V}^*$ is chosen by the state. As *Figure 3-1* illustrates, the grant bases **X** (and their associated rates **r**) for the foundation grant structure are the local school district itself (which takes trivially the value of 1 and which has the associated grant rate of F^*) and the per-pupil property value $\overline{V}^i$ of the local school district (with its associated grant rate of t^*). For the district power equalization grant structure, the grant bases **X** (and their associated rates **r**) are the local

---

[37] A district power equalization grant structure also goes by the name of a guaranteed tax base (GTB) grant structure.

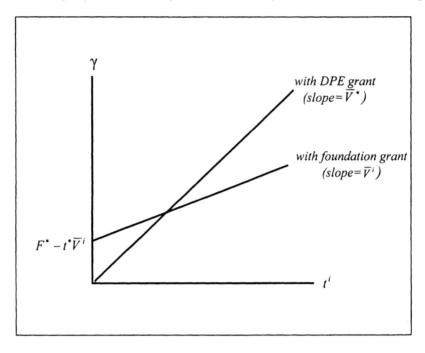

Figure 3-3. Local School District Per-Pupil Expenditures with a Foundation versus a District Power Equalization Grant Structure

school district's property tax rate t^i (which has the associated grant rate $\overline{V}^*$) and the local school district's per-pupil property tax revenue $\overline{V}^i t^i$ (which has the associated grant rate of -1).

While local school districts with greater per-pupil property wealth $\overline{V}^i$ receive a lower grant G^i that do poorer school districts under both a foundation and a district power equalization grant structure, they do not have control over local property wealth and hence cannot exploit that relationship. What local school districts do have control over is the local property tax rate, and, as *Figure 3-2* reveals, the foundation grant structure and the district power equalization grant structure are quite different in that respect. With the foundation grant structure, local school districts have no ability to manipulate the grant they receive though they are at least guaranteed a grant regardless of how much they tax themselves. However, with a district power equalization grant structure, local school districts have a significant ability to affect the amount of grant money that they receive from the state though they also run the risk, if they choose to impose a local property tax that is sufficiently low, of receiving grants that are below the level provided by a foundation grant structure.

As a result of these differences in the two types of educational grant structures, local school districts that prefer relatively low local tax rates will, as *Figure 3-3* illustrates, be able to provide a higher level of expenditures γ^i with a foundation grant structure and therefore will prefer it over a district power equalization grant structure. Likewise, local school districts that are willing to set their local property tax rate at a relatively high level will be able to provide a higher level of expenditures with a district power equalization grant structure and therefore will prefer it over a foundation grant structure.

Given the plebiscite form of government, there exists for each local school district a median voter whose ideal level of per-pupil expenditures γ^i will be the level chosen by the local school district. Assume that the median voter for school district i receives utility both from per-pupil educational expenditures γ^i in the median voter's local school district and from the consumption of other goods C^i that are purchased with income that is not provided to the state or the local school district in the form of taxes, and that both γ^i and C^i are considered normal by the median voter.[38] If we allow for the possibility that the median voter in school district i may also receive utility from the per-pupil educational expenditures in other districts (thus reflecting spillover effects),[39] this median voter's preferences can be represented mathematically by the (strictly quasi-concave) utility function:

$$U^i = U(C^i, \gamma) \tag{3-5}$$

where γ is the vector of per-pupil expenditures across all local school districts.

Let the median voter also be characterized by an exogenous level of income I^i and assessed property value H^i.[40] Assuming that income is taxed by the state at the flat rate s, the ith school district's median voter will have a budget constraint in which income must be fully divided between

---

[38] A normal good is one for which higher income results in a desire for a higher quantity of the good.

[39] Most economists believe that education provides positive spillovers, though the nature of those spillovers and their sizes are often disputed. See Clive Belfield's (2000) chapter on the aggregate effects of education for an overview of the issue. The existence and size of such spillovers may have important implications for education funding policy. See, for example, Robert Wassmer and Ronald Fisher's (2002) study of the use of fees in public education.

[40] The assumption that income and housing are exogenous is restrictive. In general, both are functions of governmental expenditures and tax rates. See Wildasin (1989) for a fuller discussion.

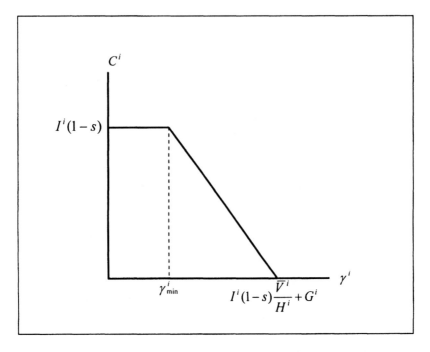

Figure 3-4. The Median Voter's Budget Constraint

private consumption C^i, state income taxes sI^i, and local property taxes t^iH^i:

$$I^i = C^i + sI^i + t^iH^i. \tag{3-6}$$

When combined with the local school district's budget constraint (*Equations 3-1* and *3-2*), this personal budget constraint implicitly defines a budget constraint for the median voter that describes the combinations of private consumption C^i and local per-pupil educational spending γ^i from which the median voter can choose. As *Figure 3-4* illustrates, the maximum amount of private consumption C^i that is possible will be equal to the amount of income left after deducting state income taxes and assuming that the local property tax is zero.   Whether local per-pupil educational expenditures are zero in that situation, however, depends on the form of the state's educational grant structure. If, as represented in *Figure 3-4*, the local school district receives an educational grant from the state even if it does not impose a local property tax (as would be the case for the foundation grant structure described in *Equation 3-3*), then local per-pupil educational expenditures would be equal to some minimum level γ^i_{min} (which, for

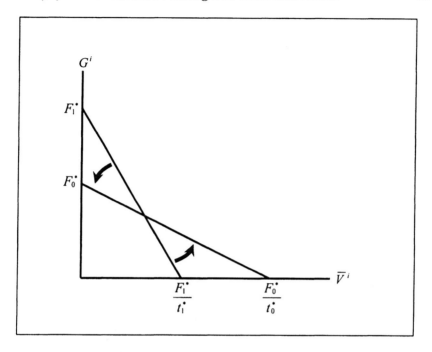

Figure 3-5. The State's Ability to Manipulate Grants to Local School Districts

example, would equal F^* if the foundation grant described in *Equation 3-3* were in place). Of course, if the state's educational grant structure does not provide a grant for local school districts that do not impose local property taxes (as is the case for the district power equalization program described in *Equation 3-4*), then the minimum level γ^i_{min} would equal zero. Median voters who wish to have a greater level of per-pupil educational expenditures than the minimum γ^i_{min} will have to impose a local property tax that will result, as shown in *Figure 3-4*, in greater per-pupil educational expenditures and lower private consumption C^i. The maximum local property tax rate would be that rate which results in private consumption C^i being zero, at which point, local per-pupil educational expenditures would be $I^i(1-s)\overline{V}^i / H^i + G^i$.

The median voter, of course, seeks to maximize utility (*Equation 3-5*) subject to the constraints embodied in *Equations 3-1, 3-2,* and *3-6*. Intuitively, the unique solution to that problem requires that the level of local per-pupil educational expenditures γ^i be increased so long as the increase in utility to the median voter as a result of that increase is no less than the reduction in utility (due to reduced private consumption C^i) associated with the higher local property taxes needed to fund the increase in γ^i.

Mathematically, this condition can be expressed by the requirement that the median voter's choice obey the first-order condition:

$$\frac{\partial U}{\partial C^i} \cdot \frac{H^i}{\overline{V}^i} \cdot \left(\frac{\partial G^i}{\partial \gamma^i} - 1 \right) + \frac{\partial U}{\partial \gamma^i} = 0 . \qquad (3\text{-}7)$$

Given this decision-making process and the fact that the state legislature is aware of how it is conducted, the state legislature can manipulate local per-student expenditures through the choice of particular educational grant structures and the adjustment of the parameters of those structures. Thus, for example, if the state legislature chooses to employ the foundation grant structure defined in *Equation 3-3*, it can alter the size of the per-pupil grant G^i going to local school districts through the adjustment of the foundation grant parameters F^* and t^*. Increases in F^* will result in an equal increase in the grant given to all local school districts, but increases in t^*, while reducing all local school district grants, will hurt property-rich school districts more than property-poor districts. Hence, as is illustrated in *Figure 3-5*, it is possible for the state legislature to reduce the per-pupil grant for local school districts with relatively high property wealth and increase the per-pupil grant for local school districts with relatively low property wealth by increasing F^* from F_0^* to F_1^* and increasing t^* by a proportionately greater amount from t_0^* to t_1^* such that $F_1^* / F_0^* > t_1^* / t_0^*$. There are, however, limits to the use of such manipulations to effect changes in local per-pupil educational expenditure levels. As Fisher (1996; pp. 87-89) notes, empirical measures of income and price elasticities (which implicitly measure the responsiveness of local per-pupil expenditure levels to changes in these parameters) suggest that local per-pupil expenditures tend to be rather unresponsive to such changes. To the extent that this is true, there may be limits to the ability to induce large changes in local school district spending patterns through the manipulation of grant structure parameters.

1.2   State Choice of Grant Structure

As noted more fully in the previous chapter, state decision making, while typically more complex than decision making at the local school district level, can be usefully modeled as being made by a unicameral legislature composed of M members, each of which represents a single local school district and seeks to maximize the probability of reelection through the provision of intergovernmental grants, the taxation of some statewide tax base, and the requirement that it balance its budget.[41] For the purposes of the model in this chapter, all intergovernmental grants are assumed to be for local public education and the statewide tax base is assumed to be personal income which is exogenous and taxed at a single uniform rate s.

The probability of reelection can be represented by a positive function of the political support ψ^i provided by the representative's constituents with political support coming in a variety of forms including active campaigning, cash contributions, and favorable voting. The level of political support for each representative in the legislature is determined by the conflicting political repercussions associated with providing educational grants to local school districts and imposing a state income tax to fund the educational grant program. As already discussed, educational grants alter the level of per-pupil educational spending at the local level. Any change in the state education grant to local school districts that results in greater spending at the local level will increase the utilities of individual constituents and hence the willingness of these individuals (all other things constant) to provide greater political support. However, individuals are also made worse off by the state income tax that they pay because it reduces the amount of disposable income available to engage in private consumption C^i and to support local public education through the local property tax. As a result, individuals will (all other things constant) provide a lower level of political support to their representatives in the state legislature as the state income tax rate s increases. Overall, then, and given a particular grant structure, the net political support that an individual α residing in the ith school district will be willing to provide can be written as the function:

$$\psi_\alpha^i = b_\alpha^i(\gamma) - c_\alpha^i(s) \tag{3-8}$$

where γ is the $M \times 1$ vector of educational expenditure levels in all M local school districts, $b_\alpha^i(\cdot)$ is assumed to be a positive, concave function of γ, and $c_\alpha^i(\cdot)$ is assumed to be a positive, convex function of s. Note that $b_\alpha^i(\cdot)$ is a function of the entire vector γ and not just the educational expenditures γ^i in the voter's own school district. This allows for the possibility of spillover effects across local school districts.

---

[41] Meier (2002) notes that while the interest that governors have in public education may vary, state legislators are always likely to care about public education because of the need to appropriate state funds for public education on an annual basis, the constant anxiety associated with taxing constituents, the perceived connection between education and economic development, and (for some states) the possibility of citizen initiatives.

The total amount of net political support ψ^i that the representative from the ith local school district receives is simply the aggregate political support across all individuals in district i:

$$\psi^i = b^i(\gamma) - c^i(s) = \sum_\alpha b_\alpha^i(\gamma) - \sum_\alpha c_\alpha^i(s). \tag{3-9}$$

Note that ψ^i is defined for a *particular* grant structure. However, given that the ability to target educational grants to particular constituencies and thus generate political support is limited by the number K of grant bases (see *Equation 3-2*) used to allocate the grant, any increase in the number of allocation criteria can be expected to increase the ability of the state legislature to target the grant to particular constituencies. Hence, a more complex grant structure will generate a greater level of political support b^i, and hence *Equation 3-9* can be made more general by rewriting it as:

$$\psi^i = b^i(\gamma, K) - c^i(s) \tag{3-10}$$

where the benefit function b^i is assumed to be a positive, strictly concave function of both local school district expenditure levels γ and the number K of grant bases used.

An individual representative in the state legislature receives the net political benefit ψ^i only if a majority of fellow representatives support a particular educational grant structure and a particular state income tax rate. Following the structure developed in the previous chapter, I assume that the state legislature's decision-making structure is characterized by a dominant political coalition that has sufficient power to design and adopt a particular educational grant structure. As a result, only the preferences of those legislators who are members of the dominant political coalition will be considered in the design of the program. Defining $\mathcal{C}$ to be the set of representatives in the coalition, the objective of the coalition will be to maximize a sum Ψ of net political benefits across all members of the coalition:

$$\Psi = \sum_{i \in \mathcal{C}} [b^i(\gamma, K) - c^i(s)] \tag{3-11}$$

As noted earlier, the state legislature is required to balance the state's budget. Revenues are derived from the proportional tax on income. Expenditures, however, while including the sum of all grants disbursed, also include the administrative costs associated with enacting and running the educational grant structure. Because administrative costs must be paid for out of the same pool of revenues used to fund the educational grants, they will reduce the ability of the state to distribute all of each tax dollar in the form of educational grants. These administrative costs include such items as the cost of legislative debate over the appropriate educational grant structure, the cost of gathering information on the political preferences of individual constituents and fellow representatives, the cost of administering the income tax, and the cost of processing the educational grants and enforcing restrictions. While the determination of these costs is a complex process, they will in general rise with the complexity of the grant structure. As a result, they can be modeled as a positive, strictly convex function of the number K of grant bases used to decide how to allocate the educational grants. Thus, the state's budget constraint can be written:

$$\sum_{i=1}^{M} G^i + A(K) - sB = 0 \qquad\qquad (3\text{-}12)$$

where $A(\cdot)$ represents administrative costs and B represents aggregate income across all constituents and across all school districts.

The dominant political coalition's problem, then, is to choose a particular educational grant structure and income tax rate s that will maximize its aggregate net political benefit function Ψ, subject of course to the balanced budget constraint described in *Equation 3-12*. More specifically, it means choosing the optimal set of grant bases, the optimal set of grant rates $\mathbf{r}$ to use with those K bases, and the optimal state tax rate s used to fund the educational grant structure.

The choice of the optimal set of grant bases involves choosing both the number of bases K as well as deciding what each base should be, that is, choosing the $\mathbf{X}$. Assuming that the latter problem can be solved for any given number of bases, increasing the number of bases will allow the dominant political coalition to more finely target the educational grants to constituents from whom it wishes to get political support. However, because an increase in the number of bases also increases the administrative costs A associated with the educational grant structure, any increase in the number of criteria will also require (all other things constant) a higher state income tax rate s, thus reducing the net aggregate political support for the dominant political coalition. As a result, the number of bases used will only increase up to the point where the additional political benefits associated with an increase in the number of bases is not exceeded by the additional political cost associated with increasing the state income tax rate still again.

Likewise, the optimal choice of the optimal set of grant rates **r** (one for each grant base chosen) can be thought of in a similar way. An increase in a particular grant rate r_k increases the political benefits b^i that the dominant political coalition receives as a result of better targeting of educational grants in a way that pleases constituents. But because a higher grant rate requires a higher income tax rate s, the dominant political coalition will find there are limits to the advantage of raising a particular grant rate, and will end up with grant rates for which the political benefit of increasing them some small amount is just offset by the associated increased political costs c^i associated with the higher state income tax rate s that is necessary to fund the higher grant rates. Alternatively, we can also think of the choice of grant rates **r** as arising within the context of a fixed state income tax rate s (that is, given a fixed pool of funds available for educational grants). Within that context, the choice of the optimal set of grant rates **r** becomes an issue of finding the right distribution of educational grants G^i across school districts with an increase in the value of one grant rate requiring that some other grant rate be reduced. Hence, the optimal set of grant rates **r** will be the one for which the political benefit of increasing one grant rate by some small amount will be the same across all grant rates. If this were not true, the dominant political coalition could always increase its aggregate net political benefit Ψ by raising the grant rates for which the political payoff was relatively high and lowering the grant rates for those associated with a relatively small political payoff.

Given the above analysis, the optimal state income tax rate s, and hence the choice of the total amount of money to be distributed to local school districts, is characterized by the obverse of the above conditions. The ideal state income tax rate for the dominant political coalition is one at which the political cost of raising the rate some small amount is just equal to the political benefit of distributing some additional, small amount of money optimally.

Mathematically, these conditions can be expressed as a set of $K + 2$ first-order conditions plus the balanced budget constraint described by *Equation 3-12* that come from solving the implied Lagrangian problem:[42]

$$\sum_{i \in \mathscr{S}} \frac{\partial b^i}{\partial K} - \lambda \frac{\partial A}{\partial K} = 0 \qquad\qquad (3\text{-}13)$$

[42] These conditions represent a simplified application of the more general set of first-order conditions described in *Chapter 2*. For a more general discussion of these first-order conditions and the nature of a Lagrangian problem, see the discussion in that chapter surrounding *Equation 2-11*.

$$\sum_{i\in\mathscr{C}}\sum_{n=1}^{M}\frac{\partial b^i}{\partial\gamma^n}\cdot\frac{\partial\gamma^n}{\partial r_k} - \lambda\sum_{n=1}^{M}x_k^i = 0 \qquad k = 1,2,\ldots,K \qquad (3\text{-}14)$$

$$\sum_{i\in\mathscr{C}}\frac{\partial c^i}{\partial s} - \lambda B = 0. \qquad (3\text{-}15)$$

Rewriting *Equations 3-13* and *3-15* and defining T to be total state tax revenue sB reveals that the optimal number of education grant bases will be characterized by the equation:

$$\frac{\partial\Psi}{\partial K} = \frac{\partial\Psi}{\partial T}\cdot\frac{\partial A}{\partial K} \qquad (3\text{-}16)$$

that is, the optimal number of educational grant bases K will be that number at which the marginal political benefit of adding the last grant base is equal to the marginal political cost of increasing taxes just enough to cover the administrative cost of adopting and using that grant base.

Likewise, *Equations 3-14* and *3-15* together characterize the optimal set of grant rates $\mathbf{r}$. Given the choice of grant bases $\mathbf{X}$, these equations imply both that the marginal political benefit to the dominant coalition of increasing grant spending by one dollar through an increase in some individual rate r_k should be equated across all bases:

$$\frac{\sum_{i\in\mathscr{C}}\sum_{n=1}^{M}\frac{\partial b^i}{\partial\gamma^n}\cdot\frac{\partial\gamma^n}{\partial r_k}}{\sum_{n=1}^{M}x_k^i} = \frac{\sum_{i\in\mathscr{C}}\sum_{n=1}^{M}\frac{\partial b^i}{\partial\gamma^n}\cdot\frac{\partial\gamma^n}{\partial r_l}}{\sum_{n=1}^{M}x_l^i} \qquad \textit{for all } k,l \qquad (3\text{-}17)$$

and that the marginal political benefit of spending one dollar through an increase in some individual rate r_k should be equated to the marginal political cost of raising state taxes by one dollar:

$$\frac{\sum_{i\in\mathscr{C}}\sum_{n=1}^{M}\frac{\partial b^i}{\partial\gamma^n}\cdot\frac{\partial\gamma^n}{\partial r_k}}{\sum_{n=1}^{M}x_k^i} = \frac{\sum_{i\in C}\frac{\partial c^i}{\partial s}}{B} \qquad k = 1,2,\ldots,K. \qquad (3\text{-}18)$$

Note that the double sum in *Equation 3-14* allows for the possibility of spillover effects. An increase in an individual grant rate r_k has two effects on members of the dominant political coalition – directly through its effect on the educational grants going to member districts and indirectly through spillover effects due to changes in the level of educational grants going to non-member districts.

As with the general structure of intergovernmental grants, the structure of a system of educational grant programs is the result of a tension between a desire for more complexity and a desire for less complexity. The diversity of economic and political circumstances across districts and across constituents argues for greater complexity, and in the absence of administrative costs, *Equation 3.13* reveals that the complexity of the educational grant program would only be limited by the condition that complexity not be pushed to the point where the marginal political benefit of adding another grant base is negative. However, administrative costs do exist, and their presence argues for a less complex educational grant structure so that a greater proportion of tax dollars make their way into educational grants received by the local school districts.

The particular form of the grant (foundation grant, guaranteed tax-base grant, etc.) will depend on the existence of other factors such as spillovers, fiscal illusion, and political asymmetry as discussed in more detail in *Chapter 2*. The classic argument for explaining the existence of educational grants is to correct for spillovers. However, parochial local views not reflected politically at the state level can result in political asymmetries that also give rise to educational grants.

Finally, it should be noted that in practice there may be limits to increasing the number of bases K, not so much because of the administrative costs A, but rather because of the correlation between bases and the target constituencies. Take, for example, a state legislature that currently distributes per-pupil educational grants on the basis of mean household income in order to assure a more even local property tax burden across school districts. If that legislature were then to decide to target school districts with large numbers of students from low-income families for additional support, it might consider using an additional grant base such as the proportion of students receiving subsidized lunches. However, it is possible that the proportion of students receiving subsidized lunches would be positively correlated with mean household income in the school district. To the extent that is true, there may be little difference in the distribution of educational grants whether this additional grant base is used or not used. As a result, we might expect the legislature to forgo the use of this additional grant base and concentrate its efforts instead on fine tuning the set of grant rates **r** to better target grants to those school districts with high proportions of students from low-income families.

1.3 Aggregate Statewide Support for Public Education and the Distribution of School District Expenditure Levels

One of the many concerns that typically surround public education funding reform is the effect on the aggregate statewide level of support for public education. While some (Fernández and Rogerson (1999)) cite California's experience in which aggregate statewide support for public education seemed to fall as a result of funding reforms,[43] others (Evans, Murray, and Schwab (1997), Murray, Evans, and Schwab (1998)) using data from other states find support for the conclusion that funding reforms result in increases in aggregate statewide support for public education.

To examine the aggregate statewide level of support for public education and the distribution of per-pupil educational expenditure levels across local school districts, consider a restatement of the above model using spatial voting theory.[44] Using spatial voting theory, the dominant political coalition's constrained maximization problem can be expressed in an equivalent unconstrained form as a weighted Euclidean distance function L that represents the political loss to the dominant political coalition associated with deviating from the ideal educational grant structure and hence the ideal mix of local school district per-pupil expenditure levels associated with that ideal educational grant structure. Thus:

$$L = \left[\sum_{i \in \gamma} w^i (\gamma^i - \gamma^{i*})^2 + \sum_{i \notin \gamma} w^i (\gamma^i - \gamma^{i*})^2 \right]^{\frac{1}{2}} \tag{3-19}$$

with the γ^{i*} representing the ideal per-pupil spending levels implied by *Equations 3-12, 3-13, 3-14,* and *3-15,* and with the weights w^i reflecting the political importance (or salience) of local school district spending in

---

[43] California's experience is complicated by the passage of Proposition 13 in 1976 that put a cap on the ability of local governments to raise revenues through property taxes. For argument and evidence that Proposition 13 was the result of California's *Serrano* decisions, see Fischel (1989, 1996), Leyden (1988), and Silva and Sonstelie (1995).

[44] Spatial voting theory is a set of tools that allow complex voting processes to be expressed in geometric form using variants of the Euclidean distance function to represent preferences. For an introduction to the spatial theory of voting, see James Enelow and Melvin Hinich's (1983) or Kenneth Shepsle and Mark Bonchek's (1997) textbook on rational political choice theory.

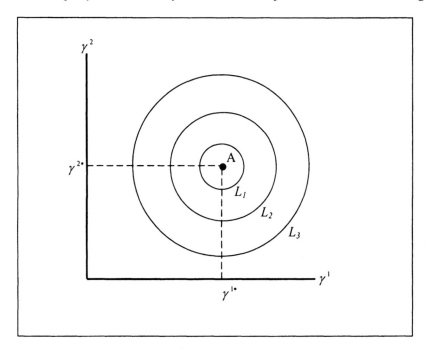

Figure 3-6. Preferences of a State Legislature's Dominant Political Coalition Assuming Equal
Political Saliency Across all School Districts

generating political support for the dominant political coalition. *Figure 3-6*
provides a visual illustration of these preferences for the simple case of a
state composed of two school districts and for which the political saliency of
each school district is the same, that is, $w^1 = w^2$. The dominant political
coalition's ideal mix of per-pupil educational expenditures in the two school
districts (that is, the mix of expenditure levels for which the political loss L
is zero) is located at point A (recall that because the dominant political
coalition knows how local school districts will react to various educational
grant structures, the choice of a particular grant structure implies a choice of
local school district per-pupil expenditure levels). The circle labeled L_1
represents those combinations of per-pupil expenditures that result in the
same political loss L_1. Likewise, the circles labeled L_2 and L_3 represent
similar sets of per-pupil expenditure combinations that result in the political
loss L_2 or L_3 with L_1, L_2, and L_3 representing increasing levels of
political loss associated with deviating from the ideal γ^* at point A, that is,
$L_1 < L_2 < L_3$.

Because spillover effects are possible across school district lines,
members of the dominant political coalition will get political support for
providing grants to both member and non-member school districts. Thus,

the weights w^i will be positive for all i. Moreover, we would expect (everything else constant) that school districts whose state representatives belong to the dominant political coalition would have greater influence on the political process, and we would expect (everything else constant) that school districts with larger populations would have greater influence on the political process. As a result, let the political salience w^i of a school district's spending be proportional to the number of students N^i in each school district, but that among local school districts with the same number of students assume that those with state representatives in the dominant political coalition have the greater political salience w^i. Thus, for districts in the coalition:

$$w^i = a_\gamma N^i \tag{3-20}$$

and for districts not in the coalition:

$$w^i = a_{\neg\gamma} N^i \tag{3-21}$$

with $a_\gamma > a_{\neg\gamma}$. Note that because non-member school districts can create spillovers, it is possible for a particularly large non-member district j to be politically more salient than some member district i, that is, $a_{\neg\gamma} N^j > a_\gamma N^i$, despite $a_\gamma > a_{\neg\gamma}$. Thus, for example, per-pupil spending in the large Los Angeles school district is likely to be highly salient for the dominant coalition in the California state legislature even if state representatives from Los Angeles are not members of the dominant coalition.

Assuming the optimal choice of grant allocation criteria as noted in *Equation 3-16*, minimizing the political loss function L requires that the dominant political coalition choose that mix of grant rates **r** and that state tax rate s where it is no longer possible to reduce the political loss L any further, that is, until the marginal political losses associated with changing **r** and s are zero. Mathematically, this requirement can be represented by the $K+1$ first-order conditions:

$$\frac{\left[a_\gamma \sum_{i \in \gamma} N^i (\gamma^i - \gamma^{i*}) \frac{\partial \gamma^i}{\partial r_k} + a_{\neg\gamma} \sum_{i \notin \gamma} N^i (\gamma^i - \gamma^{i*}) \frac{\partial \gamma^i}{\partial r_k} \right]}{\sqrt{L}} = 0 \quad \forall k \tag{3-22}$$

$$\frac{\left[a_{\gamma} \sum_{i \in \gamma} N^i (\gamma^i - \gamma^{i*}) \frac{\partial \gamma^i}{\partial s} + a_{\neg \gamma} \sum_{i \notin \gamma} N^i (\gamma^i - \gamma^{i*}) \frac{\partial \gamma^i}{\partial s} \right]}{\sqrt{L}} = 0 \qquad (3\text{-}23)$$

These first-order conditions are equivalent to the first-order conditions *Equations 3-14* and *3-15* that are associated with the original specification of the dominant political coalition's problem, and imply that $\gamma^i = \gamma^{i*}$ for all i. Thus, as we would expect, the dominant political coalition will choose its ideal as characterized previously.

The aggregate support for public education can then be defined as the student-weighted sum of local per-pupil educational expenditure levels across all local school districts, that is, by the level of per-pupil educational expenditures statewide:

$$\bar{\gamma} = \frac{\sum_{i=1}^{M} N^i \gamma^{i*}}{N} \qquad (3\text{-}24)$$

where N represents the total number of students statewide.

Figure 3-7 provides a two school district illustration under the assumptions that per-pupil expenditures in the first school district are greater than they are in the second school district (that is, $\gamma^{1*} > \gamma^{2*}$), and that per-pupil expenditures in the first school district are politically more salient than per-pupil expenditures in the second school district. (that is, $w^1 > w^2$). The dominant political coalition's ideal mix of per-pupil educational expenditures in the two school districts (that is, the mix of expenditure levels for which the political loss L is zero) is located at point A. Note also that because of the greater salience of expenditures in the first school district, the political loss circles L_1 and L_2 (with $L_1 < L_2$) are elliptical with a vertical long axis. Per-pupil educational expenditures statewide is represented by downward sloping $\bar{\gamma}$ lines, with each line having a slope equal to the negative of the ratio of the number of students in the two school districts, $-N^1/N^2$, and with lines further from the diagram's origin indicating a greater level of aggregate support for public education. The ideal level of per-pupil educational expenditures statewide is noted by $\bar{\gamma}^*$ with the $\bar{\gamma}^0$ line indicating a higher, but less desirable, level of per-pupil educational expenditures statewide.

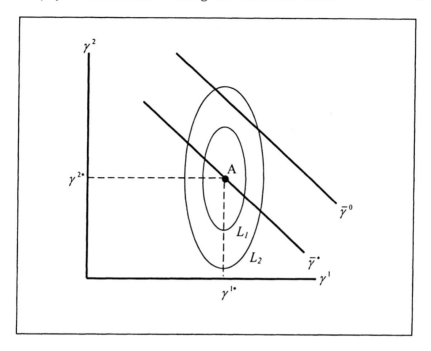

Figure 3-7. A The Ideal Mix of Local School District Per-Pupil Expenditure Levels and the Ideal Level of Aggregate Educational Expenditures

2. STATE FUNDING OF PUBLIC EDUCATION IN THE PRESENCE OF COURT INTERVENTION

The above discussion is based on the assumption that the state legislature makes its educational funding decisions unconstrained by outside influences. But, as recent history attests, state legislatures are often confronted with a judiciary that attempts to influence educational funding decisions. The effect of such attempts on state legislative behavior is examined below. Because most court interventions have historically focused on reducing educational spending disparities or increasing educational spending for the lowest spending local school districts, analysis below looks at two cases – the effect of a court mandate to reform the legislature's educational grant structure through the reduction of per-pupil educational expenditure disparities among local school districts, and the effect of a court mandate to reform the legislature's educational grant structure through an increase in per-student educational expenditures for local school districts with per-pupil educational expenditures below some defined level.

2.1   Legislative Response to an Order to Reduce Spending Disparities

Suppose, that a court finds that the optimal educational grant structure (characterized by the first-order conditions in *Equations 3-22* and *3-23*) to be unconstitutional under the state constitution and orders the state legislature to change the existing educational grant structure to one that reduces the disparity in local school-district spending levels. For simplicity, let the acceptable level of disparity be zero so that the order amounts to requiring that per-pupil expenditure levels γ^i be the same for all districts, and define $\hat{\gamma}$ to be the common level of per-pupil spending that eventually results.

2.1.1   Assuming Full Compliance

Assuming that the state legislature is able and willing to fully comply with the court order, the problem for the state legislature's dominant political coalition is one of minimizing the political loss function L (recall *Equation 3-19*) subject to the requirement that per-pupil expenditures in every school district take some common value $\hat{\gamma}$. As a result, the dominant political coalition's political loss function can be rewritten to reflect this constraint:

$$L = a_\gamma \left[\sum_{i \in \gamma} N^i (\hat{\gamma} - \gamma^{i*})^2 + a_{\neg \gamma} \sum_{i \notin \gamma} N^i (\hat{\gamma} - \gamma^{i*})^2 \right]^{\frac{1}{2}} \qquad (3\text{-}25)$$

The solution to this problem requires that the dominant political coalition choose that mix of grant rates $\mathbf{r}$ and that state tax rate s for which it is no longer possible to reduce the political loss L any further, that is, until the marginal political losses associated with changing $\mathbf{r}$ and s are zero. Mathematically, this results in the $K+1$ first-order conditions:

$$\frac{a_\gamma \sum_{i \in \gamma} N^i (\hat{\gamma} - \gamma^{i*}) \dfrac{\partial \hat{\gamma}}{\partial r_k} + a_{\neg \gamma} \sum_{i \notin \gamma} N^i (\hat{\gamma} - \gamma^{i*}) \dfrac{\partial \hat{\gamma}}{\partial r_k}}{\sqrt{L}} = 0 \quad \forall k \qquad (3\text{-}26)$$

$$\frac{a_\gamma \sum_{i \in \gamma} N^i (\hat{\gamma} - \gamma^{i*}) \dfrac{\partial \hat{\gamma}}{\partial t^s} + a_{\neg \gamma} \sum_{i \notin \gamma} N^i (\hat{\gamma} - \gamma^{i*}) \dfrac{\partial \hat{\gamma}}{\partial s}}{\sqrt{L}} = 0 \qquad (3\text{-}27)$$

Letting N_γ and $N_{\neg\gamma}$ represent the total number of students in coalition and non-coalition school districts, and letting $\bar{\gamma}_\gamma^*$ and $\bar{\gamma}_{\neg\gamma}^*$ be the student-weighted mean ideal expenditure level for coalition and non-coalition school districts,[45] the optimal level of per-pupil educational expenditures statewide assuming full compliance with the court's order will be:

$$\hat{\gamma}^* = \frac{a_\gamma N_\gamma \bar{\gamma}_\gamma^* + a_{\neg\gamma} N_{\neg\gamma} \bar{\gamma}_{\neg\gamma}^*}{a_\gamma N_\gamma + a_{\neg\gamma} N_{\neg\gamma}} \qquad (3\text{-}28)$$

Thus, the optimal common level of per-pupil spending statewide, $\hat{\gamma}^*$, will be a weighted average of the original optimal spending levels, γ^*. To determine the effect of the court order on per-pupil educational expenditures statewide, subtract the ideal level of per-pupil educational expenditures statewide $\bar{\gamma}^*$ (recall *Figure 3-7*) from this new level of per-pupil educational expenditures statewide $\hat{\gamma}^*$:

$$\hat{\gamma}^* - \bar{\gamma}^* = \frac{N_\gamma N_{\neg\gamma} [a_C - a_{\neg\gamma}(\bar{\gamma}_\gamma^* - \bar{\gamma}_{\neg\gamma}^*)]}{N(a_\gamma N_\gamma + a_{\neg\gamma} N_{\neg\gamma})} \qquad (3\text{-}29)$$

The result reveals that the change in the level of per-student educational expenditures statewide will depend on which school districts dominate the state legislature.[46] If, in the absence of the court order, the school districts that belong to the dominant political coalition would spend more on average per-pupil than non-member districts, that is, if $\bar{\gamma}_\gamma^* > \bar{\gamma}_{\neg\gamma}^*$, then the legislature will obey the court order by leveling up, that is, by increasing the aggregate level of support for public education. However, if the opposite is true, that is, if school districts in the coalition would spend on average less than school districts not in the coalition ($\bar{\gamma}_\gamma^* < \bar{\gamma}_{\neg\gamma}^*$), then the legislature will choose to level down, that is, reduce aggregate support for education. Only if there is no difference on average between the spending

---

[45] That is, $\bar{\gamma}_\gamma^* = \sum_{i \in \gamma} N^i \gamma^{i*} \Big/ \sum_{i \in \gamma} N^i$ and $\bar{\gamma}_{\neg\gamma}^* = \sum_{i \in \gamma} N^i \gamma^{i*} \Big/ \sum_{i \in \gamma} N^i$.

[46] Robert Manwaring and Steven Sheffrin (1997) provide empirical evidence in support of this conclusion that states may level up or level down as a result of litigation and public education funding reform.

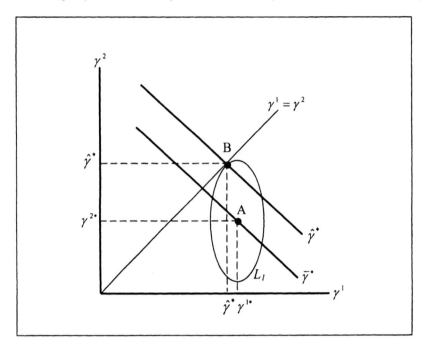

Figure 3-8. The Effect of a Court Order to Equalize Per-Student Spending under Full
Compliance

levels of school districts in and out of the dominant political coalition, that
is, only if $\bar{\gamma}^*_\gamma = \bar{\gamma}^*_{-\gamma}$, will overall statewide educational expenditures per
pupil remain unchanged.

Figure 3-8 illustrates this point for the two school district case examined
above. The court order requires that the state legislature move from its ideal
γ^* at point A to some point on the equal-spending curve (the ray labeled
$\gamma^1 = \gamma^2$). The ideal mix of educational expenditures in the two school
districts that fulfills the court order will be that point on the equal spending
curve which is just tangent to one of the dominant political coalition's
indifference curves. If, as is illustrated by the indifference curve L_1, the
higher-spending school district 1 controls the legislature, that tangency point
will be at some point B above the original, ideal level of per-pupil
educational expenditures statewide $\bar{\gamma}^*$ regardless of the relative populations
of the two districts.[47] Likewise, if the lower-spending school district 2 were

[47] Although the tangency point noted by point B moves to the southeast as the population of
the second school district increases relative to the population of the first school district, the
tangency point never moves below the original $\bar{\gamma}^*$ curve because the slope of that curve
is $-N^1/N^2$.

to control the legislature, the tangency point would be at some point below the original $\bar{\gamma}^*$ curve regardless of the relative populations of the two districts.

The degree to which the state legislature will choose to level up or level down through the appropriate choice of educational grant program structure will depend on the average (per-pupil weighted) gap between per-pupil spending in coalition and non-coalition school districts, $\left|\bar{\gamma}^*_r - \bar{\gamma}^*_{\neg r}\right|$, the relative per-pupil salience of coalition to non-coalition school districts, $a_r / a_{\neg r}$, and the relative number of students living in coalition versus non-coalition school districts, $N_r / N_{\neg r}$. The greater the gap in per-pupil expenditures $\left|\bar{\gamma}^*_r - \bar{\gamma}^*_{\neg r}\right|$ or the relative salience $a_r / a_{\neg r}$ of coalition versus non-coalition school districts, the larger will be the degree to which the state legislature will level up (or down). Likewise, the larger is $N_r / N_{\neg r}$, the smaller will be the size of increase (or decrease).[48]

2.1.2   Assuming Partial Compliance

The above analysis assumes that the state legislature is able and willing to fully comply with the court order. In practice, however, as New Jersey's experience bears witness to (Peters (1996)), there are often limits to the ability and/or the willingness of the legislature to fully comply with a court order to reduce disparities in per-pupil educational expenditure levels across local school districts. In part, the failure of a state legislature to fully comply with a court order may be tied to limitations inherent in the use of intergovernmental grants as a mechanism for effecting changes in local school district expenditure patterns. As observed at the beginning of this chapter, there are limits to the willingness of a state legislature to adopt complex educational grant structures because of the added administrative costs A that accompany such complexity. Moreover, there are sometimes

---

[48] Intuitively, this last observation is due to the fact that when the proportion of students who live in coalition school districts is higher (all other things constant), the coalition's average level of per-pupil spending will be closer to the statewide average and non-coalition school districts will contribute less to the determination of the statewide level of per-pupil expenditures. Hence, any change that the coalition adopts as a result of a court order, while perhaps having a significant effect on the spending levels of non-coalition school districts, will not change the overall statewide level of per-pupil expenditures (up or down) much. In the limit, if the legislature is dominated by a coalition of the whole, that is, the proportion of students living in coalition school districts is 100%, there would be no change in pupil spending statewide, though there may be significant changes in the spending levels of individual school districts.

ethical restrictions (often embodied in law) that prohibit the use of certain types of grant bases as criteria for the distribution of educational grants.[49]

Finally, political considerations may prohibit the use of grant structures that are overly complicated (and thus incomprehensible to large segments of the population) or that require a state tax rate above some critical level. A legislature forced by the courts to consider such politically untouchable options may decide to take its chances with defying the courts rather than choosing the certain political cost of facing the electorate. Thus, for reasons inherent in the nature of intergovernmental grants and for reasons tied to political realities, a state legislature will typically be limited to the use of fairly simple, often linear, grant formulae that do not result in spending or taxation outcomes that are unacceptable to its constituencies. Given the nonlinear distribution of local school district per-student expenditure levels, it should therefore not be surprising if the set of politically acceptable educational grant structures does not include ones that would allow a legislature to fully comply with a court order to equalize per-pupil expenditures across all school districts.

An example of a physical limitation in the ability of the state legislature to fully comply with a court's order to fully equalize per-student expenditures across all school districts is provided in *Figure 3-9*.[50] Assume that among the set of possible educational grant structures, no structure can reduce the ratio γ^1/γ^2 of per-pupil educational expenditures in school districts 1 and 2 to less than some $\beta > 1$. Thus, the legislature in trying to fulfill the court order will be unable to go beyond the line labeled $\gamma^1 = \beta\gamma^2$. Given an ideal mix γ^* of per-pupil educational expenditures in school districts 1 and 2 at point A, and a full-compliance outcome at point B, the outcome under partial compliance will be at some intermediate point C that lies at that point on the $\gamma^1 = \beta\gamma^2$ line which is just tangent to the lowest possible indifference curve (noted by the dashed ellipse) of the dominant political coalition.

Note that at this outcome, the state legislature will still choose to level up, though not enough to completely fulfill the court's order. *Figure 3-10* illustrates the case of a state legislature being unwilling for political reasons to fully comply. Though in general a state legislature's dominant political

---

[49] Among the examples that come to mind are the general use of racial, ethnic, or religious population figures. But such ethical/legal restrictions also generally make it politically difficult (though not always impossible) to use more ad hoc grant bases such as designating a state's largest city for special consideration.

[50] In practice, it is difficult to think of a situation where a simple, linear grant structure could not result in equal per-student expenditures in a two school district case. Hence, *Figure 3-8* is intended to reflect, in a simple context, problems that actually only arise with a larger number of local school districts.

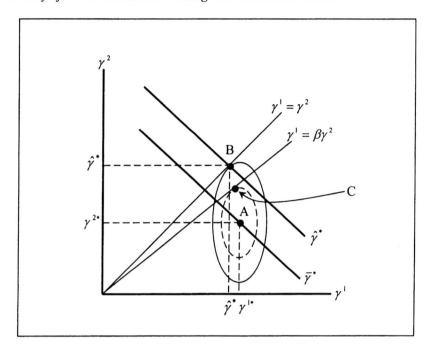

Figure 3-9 The Effect of a Court Order to Equalize Per-Student Spending under Partial Compliance Due to Physical Limitations

coalition will be willing to accept lower levels of political support rather than refuse to obey the court order, there may be limits to such willingness because of the unacceptable risk it presents to being reelected. As a result, the state legislature may refuse to incur a political loss L greater than some level L_{max} despite a court order to the contrary. If that maximum level of political loss (and its associated indifference curve) defines a set of per-pupil expenditure levels that does not include combinations where per-pupil expenditures are the same in all school districts (as is the case in *Figure 3-10*), then the best that the state legislature will be willing to do to comply with the court's order is move to some intermediate point D where the gap between per-pupil expenditures in the first and second school district is minimized.

2.2 Legislative Response to an Order to Increase Spending in the Lowest Spending School Districts

A similar analytical approach can be used to analyze the effects of a court order that finds that the optimal educational grant structure (characterized by

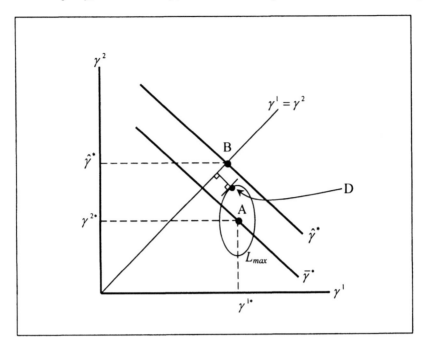

Figure 3-10 The Effect of a Court Order to Equalize Per-Student Spending under Partial
Compliance Due to Political Limitations

the first-order conditions in *Equations 3-22* and *3-23*) is unconstitutional
under the state constitution and orders the state legislature to increase per-
pupil educational expenditures for all local school districts to no less than
some minimum acceptable level γ_{min} .

2.2.1   Assuming Full Compliance

Assuming that the state legislature is willing to fully comply with the
court order, the problem for the state legislature's dominant political
coalition is one of minimizing its political loss function L subject to the
requirement that per-pupil expenditures in every school district be no less
than γ_{min} . Define the set of local school districts for which the state
legislature's ideal per-student expenditure level is less than or equal to this
minimum (that is, for which $\gamma^i \leq \gamma_{min}$) to be $\mathscr{R}$. Then the dominant political
coalition's political loss function can rewritten to incorporate that constraint
as:

$$L' = \left[a_{\curlyvee} \left(\sum_{i \in (\curlyvee \cap \mathscr{r})} N^i (\gamma_{\min} - \gamma^{i*})^2 + \sum_{i \in (\curlyvee - \curlyvee \cap \mathscr{r})} N^i (\gamma^i - \gamma^{i*})^2 \right) \right.$$

$$\left. + a_{\neg\curlyvee} \left(\sum_{i \in (\neg\curlyvee \cap \mathscr{r})} N^i (\gamma_{\min} - \gamma^{i*})^2 + \sum_{i \in (\neg\curlyvee - \neg\curlyvee \cap \mathscr{r})} N^i (\gamma^i - \gamma^{i*})^2 \right) \right]^{\frac{1}{2}} \qquad (3\text{-}30)$$

As with previous analysis, the solution to this problem requires that the dominant political coalition choose that mix of grant rates **r** and that state tax rate *s* for which it is not possible to reduce the political loss further, that is, for which the marginal political losses associated with changing **r** and *s* are zero. Hence, the $K + 1$ first-order conditions:

$$\left[a_{\curlyvee} \sum_{i \in (\curlyvee - \curlyvee \cap \mathscr{r})} N^i (\gamma^i - \gamma^{i*}) \frac{\partial \gamma^i}{\partial r_k} \right.$$

$$\left. + a_{\neg\curlyvee} \sum_{i \in (\curlyvee - \neg\curlyvee \cap \mathscr{r})} N^i (\gamma^i - \gamma^{i*}) \frac{\partial \gamma^i}{\partial r_k} \right] \Big/ \sqrt{L'} = 0 \quad \forall k \qquad (3\text{-}31)$$

$$\left[a_{\curlyvee} \sum_{i \in (\curlyvee - \curlyvee \cap \mathscr{r})} N^i (\gamma^i - \gamma^{i*}) \frac{\partial \gamma^i}{\partial s} \right.$$

$$\left. + a_{\neg\curlyvee} \sum_{i \in (\curlyvee - \neg\curlyvee \cap \mathscr{r})} N^i (\gamma^i - \gamma^{i*}) \frac{\partial \gamma^i}{\partial s} \right] \Big/ \sqrt{L'} = 0 \quad \forall k \qquad (3\text{-}32)$$

The result is that per-pupil educational expenditures in all school districts for which the state legislature's ideal was less than the court mandated minimum, that is, for all districts for which $\gamma^i \leq \gamma_{\min}$, will be increased to the amount $\gamma_{\min}$ mandated by the court; for all other school districts, there will be no change in per-pupil expenditure levels. Thus:

$$\gamma = \begin{cases} \gamma^{i*} & \text{if } \gamma^{i*} > \gamma_{\min} \\ \gamma_{\min} & \text{if } \gamma^{i*} \leq \gamma_{\min} \end{cases} \qquad (3\text{-}33)$$

The effect of this court order on per-pupil educational expenditures statewide will clearly be positive, though how much depends on how far

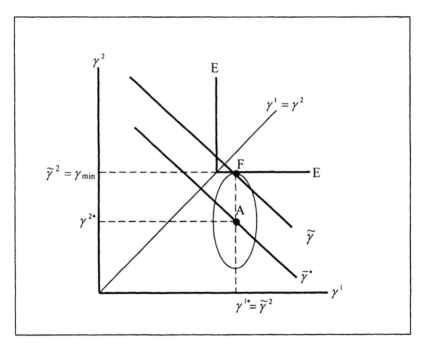

Figure 3-11. The Effect of a Court Order to Require Minimum Per-Student Spending under Full Compliance

from γ_{min} the per-student spending levels are for those school districts whose spending is increased. In general, defining $\widetilde{\widetilde{\gamma}}$ to be per-pupil expenditures statewide after the court order takes effect, the rise in per-pupil expenditures statewide will be :

$$\widetilde{\widetilde{\gamma}} - \overline{\gamma}^* = \frac{1}{N} \sum_{i \in \mathcal{I}'} N^i (\gamma_{min} - \gamma^{i*}) \tag{3-33}$$

Figure 3-11 illustrates this outcome for the same two school district case examined previously. The court order requires that the state legislature move from its ideal γ^* at point A to some point on the minimum expenditure line EE. The ideal mix of educational expenditures in the two school districts that fulfills the court order will be that point F on the minimum expenditure constraint EE that is just tangent to one of the coalition's indifference curves.

Thus the solution for the dominant political coalition is to simply increase per-student spending in those school districts that would otherwise be below the minimum per-pupil expenditure level γ_{min} mandated by the

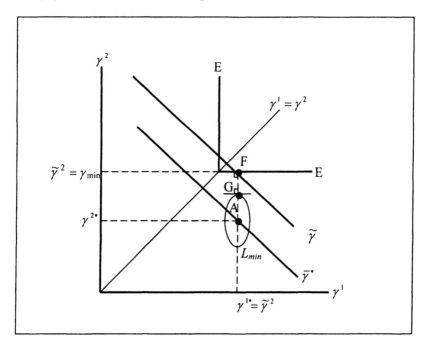

Figure 3-12. The Effect of a Court Order to Require Minimum Per-Student Spending under Partial Compliance

court, and leave the other school districts at their original per-pupil expenditure levels γ^{i*}. Notice that this result does not depend on the higher spending school districts having the greater political saliency. In terms of the diagram, even if school district 2 controlled the state legislature and had the greater political saliency, the outcome would be the same. Finally, notice that per-pupil expenditures statewide will clearly increase, as shown by the line $\tilde{\gamma}$.

2.2.2 Assuming Partial Compliance

Suppose, however, that the state legislature is unable or unwilling to fully comply with the court order to raise all per-pupil expenditures that are less than the court defined minimum γ_{min} up to that minimum. In such a case, there exists some maximum political loss L_{max} that represents either the political loss that the dominant political coalition is able to incur given the limitations to the use of intergovernmental grants, or the maximum political loss that it is willing to incur given political realities. If, as is illustrated in *Figure 3-12*, that maximum political loss L_{max} defines a set of per-pupil expenditure levels for school districts that does not include expenditure levels at or above γ_{min} for all school districts, the result will be much the same as the case of full compliance – for those school districts with per-pupil spending below the court defined minimum, per-pupil educational expenditures would increase, while for those school districts with per-pupil educational expenditures above the court defined minimum, there would be no change. However, unlike the case of full compliance, the outcome would not result in all districts having per-student expenditures of at least γ_{min}. Rather, the outcome, again as illustrated in *Figure 3-12*, would be at some point G intermediate between A and F.

3.   CONCLUSION

This chapter has provided a theoretical model of the decision making process used by state legislatures to fund public education, and how that process is affected by judicial interventions intended to remedy inequities in that same funding process. Based on a two-tiered model of governmental decision making in which state decisions are made by a dominant political coalition in the state legislature and local decisions are made through majority rule, the effect of a court order on the aggregate support for public education as well as the distribution of per-pupil expenditure levels across local school districts is shown in general to depend on the specifics of the court's order, on the relative level of per-pupil spending in school districts whose representatives control the state legislature through a dominant political coalition versus school districts whose representatives do not belong to the dominant political coalition.

The reason for such dependence comes fundamentally from a desire on the part of the state legislature's dominant political coalition to preserve as much as is politically and economically possible the levels of public education funding it considers to be ideal for its members. Hence, if the state legislature is dominated by relatively high spending school districts and if the state legislature is both able and willing to fully comply, then, as *Table 3-1* summarizes, a court order to reduce disparities in per-pupil expenditures across school districts will result in aggregate spending on public education statewide going up with that rise coming about as the result of relatively large increases in per-pupil spending in the lower spending, non-coalition member school districts and relatively low reductions in per-pupil spending in the higher spending coalition member school districts. In short, the dominant political coalition through the mechanisms of a statewide income tax and the educational grant structure will redistribute relatively large amounts of resources from themselves to the lower spending, non-coalition

*Table 3-1.*Effect of Court Orders to Equalize or Raise Minimum Expenditure Levels on Local School District Educational Expenditures

		State legislature dominated by school districts with …	
		low per-pupil expenditures	high per-pupil expenditures
Effect of court order to equalize per-pupil expenditures on …	aggregate support for education statewide	−	+
	per-pupil expenditures in low spending districts	+	+ +
	per-pupil expenditures in high spending districts	− −	−
Effect of court order to raise minimum per-pupil expenditures on …	aggregate support for education statewide	+	+
	per-pupil expenditures in low spending districts	+ +	+ +
	per-pupil expenditures in high spending districts	no change	no change

member school districts in order to keep the reductions in per-pupil expenditures in their own school districts relatively small.

Likewise, if the state legislature is dominated by relatively low spending school districts, then a court order to reduce disparities in per-pupil expenditures across school districts will result in aggregate spending on public education statewide falling. That fall is the result of relatively large reductions in per-pupil spending in the higher spending, non-coalition member school districts and relatively small increases in per-pupil spending in the lower spending, coalition member school districts. Thus, in this case, the dominant political coalition will choose to reduce the overall burden of state income taxes while engaging in sufficient redistribution from the wealthier, non-coalition school districts to themselves in order to satisfy the court's order.

In the case of a court order to raise minimum per-pupil expenditures to some level acceptable to the court, the effect (assuming full compliance) will be the same regardless of who controls the state legislature – aggregate spending on public education will rise, per-pupil spending in school districts that are currently spending less than the court-defined minimum will rise to that court-defined minimum, and school districts with per-pupil spending above the court-defined minimum will be able to preserve their level of spending.

Of course, it is possible that for institutional or political reasons, the state legislature will either not be able or unwilling to fully comply with the court's order. In such a case, the outcome will lie between the outcome associated with full compliance and the original outcome that would occur in the absence of court intervention. *Chapter 6* examines the likelihood and implications of this situation in more detail.

Chapter 4

ASSESSING THE EMPIRICAL VALIDITY OF
THE THEORY
A Case Study of 1980 Funding Reform in Connecticut

The ultimate goal of a positive science is the development of a "theory" or "hypothesis" that yields valid and meaningful (i.e., not truistic) predictions about phenomena not yet observed.
— Milton Friedman, *The Methodology of Positive Economics*[51]

The previous chapter provided a theoretical model of the decision making process used by state legislatures to fund public education and how that process is affected by judicial interventions intended to remedy inequities in the same funding process. Later chapters will use that model to examine the history of the public education funding process over the past half century particularly with regard to the effect of various judicial interventions during that period and to suggest the likely future of public education funding over the next decade or so. However, before turning to such material it will prove useful to provide empirical evidence of the consistency of the theoretical model with actual behavior so that the reader may have some confidence in the use of that model to explain and predict behavior.

This chapter provides an empirical analysis of Connecticut's 1980 experience with public education funding reform and, in particular, an examination of its decision to use a district power equalization (DPE) grant structure to distribute grants to its local school districts. This analysis allows for both an assessment of the consistency of the model with a state legislature's behavior as well as an assessment of the consistency of the model's predictions for public education grant structure choice.

Because state legislatures have resisted employing a single statewide school district that is administered centrally (Hawaii being the lone exception), state legislatures have typically governed local school districts at

---

[51] Friedman (1953; p. 7).

arms length, distributing funds through intergovernmental grant structures. Thus, the issue of grant structure choice is a significant one. Historically, the economic literature on this issue has focused on assessing the effect of alternative education grant structures on local school-district spending behavior but not on the choice of education grant structures themselves. Early work concluded that DPE grant structures were neither neutral in their effects (Feldstein (1975)) nor successful in reducing disparities in per-pupil expenditures across school districts (Carroll and Park (1983), Murnane (1985)). As a result, later work investigated alternative, and what were sometimes argued superior, grant structures. Feldstein (1975, 1984), for example, offered (and defended against Perkins' (1984) criticism) a grant structure that he argued was fiscally neutral. However, the more common argument was that some version of a foundation grant structure would be more effective, less expensive, and therefore more desirable (Ladd and Yinger (1994), Reschovsky (1994), and Fisher (1996)).[52]

More recent empirical work (Evans, Murray, and Schwab (1997), Murray, Evans, and Schwab (1998)) found that what success there has been in reforming educational grant structures has been tied to court-mandated changes[53] and not to educational grant structure changes in general. This suggests that legal constraints are a critical factor in the choice, and hence the outcome, of educational grant structure reform.[54] Unfortunately, the literature generally failed to take such constraints into account, thus calling into question the argument that foundation grants are more desirable than DPE grants.[55]

Building on the theoretical model developed in *Chapter 3*, this chapter lays out the conditions under which a legislature, confronted with a court order to reform its educational grant structure, prefers a DPE grant structure

---

[52] The debate over the appropriate grant structure took place within the larger and more general debate over school reform. For contributions to this larger literature, see Downes (1992), Oakland (1994), and Downes, Dye, and McGuire (1998). For an overview of this literature and the contributions of economic research, see Hoxby (1998a).

[53] Even with court intervention, success is by no means guaranteed. See for example Silva and Sonstelie (1995), Underwood (1995), and Fischel (1996).

[54] Hoxby (1998b) suggests that the push for greater inter-district spending equality may be due to a change in the demand for public education, not a failure of existing public finance systems. If true, it raises the question as to why such a change has not manifest itself in the decisions of legislatures not under court order to change their educational grant structure.

[55] James Buchanan and Gordon Tullock (1975) provide general support for including the political dimensions of economic policy issues into economic analysis. For rather different examples of analyses that emphasize the political dimensions in intergovernmental grants and public education funding, see Brennan and Pincus (1990), Hoyt and Toma (1993), and Poterba (1998).

over a foundation grant structure. That theoretical model is a useful foundation for such analysis because it allows the choice of grant structure to affect a legislature's willingness to fund public education in general and thereby affect both the level of state taxes as well as the distribution of spending across local school districts.[56] Then, using data from Connecticut's 1980 experience with educational grant structure reform, the empirical validity of the model is tested by (1) estimating a separately derived model of local school district expenditures based on Geoffrey Turnbull's (1992) and Robert Moffitt's (1984, 1986) analyses of intergovernmental grants, and (2) using the results of that estimation to simulate 1980 Connecticut public education expenditures under alternative grant structure regimes. The empirical results confirm the theoretical analysis – a state legislature's choice of public education grant structure depends on incentives inherent in the legal standard used by the court in evaluating the constitutionality of that state's educational grant structure.[57] If the court bases its ruling on a state equal-protection clause, then the state legislature will choose a DPE grant structure; if the court bases its ruling on a state thorough-and-efficient education clause, then the state legislature will prefer a foundation grant structure. Interestingly, a DPE grant structure turns out to be more cost effective than a foundation grant structure when satisfying a court's order, regardless of the legal standard used. When an equal protection standard is used, this advantage of the DPE structure is consistent with the legislature's preference for a DPE structure. However, when a thorough-and-efficient standard is used, the cost savings associated with the DPE grant structure is more than offset by other virtues of a foundation structure. Hence, the foundation structure is preferred.

These conclusions, because they contradict the view that a foundation grant structure would be less expensive and more effective than a DPE grant structure,[58] point to the value of incorporating state legislative behavior and legal constraints into the analysis of educational grant structures. More broadly, such conclusions, because they derive from the theoretical model

---

[56] For general evidence of the connection between a donor government's taxing and spending decisions and recipient governments' tax and spending decisions see Hettich and Winer (1988), and Nechyba (1996). For more direct evidence of the link between changes in a grant structure and the level of taxes, see Addonizio (1991), Manwaring and Sheffrin (1997), Evans, Murray, and Schwab (1997), and Murray, Evans, and Schwab (1998). Finally, for evidence of the influence of these connections on the economic effect of alternative grant structures (and hence their political desirability), see Brennan and Pincus (1990) and Munley (1995).

[57] For a broader perspective on the legal rationales for public education funding reform, see *Chapter 5*.

[58] Interestingly, theoretical work by Raquel Fernández and Richard Rogerson (2003) finds that a DPE system would dominate other grant structures in statewide plebiscite.

presented in *Chapter 3* and are consistent with observed behavior, provide reason for the reader to accept the use of that model in explaining public education funding behavior over the past half century and in suggesting what the future of public education funding is likely to be.

1.   LEGALLY CONSTRAINED GRANT STRUCTURE CHOICE

1.1   A spatial-voting representation of public education expenditure levels

Following the model in *Chapter 3*, let public education expenditures be determined in a two-tiered federal governmental structure in which a state legislature, through the decisions of a dominant political coalition, chooses a particular grant structure and provides per-pupil grants A^i to each of its M local school districts, and in which the M local school districts choose the level of per-pupil educational expenditures γ^i for their districts. This decision problem can be modeled as a spatial voting problem in which the dominant political coalition of the state legislature chooses the per-pupil expenditures γ^i of the M local school districts so as to minimize a political loss function L that is a positive function of deviations in actual district per-pupil expenditure levels γ^i from the coalition's ideal expenditure levels, γ^{i*}. Letting the political loss function take the form of a weighted Euclidean distance function, L can then be written as:

$$L = \left[\sum_{i=1}^{M} w^i (\gamma^i - \gamma^{i*})^2 \right]^{\frac{1}{2}} \qquad (4\text{-}1)$$

where $w^i > 0$ represents the political importance (or salience) of district spending in generating political support for the dominant political coalition. Because it is reasonable to believe that there are spillover effects across districts and that, therefore, coalition members get political support for providing grants to both member and non-member districts, let $w^i > 0$ for all i. In general, w^i will be higher for districts that are in the dominant political coalition.

Graphically, this problem can be illustrated by a set of indifference curves representing the coalition's loss function L. These indifference curves will take the form of M-dimensional ellipses with their direction and shape

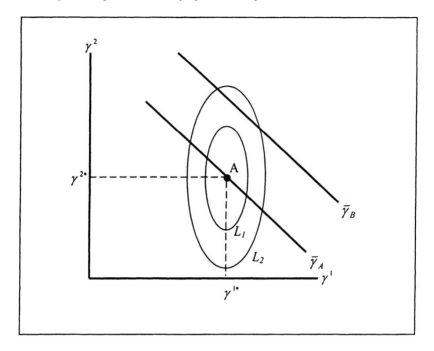

Figure4-1. The Ideal Mix of Local School District Per-Pupil Expenditure Levels and the Ideal Level of Aggregate Educational Expenditures in a State with Two School Districts

determined by the w^i, and with the level of the political loss L associated with deviating from the coalition's ideal γ^{i*} decreasing in the direction of those ideal levels. In addition, per-pupil spending statewide, $\bar{\gamma}$, can (assuming N^i is the number of students in school district i) be noted by iso-spending planes composed of all the γ^i that satisfy the equation:

$$\bar{\gamma} = \frac{\displaystyle\sum_{i=1}^{M} N^i \gamma^i}{\displaystyle\sum_{i=1}^{M} N^i} \qquad (4\text{-}2)$$

for a given value of $\bar{\gamma}$. *Figure 4-1* provides an illustration of the legislature's problem for the two-district case with ideal spending levels noted by γ^{1*} and γ^{2*}, per-pupil spending statewide noted by the iso-spending lines $\bar{\gamma}_A$ and $\bar{\gamma}_B$ (where $\bar{\gamma}_A < \bar{\gamma}_B$), and the political loss associated with different combinations of spending γ^1 and γ^2 noted by the indifference curves L_1 and L_2 (where $L_1 < L_2$).

1.2   The effect of the courts

While public education is mandated by a state's constitution, the standard used to judge whether the state is in compliance with that mandate varies. In some states, the standard is based on an equal-protection clause in the state constitution. In other states, the standard is based on a state constitutional requirement that the state provide a "thorough and efficient" system of free public schools.

Suppose that a state's existing educational grant structure is declared to be unconstitutional under one of those two standards, and suppose that the legislature has been ordered to bring that structure into compliance with the state's constitution. For simplicity, let the legislature's choice be restricted to two possible grant structures – an archetypal foundation grant structure and an archetypal DPE grant structure. The intended purpose of an archetypal foundation grant structure is to assure that all districts will be able to spend at least some minimum per-pupil amount, γ^{min}, if they set their local tax rate at some minimum level t^{min}. As a result, the archetypal foundation grant structure will take the form:

$$A^i = \begin{cases} \gamma^{min} - t^{min} V^i & if \quad \gamma^{min} - t^{min} V^i > 0 \\ 0 & if \quad \gamma^{min} - t^{min} V^i \leq 0 \end{cases} \qquad (4\text{-}3)$$

where A^i is the per-pupil value of the state legislature's grant to school district i and where V^i is the per-pupil tax base of that same school district. Note that districts with a sufficiently large tax base (that is, $V^i > \gamma^{min} / t^{min}$) will receive no grant from the state. Note also that the parameters γ^{min} and t^{min} are policy variables chosen by the legislature.

By contrast, the intended purpose of the archetypal DPE grant structure is to assure more equal per-pupil revenue for equal local tax effort. To accomplish this, the legislature defines an ideal per-pupil district tax base V^* and provides a per-pupil grant A^i equal to some fraction of the difference between the amount of revenue per pupil that the district could raise were it to have a per-pupil tax base equal to V^* and the actual amount of revenue it raises:

$$A^i = \rho t^i (V^* - V^i) \qquad (4\text{-}4)$$

where ρ is a positive, calibration parameter that is set by the state legislature and that allows the state legislature to choose the degree to which effective tax bases are equalized across school districts. If the state legislature chooses to completely equalize the effective tax base across school districts, then ρ would equal one (compare *Equation 3-3* in the previous chapter). Note also that for districts with $V^i > V^*$, the grant would be negative.

1.2.1 Choice Under an *Equal-Protection* Standard

Though defensible from a macroeconomic growth perspective (Hoxby (1998b)), the use of a state constitutional equal protection clause to attack existing educational grant structures is generally based on distributive justice arguments (Zajac (1995), Hoxby (1998b)). As a result, courts that find an existing structure unconstitutional under an equal-protection clause tend to focus on a reduction in per-pupil spending disparities across school districts. Assume that disparity can be measured by the standard deviation in per-pupil spending across districts:

$$\sigma = \frac{1}{N} \sum_{i=1}^{M} N^i (\gamma^i - \bar{\gamma})^2 \qquad (4\text{-}5)$$

and that the court insists that the state legislature reduce the level of disparity to some level σ^{max}. Because the standard deviation measures the minimum (pupil-weighted) Euclidean distance between the actual γ^i and the hyperplane defined by $\gamma^i = \gamma^j$ for all i and j, this constraint can be represented graphically (see *Figure 4-2*) for the 2-district case by the requirement that the pair (γ^1, γ^2) be within the space defined by two lines that are σ^{max} away from, and parallel to, the line where $\gamma^1 = \gamma^2$.

If the legislature employs the archetypal DPE grant structure, it can reduce per-pupil spending in the wealthier, more politically salient districts and increase per-pupil spending in the poorer, less politically salient districts through the choice of V^* and ρ. As a result, by choosing V^* and ρ appropriately, it can generate an outcome such as noted in *Figure 4-2* by the point B where the political cost of complying with the court's order is minimized. On the other hand, if it uses the archetypal foundation grant structure, it can increase spending in those districts that fall below the foundation level, but it cannot lower spending in other districts. Hence, it must move to some point C in order to satisfy the court's order.[59]

---

[59] Strictly speaking, implementation of either grant structure would require additional state funds. If these funds were raised via an increase in state taxes (rather than reducing the spending in some other state governmental program), spending in all districts would fall somewhat because of the greater state tax burden. However, empirically this effect is quite small because of the small income elasticity of the demand for school district expenditures and because of the small tax rate used to fund public education. Using data

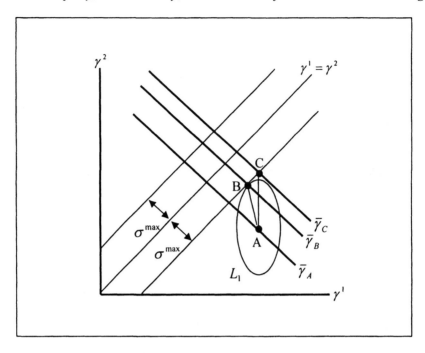

Figure 4-2. Conditions Under Which a DPE Grant Structure is Preferred to a Foundation Grant Structure

As *Figure 4-2* reveals, use of the foundation grant structure is less preferred by the state legislature to the DPE grant structure because, while it allows the wealthier, more politically salient districts to maintain their level of per-pupil spending, it does so at too high a monetary, and therefore, political cost.[60] Indeed, in addition to per-pupil spending statewide being higher under a foundation grant structure than a DPE grant structure, the legislature's budget (and therefore the state tax rate *s*) will be higher because of the foundation grant structure's reliance on only income effects to raise the spending in lower-spending districts; the DPE grant structure, by

---

from Connecticut, for example, the result is a fall in per-pupil expenditures of less than a dollar. As a result, I have for expository reasons omitted this effect from the formal analysis.

[60] In general, as discussed in *Chapter3*, for any given reduction in disparity in spending across districts, the change in the average level of spending across all districts will depend on whether the state legislature is dominated by higher spending districts (in which case state average spending will rise) or lower spending districts (in which case state average spending will fall). Because higher spending districts typically tend to dominate state legislatures, only that case is illustrated here.

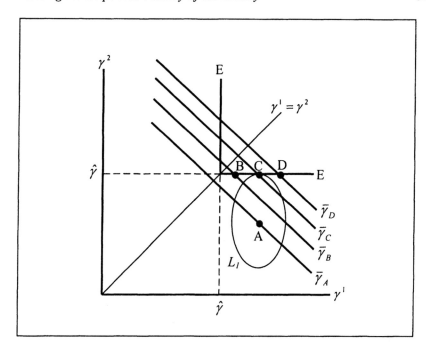

Figure 4-3. Conditions Under Which a Foundation Grant Structure is Preferred to a DPE Grant Structure

contrast, uses both income and substitution effects (by effectively lowering the price of education) for lower-spending districts.

1.2.2 Choice Under a *Thorough-and-Efficient* Standard

The use of a state constitutional thorough-and-efficient education clause to attack existing educational grant structures is typically based on a right-to-necessities argument (Zajac (1995)) or a Rawlsian perspective (Rawls (1971), Ladd and Yinger (1994)). Hence, courts that find a state's public education funding structure unconstitutional under this standard will focus on increasing per-pupil spending in the lowest spending, and typically poorest, local school districts. Thus, court orders based on this standard can be thought of as imposing a constraint that per-pupil spending in all local school districts be no less that some $\hat{\gamma}$:

$$\gamma^i \geq \hat{\gamma} \quad \forall i \tag{4-6}$$

which graphically can be represented for the 2-district case by an L-shaped constraint such as show by the line EE in *Figure 4-3*.

If the legislature employs the archetypal foundation grant structure, it can increase spending in those districts whose per-pupil spending is below the court-imposed $\hat{\gamma}$ while leaving the spending in all other districts unchanged. Graphically, this can be illustrated for the 2-district case by the point C in *Figure 4-3*. Alternatively, the legislature can use the archetypal DPE grant structure. While it is theoretically possible that a DPE grant structure could achieve the same result, it is unlikely because of the less than perfect correlation between V^i and γ^i. As a result, the outcome will depend on the level of V^*.

If V^* is set below the V^i of the highest spending local school districts, the result (as point B in *Figure 4-3* shows) will be a reduction in spending by the wealthier, politically more salient districts. In addition, while it is true that per-pupil spending statewide (as well as the legislature's budget) will be lower with the DPE structure (compare the iso-spending lines $\bar{\gamma}_B$ and $\bar{\gamma}_C$), it is not sufficient to compensate for the lower political support associated with the reduction in spending among the wealthier, politically salient districts. As a result, the foundation grant structure will be preferred.

Likewise, if V^* is set above the V^i for all local school districts, per-pupil spending in all districts (see point D in *Figure 4-3*) will rise, thus making per-pupil spending statewide higher under the DPE grant structure than under the foundation grant structure (compare the iso-spending lines $\bar{\gamma}_C$ and $\bar{\gamma}_D$). Given that the foundation grant structure allows the legislature to satisfy the court's order with a level of per-pupil spending statewide that is closer to its ideal , $\bar{\gamma}_A$, the result once again is that the foundation grant structure will be preferred.

2.   EMPIRICAL ANALYSIS

Empirical evidence in support of the above arguments can be found in Connecticut's 1980 experience with educational grant reform. Connecticut's educational grant structure through most of the 1970s primarily took the form of a flat $250 per-pupil grant with district spending ranging from $1000 to $3000 per-pupil (1980 dollars). See *Table 4-1*. In 1977, the Connecticut Supreme Court in *Horton v. Meskill* ruled that the educational finance system violated the Connecticut constitution's equal protection clause.[61] While the Court left the ultimate solution up to the legislature, it was clear that the Court envisaged a grant structure that provided "a

---

[61] Full legal citations are provided in the *Reference* section at the end of the book.

Table 4-1. Connecticut before and after *Horton* (1980 dollars)

	1974-5	1980-1	Change
Number of districts	169	169	0
Number of pupils	649,608	533,836	-115,772
Expenditures statewide			
• Aggregate	$1,392,964,280	$1,385,373,312	-$7,590,970
• Per-pupil	$2,144	$2,595	+$451
District per-pupil expenditures			
• Mean	$2,003	$2,480	+$477
• Minimum	$1,302	$1,753	+$451
• Maximum	$3,066	$3,550	+$484
• Range	$1,763	$1,797	+$34
• Standard deviation	$349	$388	+$39
State aid			
• Aggregate	$343,210,508	$360,967,786	+$17,757,278
• Per-pupil	$528	$676	+$148
• As proportion of aggregate educational expenditures statewide	0.25	0.26	+0.01

Sources: Data derived from Connecticut Public Expenditure Council (1976), Connecticut State Board of Education (1981), US Council of Economic Advisors (1993), and photocopies provided by the Connecticut State Department of Education.

substantial degree of equality of educational opportunity" while preserving local control and the use of the local property tax as an important source of funding (*Horton v. Meskill, 172* Conn. 650-651).

Using the theoretical arguments presented earlier in this chapter, this emphasis on equal protection suggests that the Connecticut legislature would put in place a form of DPE grant structure. In fact, that is what happened. However, while the program apparently satisfied the Court, it appears to have been a failure at reducing local school district spending disparities. As *Table 4-1* reports, by 1980 disparities in district per-pupil spending (as measured by standard deviation and by range) had risen. What makes the situation less than clear, however, is the fact that enrollments fell by nearly 1/5 over this same period while per-pupil spending statewide rose by roughly 1/5. As a result, the answer to the question of whether the Connecticut legislature acted in a manner consistent with the theoretical arguments above in its choice of a DPE grant structure is not clear.

To answer that question, and to determine whether in fact a DPE grant structure was the best choice for Connecticut state legislature, constrained as it was by the Connecticut Supreme Court, I estimated an empirical model of local school district expenditures using 1980 Connecticut data, used the results of that estimation exercise to simulate local school district expenditures under three alternative grant structure regimes, and evaluated which of those grant structure regimes would have been preferable to the Connecticut state legislature under the circumstances.

2.1   Empirical model

Because school district expenditure decisions in Connecticut are, more often than not, the result of some form of town-meeting political structure,[62] I used Geoffrey Turnbull's (1992) pivotal voter model of local expenditure as the foundation for the empirical model.   Turnbull's model has the additional virtue of incorporating the empirically ubiquitous flypaper effect into the formal structure of the model through the assumption of a risk averse pivotal voter.[63]   In addition, because Connecticut's educational grant structure generates piecewise-linear budget constraints for its local school districts, the model is also based on Robert Moffitt's (1984, 1986) work on piecewise linear demand.[64]

Following Turnbull, then, assume that the provision of education in each school district is determined by a risk-averse pivotal voter who chooses a local tax rate t and receives utility $U(\gamma, C)$ from district per-pupil education expenditures γ and other consumption C.[65]   In choosing t, the pivotal voter is constrained by the personal budget constraint:

$$I(1 - s) = C + tH \tag{4-7}$$

and the school district budget constraint:

$$\gamma = t(V + \theta^V) + G \tag{4-8}$$

---

[62] See Connecticut Secretary of State (1980). Connecticut is entirely divided into 169 school districts that are coterminous with the state's 169 towns. Funding for school districts comes from town property tax levies and from state aid. Although school districts do not levy a separate tax, the share of the town's property tax revenues dedicated to public education is known (Connecticut State Board of Education (1979, 1981)). There are also some "regional" districts.   However, these districts are essentially cooperative arrangements among two or more of the 169 town-based districts. Sometimes the purpose of such districts is to run a joint school system. Other times, it is simply to run a combined high school.

[63] It should be noted that the issue of the appropriate treatment of the flypaper effect is an unsettled question. Because exploring alternative treatments of the flypaper effect would distract from the purpose of characterizing legislative preferences for grant structure, but because some treatment of the flypaper effect is necessary given the ubiquity of the effect, I have chosen to use Turnbull's model as a reasonable solution. For examples of alternative behavioral and econometric explanations of the flypaper effect, see Filimon, Romer, and Rosenthal (1982), Fisher (1982), Hamilton (1983), Zampelli (1986), Megdal (1987), Marshall (1991), and Turnbull (1992).

[64] Paul Rothstein (1992) uses such techniques in examining local school expenditure decisions.

[65] For ease of exposition, the i superscripts have been dropped.

where I represents the pivotal voter's income, H represents the value of the pivotal voter's assessed property, $V+\theta^{v}$ represents the local per-pupil tax base, G represents the state's public education per-pupil grant-in-aid, and s represents the state income tax rate needed to fund the state's educational grant program. Because the pivotal voter does not know the size of the district's tax base when choosing t, the local per-pupil tax base is modeled as the pivotal voter's expectation concerning that tax base, V, plus a stochastic element θ^{v} (assumed to have zero mean and finite variance σ_{v}^{2}) reflecting the pivotal voter's uncertainty over that tax base.

In 1980, Connecticut state aid per pupil G was provided through a DPE program that took the form of a per-pupil block grant B and a matching grant with rate m tied to local tax effort t:[66]

$$G = B + tm. \qquad (4\text{-}9)$$

The pivotal voter's problem is to choose t so as to maximize the expected value of utility $U(\gamma, C)$ subject to the *Equations (4-7)*, *(4-8)*, and *(4-9)*. The optimal tax rate t is one at which the relative value to the pivotal voter of the last unit of public education (measured in terms of private consumption) is equal to the loss in private consumption necessary to fund that last unit of public education.[67] Because the loss in private consumption associated with increasing public education comes about through an increase in taxes, it is commonly know as the tax price. Mathematically, then, this requirement for the optimal tax rate t is reflected in the requirement that pivotal voter's choice of tax rate satisfy the first order condition:

$$\frac{\left(\frac{\partial U}{\partial \gamma}\right)^{e}}{\left(\frac{\partial U}{\partial C}\right)^{e}} = \frac{H}{V+m} - \frac{\left(\frac{\partial U}{\partial \gamma}\right)^{e}\theta^{v}}{(V+m)\left(\frac{\partial U}{\partial C}\right)^{e}}. \qquad (4\text{-}10)$$

with the superscript e being the expectations operator. The pivotal voter's optimal tax rate defines the voter's desired level of expenditures γ^{d}. This desired level of expenditures γ^{d} is assumed to be a function of the pivotal

---

[66] Because the level of state aid was widely publicized before t was chosen, I assume that this aid was known with certainty.

[67] Those familiar with microeconomic theory will recognize this as the requirement that the marginal rate of substitution in the mind of the pivotal voter equal the marginal rate of physical transformation. If, for example, the pivotal voter valued public education relative to private consumption at a greater rate than it cost to make it, the pivotal voter would prefer a higher tax rate which would increase public education more than enough to compensate for the reduction in private consumption.

voter's tax price P, effective income M, and a set of personal characteristics Z:

$$\gamma^d = D(P, M, Z). \qquad (4\text{-}11)$$

As *Equation (4.10)* reveals, the form of the pivotal voter's effective tax price P is more complex than the classic form of tax price because of the presence of uncertainty and risk aversion:[68]

$$P = \frac{H}{V+m} - \frac{\left(\frac{\partial U}{\partial \gamma}\right)^e \theta^V}{(V+m)\left(\frac{\partial U}{\partial C}\right)^e}. \qquad (4\text{-}12)$$

This effective tax price differs from the standard tax price for two reasons. First, an increase in t results in an increase in expenditures both through increased local revenue and through increased state aid, hence, $V + m$ instead of V in the denominator of the first term. Second, voter risk aversion and uncertainty over the local tax base result in a tax price that is augmented in the mind of the voter by the 'risk premium' $\varPi$:

$$\varPi = - \frac{\left(\frac{\partial U}{\partial \gamma}\right)^e \theta^V}{(V+m)\left(\frac{\partial U}{\partial C}\right)^e} > 0. \qquad (4\text{-}13)$$

Effective income M is the amount of resources that the pivotal voter would expect to have were per-pupil educational expenditures γ set to zero.[69] An examination of *Equations (4-7), (4-8),* and *(4-9)* after setting γ equal to zero reveals that the pivotal voter's budget constraint can be rewritten as:

$$I(1-s) + \frac{BH}{V+m+\theta^V} = C. \qquad (4\text{-}14)$$

Hence, the pivotal voter's expected income M is the sum of the voter's personal income net of state taxes and the voter's expected share of the district's grant income:

---

[68] The classic form of the tax price is H/V reflecting the fact that for every dollar increase in per-pupil educational expenditures, the pivotal voter's share of that increase is equal to the pivotal voter's relative share of the school district's tax base.

[69] Steven Craig and Robert Inman (1986) refer to effective income as "full fiscal income."

$$M = I(1-s) + \left(\frac{BH}{V+m+\theta^V}\right)^e. \tag{4-15}$$

The particular effective tax price P and effective income M that each school district's pivotal voter in Connecticut had in 1980 depended on the matching rate m and block grant B that the pivotal voter's school district used to calculate their state aid. Most Connecticut local school districts in 1980 used "standard" formulae, m_1 and B_1, to calculate the matching rate and the block grant, thus resulting in an effective tax price P_1 and effective income M_1.[70] However, for particularly wealthy districts and for a few other districts with sufficiently high local property tax rates, the use of these standard formulae would have resulted in a per-pupil grant less than $250 (the size of the flat per-pupil grant provided throughout most of the 1970s). Originally, the legislature had hoped to provide additional "hold-harmless" aid to ensure that no district would receive less than $250 per pupil. However, fiscal pressures eventually led to each local school district's hold-harmless aid being reduced by 25%. The net effect was that local school districts receiving hold-harmless aid had a block grant B_2 that was greater than that which they would have received under the standard formula and a matching rate m_2 that was 75% lower than the standard matching rate formula.[71] Thus, the effective tax price and effective income for these districts was some $P_2 > P_1$ and $M_2 > M_1$. For all districts, there was also a district-specific minimum expenditure requirement (MER).

Overall, this grant structure resulted in three types of local school districts. The first type of local school districts were those school districts with sufficiently low property wealth to assure that state aid was at least $250 per pupil regardless of the value of the local property tax rate t chosen. Hence, formulae B_1 and m_1 were used, and desired demand took the form:

$$\gamma_1^d = f(M_1, P_1, Z). \tag{4-16}$$

---

[70] The standard block grant was equal to a district-specific block grant for various smaller, special programs plus 68% of the previous year's DPE grant. The standard matching rate was set equal to 32% of $(V^* - \bar{H})(N+0.5W)/N$ with V^* equal to a district-specific guaranteed tax base, H equal to the district's population-mean tax base, N the district's number of students, and W the district's number of children receiving AFDC aid. Defining $\bar{I}$ to be a district's population-mean income, V^* for each district was equal to the ninth largest $\bar{H} \cdot \bar{I}$ divided by the district's own $\bar{I}$.

[71] The block grant formula with the receipt of hold harmless aid was equal to a district-specific block grant for various smaller, special programs plus the sum of $187.50 and 17% of the previous year's DPE grant.

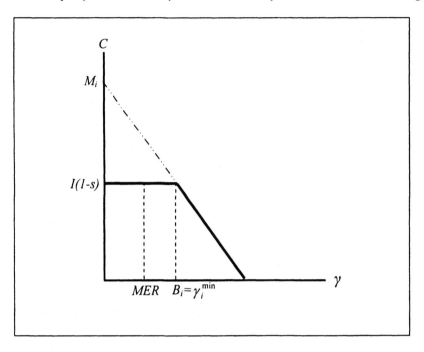

Figure 4-4. Type-1 and Type-2 School District Budget Constraint When $B_i >$ MER (i=1, 2)

The associated budget constraint for the pivotal voter in a type-1 school district depended on whether the standard block grant B_I was greater or less than the school district's MER. If, as is illustrated in *Figure 4-4*, the standard block grant B_I was greater than the school district's MER, then the minimum possible level of expenditure γ_1^{min} was equal to B_I. On the other hand, if, as is illustrated in *Figure 4-5,* the standard block grant B_I was less than the school district's MER, then the minimum possible level of expenditure γ_1^{min} was equal to the MER. Actual expenditures for these type-1 school districts then depended on whether desired demand γ_1^d was greater or less that the minimum possible level of expenditure γ_1^{min}. If desired demand γ_1^d was greater than the minimum expenditure level γ_1^{min}, actual expenditures were simply the sum of desired expenditures γ_1^d and unanticipated local property tax revenues $t\theta^v$. On the other hand, if desired demand γ_1^d was less than or equal to the minimum expenditure level γ_1^{min}, actual expenditures were set equal to the sum of the minimum expenditure level γ_1^{min} and the unanticipated local property tax revenues $t\theta^v$. Thus, following Moffitt (1984, 1986) and Rothstein (1992), actual expenditures can be defined as:

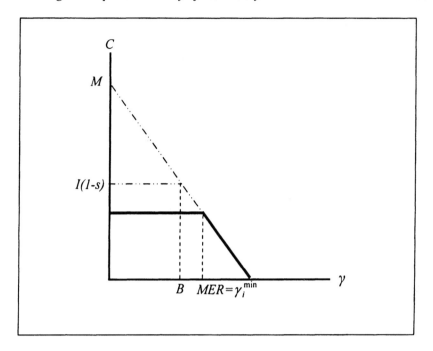

Figure 4-5. Type-1 and Type-2 School District Budget Constraint When MER > B_i (i=1, 2)

$$\gamma_1 = (1 - D_1)\gamma_1^{min} + D_1\gamma_1^d + \varepsilon_r \qquad (4\text{-}17)$$

with the random error ε_r being equal to the unanticipated property tax revenue $t\theta^v$ and:

$$D_1 = \begin{cases} 1 & if \quad \gamma_1^d > \gamma_1^{min} \\ 0 & if \quad \gamma_1^d \le \gamma_1^{min} \end{cases} \qquad (4\text{-}18)$$

The second type of district were those districts with property wealth that was sufficiently high to assure that state aid with the standard formulae would be less than $250 per pupil regardless of the value of the local property tax rate t chosen. Hence hold-harmless aid was always provided, and desired demand took the form:

$$\gamma_2^d = f(M_2, P_2, Z). \qquad (4\text{-}19)$$

Like the previous type, the associated budget constraint for the pivotal voter in a type-2 school district depended on whether the standard block grant B_2 was greater or less than the school district's MER. *Figure 4-4* illustrates the situation when the standard block grant B_2 was greater than the school district's MER, and *Figure 4-5* illustrates the situation when the standard block grant B_2 was less than the school district's MER. Actual expenditures for these type-2 school districts then depended on whether desired demand γ_2^d was greater or less that the minimum possible level of expenditure γ_2^{min}. If desired demand γ_2^d was greater than the minimum expenditure level γ_2^{min}, actual expenditures were simply the sum of desired expenditures γ_2^d and unanticipated local property tax revenues $t\theta^V$. On the other hand, if desired demand γ_2^d was less than or equal to the minimum expenditure level γ_2^{min}, actual expenditures were set equal to the sum of the minimum expenditure level γ_2^{min} and the unanticipated local property tax revenues $t\theta^V$. Thus, actual expenditures were:

$$\gamma_2 = (1 - D_2)\gamma_2^{min} + D_2\gamma_2^d + \varepsilon_r \qquad (4\text{-}20)$$

with the random error ε_r being defined as before, and with D_2 being defined as:

$$D_2 = \begin{cases} 1 & if \quad \gamma_2^d > \gamma_2^{min} \\ 0 & if \quad \gamma_2^d \leq \gamma_2^{min} \end{cases} \qquad (4\text{-}21)$$

Finally, the third type of school districts were those with property wealth between the two extremes examined above. For these districts, the receipt of hold-harmless aid depended on the value of the local property tax rate t that they chose. To facilitate the examination of this situation, let t_0 represent the value of the local property tax rate t at which the expected state aid based on the matching rate m_1 and B_1 equals the level of expected state aid expected using the matching rate m_2 and B_2. Then t_0 can be defined as:

$$t_0 = \frac{B_2 - B_1}{m_1 - m_2} \qquad (4\text{-}22)$$

with $\gamma(t_0)$ representing the associated level of per-pupil educational expenditures.

If the actual local property tax rate t chosen was less than t_0, then hold-harmless aid was provided to the school district, total state aid to the school district was defined by the matching rate m_2 and the block grant B_2, and the

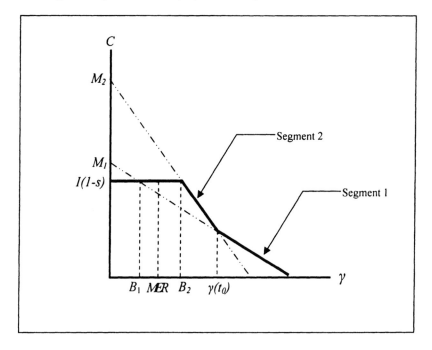

Figure 4-6. Type-3 School District Budget Constraint When MER < B_2

pivotal voter for the school district would have an effective income of M_2 and an effective tax price of P_2. However, if the actual local property tax rate t chosen was greater than or equal to t_0, then no hold-harmless aid was required, and so total state aid to the school district was defined by the matching rate m_1 and the block grant B_1, thus resulting in the pivotal voter in that school district having an effective income M_1 and a effective tax price of P_1.

Because $P_1 < P_2$ and $B_1 < B_2$, the implied budget constraint for this third type of local school district was generally convex to the origin with a kink at the expenditure level associated with $t = t_0$ (that is, at $\gamma(t_0)$) and with the minimum possible level of expenditure γ_3^{min} equal to the greater of B_2 and the school district's MER (recall that $B_1<B_2$), that is, it will be equal to γ_2^{min}. *Figures 4-6* and *4-7* illustrates this situation when the MER was less than $\gamma(t_0)$. The resulting form of the desired demand equation under this latter situation would therefore depend on which segment of the budget constraint provided the higher utility. If we allow the indirect utility function to be indicated by the function $W(P,M)$, then the first budget-constraint segment (where the pivotal voter's tax price and effective income are P_1 and M_1) would be preferred if $W(P_1,M_1) \geq W(P_2,M_2)$. On the other hand, if

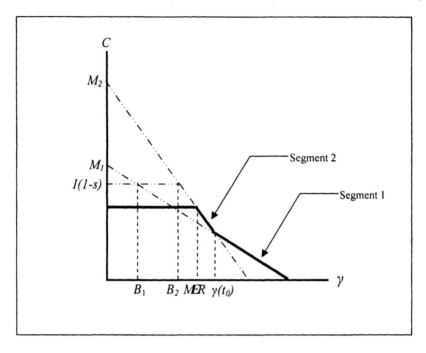

Figure 4-7. Type-3 School District Budget Constraint When $B_2 <$ MER $< \gamma(t_0)$

$W(P_1, M_1) < W(P_2, M_2)$, then the second segment would be preferred. Actual demand therefore took the form:

$$\gamma_3 = (1 - D_2)\gamma_2^{\min} + D_2(1 - D_3)\gamma_2^d + D_3\gamma_1^d + \varepsilon_r \qquad (4\text{-}23)$$

with γ_1^d, γ_2^d, and D_2 defined by *Equations (4-16), (4-19)*, and *(4-21)*, with ε_r being defined as before, and with D_3 being defined as:

$$D_3 = \begin{cases} 1 & if \quad W(P_1, M_1) > W(P_2, M_2) \\ 0 & if \quad W(P_1, M_1) \le W(P_2, M_2) \end{cases} \qquad (4\text{-}24)$$

If, however, the MER was greater than $\gamma(t_0)$, then, as *Figure 4-8* illustrates, none of Segment 2 was available to the school district and the budget constraint for the school district was essentially the same as that associated with type-1 school districts (compare *Figure 4-8* with *Figure 4-5*) with demand equal to γ_1 as defined in *Equation (4-17)*.

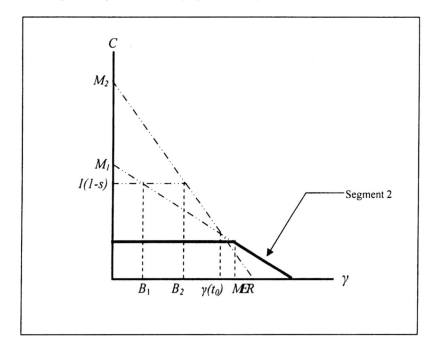

Figure 4-8. Type-3 School District Budget Constraint When MER > $\gamma(t_0)$

2.2   Estimation

The theoretical model developed in this chapter was estimated using 1980 data from all 169 Connecticut school districts.[72]   See *Table 4-2* for a summary of the variables used and their values.   Population mean and median values were used for the pivotal voter's housing, income, and other personal characteristics.[73]   To account for the pivotal voter's expectations, I used the lagged value of the local tax base to proxy for V,[74] assumed that the risk premium Π can be modeled by the function $\varphi_P/(V+m)$ with φ_P being a parameter to be estimated, and assumed that the voter's expected share of

---

[72] Data were taken from US Department of Commerce, Census Bureau (1982a), from printouts based on US Department of Commerce, Census Bureau (1982b, 1983), from Connecticut Office of Policy and Management (1980), from photocopies provided by the Connecticut State Department of Education, and from Connecticut State Board of Education (1979, 1981).

[73] The set of demographic variables available and included in the empirical analysis were median age, median household size, median education, proportion of population that was black, proportion of the population that rented, and proportion of the population that resided in US Census defined urban areas.

[74] The use of lagged property values precludes introducing an error-in-variables problem.

Table 4-2. 1980 Connecticut school district characteristics (1980 dollars)

Variable	Description	Mean	Standard deviation	Minimum	Maximum
γ	Per-pupil expenditures	2,480	388	1,753	3,550
V	Per-pupil tax base	194,039	96,830	83,020	640,614
S	Number of pupils	3,159	3,775	99	25,951
B	Per-pupil block grant	400	68	265	660
H	Median housing value	68,660	24,729	40,100	186,700
I(1-s)	Net median income	21,986	5,471	11,354	44,355
MA	Median age	32.7	3.3	21.8	41.8
MS	Median household size	2.6	0.3	2.0	3.5
ME	Median education	2.2	0.4	1	4
PB	Proportion population black	0.02	0.05	0.0	0.34
PR	Proportion population renting	0.25	0.13	0.06	0.77
PU	Proportion population urban	0.43	0.41	0.00	1.00

Notes:

γ = 1980 current educational expenses net of transportation costs, capital outlays, and debt service. This is the same variable used by Lovell (1978) in his analysis of 1970 Connecticut.

V = 1979 equalized net grand list divided by S.

S = 1980 average daily membership.

B = See footnotes 18 and 19

H = 1980 median value of owner-occupied housing

s = 1980 aggregate state educational grants divided by state aggregate personal income

ME = constructed from 1980 frequency data of the educational attainment for persons 18 years old and over (1=less than a high school degree; 2=completed high school; 3=1-3 years of college; 4=4 years of college; 5=5 or more years of college).

the district's grant income which enters into the determination of expected effective income (see *Equation (4-15)*), can be modeled by the function $BH/(V+m+\varphi_M)$ with φ_M being the parameter to be estimated. Finally, I assumed that desired demand took a log-linear form with, following Moffitt (1984, 1986) and Rothstein (1992), an additive error term ε_h (with finite variance σ_h^2) that reflects heterogeneity error.[75] This error, like the random error ε_r, is not known to the analyst. However, unlike the random error, this error is known to the pivotal voter. Thus, desired demand with this additional structure took the form:

$$\ln \gamma^d = \pi P + \mu M + \zeta Z + \varepsilon_h. \tag{4.25}$$

As Moffitt (1986) notes, two-error models such as this one generally require the use of maximum likelihood estimation methods. However, a complication arises with this particular model because the expenditure data cluster away from the minimum expenditure requirement MER. Hence, it is

[75] I also estimated the model using a linear functional form. Results were much the same.

Table 4-3. Estimation results (p-values in parentheses)

Parameter	Description	Basic Model	Demographic Model
φ_P	Risk premium parameter	145,108	31,597
		(0.34)	(0.28)
φ_M	Grant-income share parameter	-103,264	-104,393
		(0.00)	(0.00)
π	Tax price coefficient	-0.30	-0.51
		(0.21)	(0.01)
μ	Income coefficient	0.9E-5	2.0E-5
		(0.02)	(0.00)
ζ_0	Constant term	7.94	7.92
		(0.00)	(0.00)
ζ_{MA}	Age coefficient		-4.0E-5
			(0.66)
ζ_{MS}	Household size coefficient		-0.15
			(0.00)
ζ_{ME}	Education coefficient		0.02
			(0.41)
ζ_{PB}	Proportion black coefficient		0.89
			(0.00)
ζ_{PR}	Proportion renting coefficient		0.03
			(0.65)
ζ_{PU}	Proportion urban coefficient		0.01
			(0.40)
σ^2	Likelihood fn. variance	1.1E-2	0.8E-2
	parameter	(0.00)	(0.00)
Function value		-1183.80	-1154.38
Squared correlation coefficient for actual and predicted expenditures		0.50	0.65
Likelihood ratio test (demographic variables; df=6)			58.84
			(0.00)

not possible to separately identify ε_h and ε_r. The model must therefore be specified as a single-error model. While such models can be estimated with either non-linear least squares or maximum likelihood, I chose maximum likelihood using *EZClimb* (Leyden 1991), a hill-climbing program based on Goldfeld, Quandt, and Trotter's (1966, 1968) modified quadratic hill-climbing algorithm.

The results of estimating the model both with and without the set of demographic variables are presented in *Table 4-3*. Overall performance as measured by the squared correlation coefficient were generally good with both the basic model and the demographic model (0.50 and 0.65

respectively) with the coefficients on the common set of core variables $(\varphi_P, \varphi_M, \pi, \mu, \zeta_0)$ of expected sign and generally significant. The coefficient μ on the expected effective income M was positive as expected and statistically significant at standard levels for both models, while the coefficient π on the effective tax price term P was negative and, for the demographic model, statistically significant. The demographic variables as a group had a statistically significant effect as measured by a likelihood ratio test. Connecticut school districts with a greater median level of education had, ceteris paribus, greater per-pupil spending, as did districts with a greater proportion of the population that was black, that were renters, or that lived in urban areas. Districts with an older median age or greater median household size tended, ceteris paribus, to choose lower levels of spending.[76]

The 1980 Connecticut pivotal voter's attitudes about uncertainty and risk are embodied in the grant-income share parameter φ_M and the risk premium parameter φ_P. The estimate of the grant-income share parameter, φ_M, which can be interpreted as a measure of the amount by which local property wealth is discounted because of uncertainty and risk aversion, was relatively stable between the two models with a value in the neighborhood of $-100,000$. Given that mean per-pupil property value was just under $200,000 (see *Table 4-2*), it would appear that the average 1980 Connecticut pivotal voter effectively discounted the local per-pupil tax base by more than half as a result of risk aversion and the presence of uncertainty.

The parameter φ_P is less easy to interpret intuitively, but forms the critical parameter for getting a measure of the 1980 Connecticut pivotal voter's risk premium and thereby the degree to which that pivotal voter

---

[76] Bergstrom, Rubinfeld, and Shapiro (1982), Lovell (1978), and Rubinfeld and Shapiro (1989) also found education to have a positive effect on educational expenditures; Denzau (1975) found no significant effect. The proportion of the population that is black was found to affect expenditures positively by Bergstrom, Rubinfeld, and Shapiro (1982); Rubinfeld and Shapiro (1989) found no significant effect, though they cited additional microdata that black voters tend to demand more education than their white counterparts. Rothstein (1992) found an insignificant negative effect. Concerning household size, Bergstrom, Rubinfeld, and Shapiro (1982), Rothstein (1992), and Rubinfeld and Shapiro (1989) found, unlike this study, that it had a positive effect on education expenditures; Lovell (1978), Romer and Rosenthal (1982), and Filimon, Romer, and Rosenthal (1982) found that the number of children affected expenditures negatively. Concerning age, Bergstrom, Rubinfeld, and Shapiro (1982) and Rubinfeld and Shapiro (1989) found that the proportion of the population over 65 was a positive factor in educational expenditures, while Rothstein (1992) found, like this study, that age was a negative factor. Finally, Rothstein (1992) is the only study of which I am aware in which a measure of owner/renter status is used; he finds that the fraction of owner-occupied housing in a district affects expenditures negatively. See Martinez-Vazquez and Sjoquist (1988) for an analysis of the importance of distinguishing renters from homeowners in models of local public choice.

Table 4-4. Tax prices, elasticities, and derivatives (district means)

Statistic	Basic Model	Demographic Model
Risk premium Π	0.80	0.17
Actual tax price ($H/(V+m)$)	------------ 0.35 ------------	
Effective tax price ($H/(V+m)+\Pi$)	1.15	0.52
Elasticity of per-pupil expenditures with respect to ...		
• Actual tax price	-0.10	-0.18
• Effective tax price	-0.34	-0.27
• Personal income	0.20	0.44
Derivative of per-pupil expenditures with respect to		
• personal income ($\partial E/\partial I(1-s)$)	0.02	0.05
• grant-income share ($\partial E/\partial I$)	0.06	0.14
Turnbull's risk-income elasticity	-0.03	-0.06

effectively overestimated the tax price as a result of uncertainty and risk aversion. Here, the results differ remarkably between the two models. As *Table 4-4* reveals, the average actual tax price, $H/(V+m)$, was a reasonable 0.35. However, because of dramatically different measures of φ_P in the two models, the estimate of the average risk premium Π was quite different between the two models (0.80 in the basic model versus 0.17 in the demographic model), thus resulting in a rather high mean effective tax, $H/(V+m)+\Pi$, in the basic model of 1.15 versus a more reasonable value of 0.52 in the demographic model. This latter value suggests that the 1980 average Connecticut pivotal voter effectively overestimated the local tax price by just under fifty percent as a result of uncertainty and risk aversion.

Consistency of the empirical results with other studies can show by examining elasticities. The mean price elasticity with respect to the actual tax price in the more reasonable demographic model (see again *Table 4-4*) was –0.18, a value that is consistent with other studies and, as expected, smaller than the mean price elasticity with respect to effective tax price (–0.27 in the demographic model).[77] Mean income elasticity with respect to personal income with a value of 0.44 in the demographic model was somewhat lower than other studies but within the range expected and certainly more in keeping with other studies than the value (0.20) in the basic model.[78]

---

[77] Inman (1979) and Bergstrom, Rubinfeld, and Shapiro (1982), found price elasticities in the -1/4 to -1/2 range. Rubinfeld and Shapiro (1989) argue, however, that these estimates may be biased and too elastic.

[78] Inman (1979) and Bergstrom, Rubinfeld, and Shapiro (1982) found income elasticities around 2/3. Rubinfeld and Shapiro (1989) argue, however, that this value may be biased and too elastic.

Finally, note that the mean derivative of per-pupil district expenditures with respect to an increase in the pivotal voter's share of grant income $\left(BH/(V + m + \theta^V)\right)^e$ was 0.14 in the demographic model which was more than twice the value of the same derivative with respect to an equal increase in personal income (0.05 in the demographic model). This finding, that a government receiving a grant will increase its spending by more than they would have had personal income in the community risen by an amount equivalent to the amount of the grant, is know as the flypaper effect ("money sticks where it lands") and is ubiquitous in empirical studies of local government spending behavior. It is also consistent with Turnbull's (1992) argument that the flypaper effect is the result of voter risk aversion in the face of uncertainty concerning the size of the local tax base. Evidence of the consistency of these results with Turnbull's argument can be seen by calculating the risk-income effect elasticity which measures the degree to which an increase in the standard error in the tax base affects the level of expenditures. The mean risk-income effect elasticity was -0.06, thus indicating that a relatively small amount of uncertainty over the local tax base is sufficient to explain a significant portion of the flypaper effect. Turnbull's benchmark value for the risk-income effect elasticity was -0.12.

Overall, then, while both models performed reasonably well, the demographic model was significantly better at explaining Connecticut's educational expenditures in 1980 and was more consistent with expectations. An intuitive explanation for this is that there is considerable variation in behavior across local school districts that is correlated with the various demographic variables. When those demographic variables are not included in the model, the parameter estimates (particularly those associated with the tax price) provide a measure of the behavior of an "average" district but of no individual district in particular. Thus, the underlying relationship between tax price and expenditures is to some degree masked, and the power of the model reduced. Inclusion of the demographic variables allows each district to have, in essence, an unique constant term and thereby increase the power of the model.

2.3   Simulation

Using the results from the demographic model, 1980 Connecticut local school district expenditures were simulated under three alternative grant structure regimes - the actual DPE program employed by Connecticut in 1980, the archetypal foundation grant program described by *Equation 4-3* above, and a "complete" foundation program that requires school districts to levy the minimum tax rate associated with the archetypal foundation grant

Table 4-5. Predicted effects of alternative grant structures on Connecticut public school district expenditures

Effect on ...	DPE	Grant Structure Archetypal Foundation	Complete Foundation
Per-pupil spending by wealthiest districts	Fall	No change	No change
Per-pupil spending by poorest districts	Rises the most	Rises the least	Rises a middle amount
Standard deviation in per-pupil spending	Falls the most	Falls the least	Falls a middle amount
State-wide per-pupil spending		Less than associated with a complete foundation program	Less than needed to reduce disparity as much as DPE program

structure.[79] To eliminate the possible effect of differing state tax rates, I assumed for all simulations that total aid from the state, and hence the state tax rate, was fixed at actual 1980 levels. For the two foundation grant structures, the minimum tax rate t^{min} was calculated using a minimum school district tax base V^* equal to \$288,276, that is, 45% of the maximum school district tax base. Given the total amount of aid from the state, this implied $t^* = 0.0060$ (compared to the 1980 district mean of 0.0092).[80]

Table 4-5 summarizes the predicted results of this simulation exercise based on the theoretical analysis in Section 2 above. In brief, the DPE program was predicted to reduce spending disparities the greatest by raising spending in the poorest districts and reducing spending in the richest districts. Both foundation grant structures were predicted to increase spending in the poorest districts (more so with the complete foundation grant structure) but leave spending in the richest districts unchanged. Predictions about the level of per-pupil spending statewide were less straightforward. Based on the analysis in Section 1 above, it was anticipated that any foundation grant structure that reduces spending disparities to the same degree as the DPE grant structure will result in higher per-pupil spending statewide and a bigger legislative budget. Because total state aid was kept constant in the simulations, it was therefore anticipated that per-pupil spending statewide under the two foundation grant structures would be less

---

[79] See Ladd and Yinger (1994) and Reschovsky (1994).

[80] I also ran the simulations assuming V^* was \$256,246 or 40% of the maximum school district tax base. Given the fixed set of state funds, this implied $t^* = 0.0080$. Interestingly, however, the conclusions did not change, though, it should be noted, as the percentage that defines V^* fell, the foundation grant program (archetypal or complete) resulted in a higher mean expenditure and higher mean tax rate.

Table 4-6. Simulated 1980-1 Connecticut per-pupil expenditures (1980 dollars)

| | Simulated Expenditures | | | Actual Expenditures | Effect of Switching from DPE to … | |
	DPE	Archetypal Foundation	Complete Foundation		Archetypal Foundation	Complete Foundation
Mean	2,473	2,452	2,497	2,480	-21	+25
Median	2,424	2,432	2,432	2,424	-19	-19
Std dev	324	425	395	389	+255	+220
Minimum	1,957	1,238	1,831	1,753	-914	-316
Maximum	3,681	4,188	4,188	3,550	+2,918	+2,004

than the amount needed to reduce spending disparities to levels associated with the DPE structure. Moreover, because the complete foundation grant structure requires a minimum school district tax rate, it was anticipated that per-pupil spending statewide would be lower with an archetypal foundation grant structure than with a complete foundation grant.

Actual results are summarized in *Table 4-6.* As predicted, under the DPE structure, minimum spending is greater, maximum spending is lower, and spending disparity is lower than under either form of foundation grant structure. Moreover, and again as predicted, increasing the rigor of the foundation grant structure (as witnessed by the change from the archetypal foundation grant structure to the complete foundation grant structure) does not change maximum spending levels. Finally, and again as predicted, per-pupil spending statewide is less under the archetypal foundation grant structure than it is under the complete foundation structure, and per-pupil spending statewide under the two foundation grant structures is less than the amount needed to reduce spending disparities to the levels associated with the DPE structure. This last result, in particular, provides indirect evidence that had the legislature employed some form of foundation grant structure to satisfy the Court, its budget would have been larger than it was using the DPE structure. *Figure 4-9* presents these results graphically, and a comparison of *Figure 4-9* and *Figure 4-2* reveals the consistency of the simulation results with the theory.

3.   CONCLUSION

This chapter has provided empirical evidence of the consistency of the theoretical model presented in *Chapter 3* with observed state legislative behavior. The conditions under which a state legislature, confronted with a court order to reform its educational grant structure, will prefer one type of grant structure over another were derived from *Chapter 3's* theoretical

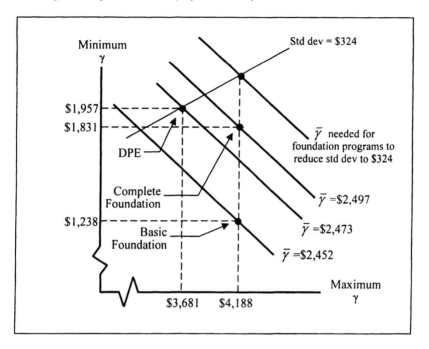

Figure 4-9. Simulated Per-Pupil Expenditures Under Alternative Grant Structures, 1980-1
(1980 dollars)

model, and these conditions were empirically evaluated using 1980 data
from Connecticut along with an independently developed econometric
model of local school district behavior. The empirical results confirmed the
predictions of the theoretical analysis, thus reinforcing the notion that a state
legislature's choice of public education grant structure depends critically on
the incentives inherent in the state's political structure and the legal
standards used by the court in evaluating the constitutionality of that state's
educational grant structure. Equally important, given the criticism that has
sometimes been levied against DPE grant structures, is the specific finding
that the choice of a DPE grant structure over a foundation grant structure
may in fact be the result of a rational calculus on the part of a state
legislature and not the result of some misapprehension about such grant
structures.

That a state legislature's choice of grant structure depends not simply on
the effect of such grant structures on local school district behavior, but on
the effects of such grant structures in the context of the political and legal
environment in which the state legislature finds itself suggests that a full
understanding of past behavior and prediction of future behavior requires a

full appreciation for the political and legal context within which state legislatures operate. It is, therefore, to that task that the next chapter turns.

Chapter 5

A LEGISLATIVE AND LEGAL HISTORY OF PUBLIC EDUCATION FUNDING

Those who cannot remember the past are condemned to repeat it.
— George Santayana, *Reason in Common Sense*[81]

The past half century has witnessed more than a five-fold increase in the real value of resources devoted to public education. While the number of students has also risen over that period, real expenditures even when adjusted for the number of students have also risen steadily so that today per-pupil educational expenditures are now about four times as large as they were in the late 1950s. Interestingly, however, educational expenditures as a percentage of GDP, while higher than the late 1950s, have remained roughly the same (in the neighborhood of four percent) since 1970. Moreover, while the percentage of the federal government's budget devoted to public education is double the level it was in 1960, it still amounts to less than two percent of all federal government expenditures. Finally, the seeming paradox of educational expenditures comprising a smaller percentage of state governmental budgets today than in 1960 is explained in large part by the addition of other activities since 1960 to the list of services that state governments provide, and not to a reduction in the level of involvement by state governments.

Within the context of these general trends, state governments have moved from a world in which its legislatures funded public education for the most part unfettered by outside forces to a world today in which virtually every state legislature finds itself under pressure from the courts, the federal government, and the general public to reform its funding of public education.[82]

---

[81] Santayana (1920).

[82] As of 2004, all but five states (Delaware, Hawaii, Mississippi, Nevada and Utah) have had legal challenges to their state educational funding systems (Advocacy Center for Children's Educational Success with Standards (2004)).

This chapter examines the history of the public education funding process with a particular focus on the courts, the effect of their interventions on state legislative funding behavior, and the legal reasoning that has underlain their actions. Using *Chapter 3*'s model of the public education funding process, particularly the spatial voting diagram developed in that chapter,[83] this chapter traces the effect of the court's initial forays in the 1970s that focused on increased funding equity between school districts, to the growing dissatisfaction with the outcome of such efforts in the late 1980s, to the attempt to reframe the problem in adequacy and accountability terms in the 1990s.   While the courts would seem to have considerable power to affect the funding of public education, in practice their ability to manipulate state legislatures has been severely constrained by the inability and/or the unwillingness of state legislatures to fully comply with court orders.   The result is that the use of the courts to effect changes in the funding of public education has been a slow (and education reform advocates would say a frustrating) process.

From a legal and economic perspective, the history of public education funding can be divided into three periods that reflect the degree and the type of intervention by the courts in the state legislative funding process.   The first period covers the time during which the courts were for the most part uninvolved in that funding process.   Though the end of that period varies from state to state, by convention that period ends with the California Supreme Court case *Serrano v. Priest* in 1971.[84]   The second period covers the time from the *Serrano* case forward during which the courts focused primarily on funding equity between school districts, that is, on equalizing per-pupil expenditures across school districts, and sorting out the legal issue of whether public education funding equity cases were essentially a federal or a state legal issue.   Again, the end of that period varies from state to state (and indeed has never ended in some states), but generally is associated with the Kentucky Supreme Court case *Rose v. Council for Better Education* case in 1989.   The final period comprises the period from the *Rose* case forward and generally deals with the attempts by the courts and legislatures to formulate and implement an alternative to the disappointing equalization efforts that is based on the notions of adequacy and accountability.

---

[83] This diagram provides a schematic representation of per-pupil spending levels γ_i in higher and lower spending local school districts that come about as the result choices the state legislature makes with regard to the providing aid to local school districts (the local school districts' reaction to such choices already incorporated into the analysis). It also provides measurement of the overall level of support for public education in the state through a line $\bar{\gamma}$ representing statewide average per-pupil expenditures. For more details, see *Chapter 3*.

[84] Full legal citations are provided in the *Reference* section at the end of the book.

1. PUBLIC EDUCATION FUNDING BEFORE SERRANO

1.1 Public Education Governance and Funding Structures

The modern provision of public education through a system of local school districts that receive grants from state governments can be traced to the Progressive Era reforms in the late 1800s and to the associated later work of Ellwood Cubberley, George Strayer, and Robert Haig. As Charles Benson (1961) and Abe Feuerstein (2002) document, prior to the Progressive Era local school districts were by and large autonomous units governed by large school boards whose members where elected by district and whose responsibilities ranged all the way from establishing general policy to taking care of such day-to-day administrative tasks as hiring individual teachers and choosing textbooks. However, in the late 1800s, the Progressive Era ushered in a variety of changes intent on removing governmental administration from political influence and instituting a professional class of governmental administrators. While perhaps the best known change during the Progressive Era was the institution of a city manager form of government, school districts were also swept up in the movement. Because of perceptions of political corruption and poor quality school administration, the size and power of school boards were reduced and general administrative power transferred to an enhanced superintendent position. Thus, from the late 1800s until the 1960s, school boards were typically relatively small bodies, often elected at large, charged with setting general local education policy, and overseeing the local school district's superintendent who was charged with administering the day-to-day affairs of the school district.

Revenues for local school districts in the late 1800s varied and were often tied to endowment funds. With the beginning of the 1900s, however, these funds, even when supplemented with tax revenues, were no longer adequate to the task of educating children at the level increasingly demanded by local constituencies.[85] Ellwood Cubberley, then a doctoral student at Columbia University's Teachers College and later dean of Stanford

---

[85] It is perhaps paradoxical that in recent decades, public *higher* education has seen state governments increasingly unwilling to provide increased funds for the delivery of education services, and that as a result, such institutions have become increasingly dependent on endowment income, provided this time not by the state government but by private sources.

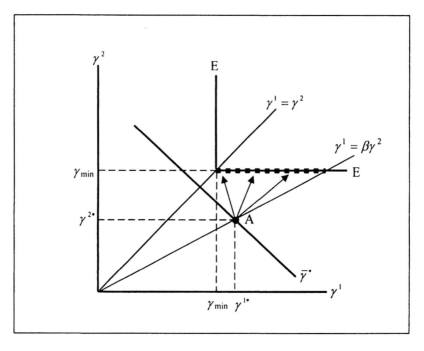

Figure 5-1. Cubberley's Pursuit of Educational Adequacy Through an Early Form of DPE Grant Structure

University's School of Education, argued in his highly influential *School Funds and Their Apportionment* (Cubberley (1905)) that all children deserved the same advantage as much as possible when it came to their education and that the primary obligation for assuring such a result rested with the state government because education, unlike sewers, is not solely a local concern, but rather a matter of the common good. Moreover, he argued that aid should not be given indiscriminately, but rather should be based on both need and effort in order to provide incentives for local school districts to provide quality education and to encourage those school districts to increase the length of the school year and attendance rates. To that end, he advocated a system of state funding based on the number of teachers and aggregate attendance over the school year (to encourage the lengthening of the school year) with an additional fund to achieve an equalization of education services that did not result from the above funding structure.

In practice, while the level of education generally improved and expanded both in terms of the length of the school year and the number of years students attended, the range of educational quality across school districts was still quite high. Such a result was not wholly unexpected. As James Ward (1990) notes, Cubberley was well aware that while all children are deserving of the same advantages, in practice that is not likely to occur. In part because of this recognition, Cubberley's proposals, as *Figure 5-1* illustrates,[86] while attempting to achieve a reduction in spending disparities across school districts, focused more on increasing the minimum level of spending.

But Cubberley's willingness to accept inequalities in the hope of improving minimum levels of spending was not shared by all. Concern over such inequalities increased, and in 1921 the National Educational Association formed a commission with the support of several philanthropic organizations including the Carnegie Corporation to determine the cost of providing quality public education, and to determine how proper funding for such education might be obtained. With the guidance of an advisory committee that included such notable academics as Edwin Seligman from Columbia University, Wesley Mitchell, director of the National Bureau of Economic Research, and James Angell, president of Yale University, the commission began its work. By 1923 the commission had finished, and issued its report *The Financing of Education in the State of New York*, authored by commission members George Strayer of Columbia University's Teachers College and Robert Haig of Columbia University's economics department. The report proposed a number of recommendations – an increase in the overall level of support for public education, the elimination of the number of teachers as a criterion for state aid, and the use of a state grant structure that we call today a foundation grant structure (Strayer and Haig (1923)).[87]

The proposal to eliminate the number of teachers as a criterion for state aid is especially interesting because it presages the current modern debate over equalization versus adequacy, and foundation versus district power equalization educational grant structures. In practice, the use of the number of teachers as a criterion for state aid, as Cubberley knew, results in state aid being a positive function of the local tax effort. But such rewards, as Strayer and Haig recognized, increases the possible disparities in per-pupil spending across school districts by creating an additional incentive for school districts to increase spending.[88] Thus, because Strayer and Haig had a greater preference for equalizing spending across school districts than did Cubberley (see *Figure 5-2*), they proposed removing that criterion and using a foundation grant structure instead. It turns out that Strayer and Haig's

---

[86] Point A indicates the initial mix of per-pupil expenditures in higher- and lower-spending local school districts; the line $\gamma^1 = \beta\gamma^2$ indicates those per-pupil expenditure combinations with the same proportional level of disparity as at point A.

[87] See *Equation 3-3* in *Chapter 3* for a simple version of this structure.

[88] See Ward (1990) for further discussion.

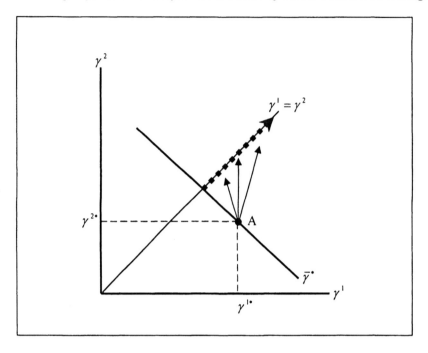

Figure 5-2. Strayer and Haig's Pursuit of Educational Equality Through a Foundation Grant
Structure

arguments were persuasive, and by the 1960s, most states had adopted some
variant of the foundation grant structure that they had proposed.[89]

The 1960s are commonly viewed as a period of relative calm in public
education funding. However, while the landscape of public education
governance and funding was relatively stable in this period immediately
preceding the modern explosion of controversy over public education
funding in the 1970s, it is important to note that as a result of increased
social advocacy tied to the civil rights movement, efforts in the 1960s had
begun to open up school board governance to a broader range of
constituencies through increases in board size and the return of election by
district. Feuerstein (2002), in fact, argues that the reforms of the Progressive
Era had in some ways put school boards under the control of a local elite,

---

[89] Strayer and Haig's report, with its focus on institutional arrangements, the notion that
socially desirable goals can be achieved through changes in such arrangements, and the
use of methodical empirical analysis, fits within the spirit of institutional economics
movement that reached its zenith in the 1920s and that counted among its founding leaders
Wesley Mitchell. Institutional economics has often been viewed as incoherent, but
Malcolm Rutherford (2000) argues otherwise and provides a coherent description of the
movement and an explanation as to why the program was so appealing in the 1920s.

thus reducing the responsiveness of school boards to the demands of minority and low-income individuals, and that these reforms reflected an effort to re-democratize the governance of public education. Paradoxically, however, the reforms intended to open up the public education governance process to minorities and low-income individuals, were accompanied by increased centralization at the state level. The result was the beginning of the gradual reduction in the power of local school boards, even as these boards became more representative of local interests, and the increase in state control of the local education process. This resulted in political asymmetry between state and local interests which set the stage for increased state intervention in the financing of local public education.[90]

1.2 Funding and Expenditure Patterns

In 1960, public education revenues totaled 2.9% of GDP (nearly $75 billion in 2002 dollars) with per-pupil public education expenditures averaging $2,382, or just over a quarter of current levels.[91] While the federal government provided almost $3.3 billion, that sum amounted to only 4% of total public education revenues and made up less than 1% of the total federal budget. By contrast, state and local governments devoted over 36% of their budgets to public education which amounted to 96% of total public education revenues. By 1970, public education revenues had risen dramatically, totaling 4.1% of GDP or $162 billion, and the federal government's contribution had risen to nearly $13 billion. Despite that rise, however, federal aid during this time was for political reasons typically provided through categorical grants that could not be used to help school districts cover their general expenses.[92] As a result, by 1970 state and local governments still provided more than 92% of all public education revenues, and even more of the funds needed for the general function of local school districts.

[90] Political asymmetry occurs when those who dominate local school boards have preferences that are different from those who dominate the state government. Because of different participation patterns in school school-board versus state-legislature elections and differences in interest group behavior and influence at the local versus the state level, such asymmetries are likely to exist. As state governments become more involved in such local decision making, this political asymmetry results in greater reason for intervention by the state government. See *Chapter 2* for more details.

[91] All dollar figures in this chapter are in 2002 dollar terms. See *Chapter 1* for details on the source of these figures.

[92] See Rossmiller (1990). As Robert Berne and Leanna Stiefel (1999) document, the federal government continues to restrict its public education aid to specific purposes, particularly for special needs students such as those who are disabled, economically disadvantaged, or economically at-risk.

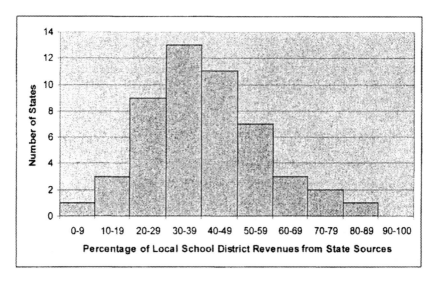

Figure 5-3. Distribution of School District Dependence on State Revenues, 1970-1[93]

While state and local governments uniformly provided the bulk of public education funding during this period, the degree of state aid to local school districts varied considerably across states. As *Figure 5-1* reveals, state support for public education ranged from less than 10% of total funding to more than 80%. On average, approximately 85% of that aid took the form of general purpose aid (the rest being intended for specific services and programs such as vocational education, transportation, and building construction) with roughly 2/3 of that general purpose aid intended to reduce disparities in available resources between low- and high-wealth school districts (Benson (1961), Reischauer and Hartman (1973)).

The effect that such equalization aid had on reducing disparities in per-pupil expenditures across school districts is not clear, and certainly considerable disparities in intra-state per-pupil expenditures still existed in most states by the late 1960s.[94] As *Table 5-1* reveals, the ratio of highest-to-lowest school district per-pupil expenditures in 1969-70 ranged from 56.2

---

[93] Derived from *Table 2-3* of Reischauer and Hartman (1973).

[94] Similar concerns exist over inequities in the distribution in resources within school districts. Historically this intra-district issue has not received much attention, no doubt, in part, because of the difficulty of getting information and data about the distribution of resources within particular school districts. However, William Camp, David Thompson, and John Crain (1990) in their examination of the issue argue that this may be changing as researchers and litigants develop more sophisticated strategies for examining the issue. For more recent documentation of intradistrict inequities, see Iatarola and Stiefel (2003).

Table 5-1. Disparities in School District Per-Pupil Property Values and Expenditures, 1968-9 and 1969-70

state	Ratio of highest-to-lowest school district per-pupil property values, 1968-9	Ratio of highest-to-lowest school district per-pupil expenditures, 1969-70	Ratio of 90th percentile-to-lowest school district per-pupil expenditures, 1969-70	state	Ratio of highest-to-lowest school district per-pupil property values, 1968-9	Ratio of highest-to-lowest school district per-pupil expenditures, 1969-70	Ratio of 90th percentile-to-lowest school district per-pupil expenditures, 1969-70
Alabama	4.5	2.0	1.6	New Hampshire	4.5	4.8	2.6
Alaska	3.9	3.8	2.6	New Jersey	10.4	5.9	2.1
Arizona	22.2	7.1	2.4	New Mexico	21.4	2.5	1.4
Arkansas	10.7	3.4	1.7	New York	84.2	11.4	1.9
California	24.6	7.9	2.3	North Carolina	3.2	1.6	1.4
Colorado	11.1	6.3	1.9	North Dakota	1.7	5.6	2.4
Connecticut	5.7	2.6	2.0	Ohio	10.7	4.1	2.1
Delaware	5.5	1.7	1.7	Oklahoma	22.4	8.3	2.1
Florida	9.3	1.8	1.4	Oregon	5.3	11.4	2.1
Georgia	4.7	2.0	1.9	Pennsylvania	10.5	7.9	2.1
Hawaii*	na	na	na	Rhode Island	2.2	2.3	2.0
Idaho	3.0	6.6	1.9	South Carolina	8.8	1.5	1.4
Illinois	20.1	5.9	2.9	South Dakota	9.7	34.2	4.3
Indiana	17.4	2.6	2.0	Tennessee	9.5	2.5	2.0
Iowa	5.2	2.0	1.5	Texas	45.1	56.2	3.4
Kansas	182.8	3.2	1.6	Utah	8.6	2.8	1.2
Kentucky	8.6	2.6	1.7	Vermont	3.3	4.2	2.5
Louisiana	13.5	1.8	1.5	Virginia	6.8	2.6	1.8
Maine	11.2	9.1	3.1	Washington	12.5	9.2	2.3
Maryland	2.8	1.6	1.6	West Virginia	3.6	1.4	1.4
Massachusetts	10.4	9.3	2.1	Wisconsin	77.9	3.4	2.1
Michigan	30.0	3.1	2.2	Wyoming	6.1	23.6	1.9
Minnesota	5.2	4.0	2.1				
Mississippi	5.2	2.6	1.7	**Maximum**	**182.8**	**56.2**	**4.3**
Missouri	29.6	9.1	3.8	**Mean**	**17.2**	**7.0**	**2.1**
Montana	3.1	18.2	2.9	**Median**	**9.3**	**3.8**	**2.0**
Nebraska	19.0	12.4	2.9	**Minimum**	**1.7**	**1.4**	**1.2**
Nevada	4.0	2.2	1.2	**Std. Deviation**	**29.1**	**9.3**	**0.7**

*Hawaii has a single statewide district.

Source: Advisory Commission on Intergovernmental Relations (1973), Tables 31-33.

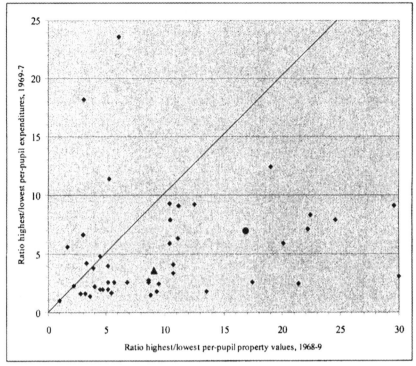

Figure 5-4. Disparities in school district property wealth and expenditures before Serrano
(mean = ●; median = ▲ ; note that five states are off the graph: Kansas (183,3), New York
(84,11), South Dakota (10,34), Texas (45,56), and Wisconsin (78,3))

(Texas) to 1.4 (West Virginia) with a median of 3.8. Because such figures
may be skewed by special circumstances associated with school districts that
are very sparsely populated, that have a particularly large geographic size, or
that primarily service children with special education needs (Advisory
Commission on Intergovernmental Relations (1973)), an adjusted ratio that
compares per-pupil expenditures at the 90th percentile level to the lowest
per-pupil expenditure level is also reported.[95]   While the ratios were
generally lower (with a median value of 2.0), there was still a reasonably
large range from a maximum of 4.3 (South Dakota) to a minimum of 1.2
(Utah and Nevada).

To get a sense of the extent to which funding mechanisms at the time
kept these disparities from being even worse, one can examine the pattern of
school district per-pupil property values and compare them to the pattern of

___

[95] Thus, 90% of all students live in school districts that have a per-pupil expenditure level that
   is at this level or lower.

Table 5-2. Disparities in School District Per-Pupil Expenditures, 1899-1970

state	Ratio of highest-to-lowest school district per-pupil expenditures, 1899-1911*	Ratio of highest-to-lowest school district per-pupil expenditures, 1969-70
Connecticut	3.0	2.6
Massachusetts	15.8	9.3
New York	5.4	11.4
Mean	**8.1**	**7.8**
Median	**5.4**	**9.3**
Standard Deviation	**6.8**	**4.6**

* The Connecticut ratio is based on all the school districts in two of the state's eight counties: Fairfield (which had the third highest county property values per child) and Windham (which had the lowest county property values per child). The New York ratio is based on a simple average of the highest-to-lowest school district per-pupil expenditures in elementary schools and high schools.

Sources: Advisory Commission on Intergovernmental Relations (1973; Table 32); Cubberley (1905; Tables 3, 7, and 8); and Strayer and Haig (1923; Tables 7, 8, and 18).

school district per-pupil expenditure levels. While school district per-pupil property values do not directly translate to school district expenditures, they do provide a general measure of the resources available to school districts. As *Table 5-1* shows, the ratio of highest-to-lowest per-pupil property values across the several states ranges even more widely than per-pupil expenditure levels with a maximum of 182.8 (Kansas), a minimum of 1.7 (North Dakota), and a median of 9.3. *Figure 5-4* provides a clearer overall picture of the relationship between per-pupil property values and per-pupil expenditure levels. As that figure reveals, most states have a lower level of per-pupil spending disparities than they have per-pupil property values, thus suggesting that the equalization efforts in the 1960s may have had some effect.

However, limited historical evidence suggests that despite such efforts, disparities may not have been much better than they were at the turn of the 20th century. *Table 5-2* provides a comparison of per-pupil expenditure levels in a select set of states using the date from *Table 5-1* in combination with data from Cubberley's (1905) and Strayer and Haig's (1923) reports. While the Cubberley, and the Strayer and Haig data are far from complete (and thus represent conservative measures of the degree of disparity in school district per-pupil expenditure levels), the overall impression of these numbers is that there hadn't been much change in spending disparities between 1900 and 1970. One of reasons for such an apparent lack of change, no doubt, is due to the rather unfocused structure of the equalization aid provided in the 1960s. However, additional data presented in *Table 5-3*, though again incomplete, suggest that another part of the explanation may be

Table 5-3. Disparities in School District Per-Pupil Property Values, 1903-4 versus 1968-80

state	Ratio of highest-to-lowest school district per-pupil property values,1903-4[*]	Ratio of highest-to-lowest school district per-pupil property values,1968-9
California	2.8	24.6
Connecticut	4.4	5.7
Indiana	5.2	17.4
Kansas	1.9	182.8
Massachusetts	3.6	10.4
Missouri	4.3	29.6
Wisconsin	5.0	77.9
Mean	**4.2**	**49.8**
Median	**4.4**	**24.6**
Standard Deviation	**1.4**	**63.3**

[*]With the exception of Connecticut and Massachusetts, ratios are based on partial samples which typically are based on averages of the state's first 8 counties (listed alphabetically) plus the largest city in the state. The Connecticut ratio is based on all the school districts in two of the state's eight counties: Fairfield (which had the third highest county property values per child) and Windham (which had the lowest county property values per child). The Massachusetts ratio is based on a complete sample of school districts.

Sources: Advisory Commission on Intergovernmental Relations (1973; Table 31); and Cubberley (1905; Tables 1, 7, 8, and 10-14).

that disparities in per-pupil property values increased over much of the 20th century.

1.3   The Role of the Courts

The decades before the *Serrano* case saw only a few court cases that dealt directly with public education funding and none that found state funding structures sufficiently wanting to require change. Despite the lack of court involvement in the pre-*Serrano* period, the period was a significant one from a legal perspective. While the debate over public education funding that arose out of the work of Cubberley and of Strayer and Haig never died out, by the 1960s the debate was certainly a muted one. The nation by this time was preoccupied with the racial desegregation of the public schools. But rather than supplant the original education finance debate, the desegregation movement energized public education finance reform efforts and provided both intellectual and legal foundations for the modern effort to reform public education finance through court action.

The effort to desegregate the public schools through court action can be traced to a long series of cases that slowly whittled away at the doctrine of "separate but equal" that was associated with the US Supreme Court's 1896 *Plessy v. Ferguson* decision and that resulted in the US Supreme Court's 1954 landmark decision *Brown v. Board of Education*. The effort to overturn *Plessy* was the result of a consciously designed plan (developed by, among others, future US Supreme Court justice Thurgood Marshall) that began with what were perceived as the most likely to succeed cases – those involving state law schools and other graduate schools where it would be easier to show that equality could not be obtained through separate facilities. Having won in those efforts, the plan was to then move to an assault on the public schools using the previous successes as precedent. Success came most notably in a 1938 case involving the law school at the University of Missouri (*Missouri ex rel Gaines v. Canada*) and in two 1950 cases involving the law school at the University of Texas (*Sweatt v. Painter*) and the graduate school at the University of Oklahoma (*McLaurin v. Oklahoma State Regents*).[96] One of the issues with which the Court grappled in these cases was how to define equity. In earlier cases (dating all the way back to the *Plessy* case), the notion of equity was defined primarily in terms of tangible resources. As a result, the Court could find that it was legal to restrict Mr. Plessy to particular railway cars so long as the cars themselvves were physically the same. Over time, however, the courts gradually accepted the view that the benefits of education, such as those associated with the prestige of the institution or the right to interact with all students, were often intangible. As a result, the courts shifted to a more general comparison of intangible resources and their impact on the quality of education. All this came to a head in 1954 when the Supreme Court confronted public school segregation in the *Brown* case.[97] Based on the notion that many of the resources important to education cannot be reduced to a counting of tangible resources, the Court concluded that "in the field of public education the doctrine of 'separate but equal' has no place" and therefore violates the Fourteenth Amendment's guarantee of equal protection (*Brown v. Board of Education* (1954) 347 US 495).

The aftermath of the *Brown* decision was one of both legal and political successes and frustrations, the most notable political success being the passage of the 1964 Civil Rights Act. However, while *Brown* signaled that the Supreme Court was willing to break from its traditional, rather passive role and adopt a policy of judicial activism when it perceived civil rights infringements, the outcome was less than civil rights advocates had hoped for. In practice there were often gaps between promise and implementation because of resistance from the lower courts and a lack of political support

---

[96] Paul Minorini and Stephen Sugarman (1999b) provide a fuller but succinct overview of this process of litigation. For a comprehensive treatment, see Wilkerson (1979).

[97] There were, in fact, two *Brown v. Board of Education* decisions, the first in 1954 dealing with the substantive issue of public education segregation, the second in 1955 dealing with issues of remedy and from which the controversial phrase "all deliberate speed" was coined.

(Bosworth (2001)). While the courts have always seen one of their roles as protecting the rights of minorities,[98] the resistance to desegregation encountered resulted in the courts having to supervise many orders on an ongoing basis.   Courts had little experience or expertise with such "administrative" supervision, and as a result many judges were hesitant to interject themselves into the process.[99]

Compounding that problem was the advent in the 1960s of new, *de facto* segregation that resulted from whites moving out of desegregated school districts and into school districts that were predominantly white (Minorini and Sugarman (1999b)). Because of concerns over whether this white flight would return the nation to the segregated situation that existed before the *Brown* decision, civil rights advocates began thinking about alternative legal strategies. Because *Brown* was for many as much about improving public education for black students as it was about desegregation, and because any new push for better public education for black students would require political as well as legal muscle, strategists began thinking in terms of funding. Though the correlation was far from perfect, many black students lived in school districts that were funded at lower per-pupil levels than many districts composed mostly of white students. As a result, any push to redress inequities in the funding of school districts held the hope that it might improve the education of black students. Moreover, because many white students from low-income families were in a similar situation, any effort to improve the equity of public education funding would help them as well, thus broadening the political constituency in favor of this new strategy.[100]

There were, however, risks to pursuing such a strategy. Beyond the fact that the correlation between black students and low funding levels was not perfect, there were concerns that such a focus, by eschewing the mantle of *Brown*, would divert the nation's attention from the fundamental issue of civil rights and racial inequities. In addition, many were concerned that a strategy of focusing on tangible resources might be interpreted as a return to the "separate but equal" doctrine of *Plessy*. Finally, the *Coleman Report,* a study commissioned by the 1964 Civil Rights Act (Coleman et al. (1966)),

---

[98] The importance of protecting the rights of minorities can be traced all the way back to the founding of the Republic. See, for example, *Federalist Papers* 10 and 51 (Hamilton, Jay, and Madison (1787)).

[99] The legal debate in the *pre-Serrano* period over how far the courts should go to protect "discrete and insular minorities" can be traced through *US v. Carolene Products Co.* (1938), *Minersville School District v. Gobitis* (1940), *Kovacs v. Cooper* (1949), and *Lucas v. Colorado General Assembly* (1964). See Bosworth (2001) for further discussion.

[100] With the advent in recent decades of an increasingly large Hispanic population, the value of the traditional distinction between black and white has come under increasing scrutiny. For background on educational reform from an Hispanic perspective, see Meier and Stewart (1991).

found that school resources were less important to student performance than the background of the student. To the extent this last observation were true, the focus on public education funding equity might result in only a dissipation of the efforts put into civil rights improvements and little improvement in the education of students in low spending school districts.

In fact, earlier efforts to employ this strategy of pursing public-education funding equity in the federal courts were not successful.[101] Because of the difficulties that the courts had had monitoring and enforcing desegregation orders, the courts in this pre-*Serrano* period refused to be drawn into issues of public education funding equity when the case was divorced from race. A prime example of this was the 1968 Illinois case *McInnis v. Shapiro*.[102] In 1968, a suit filed by public school students in Cook County, Illinois claimed that the students' rights under the Fourteenth Amendment to equal protection and to due process had been violated because of large disparities in per-pupil expenditures across Illinois, and that because of these disparities the students were deprived of an education commensurate with their needs and the level of education provided to others. The court found that there was no cause for action. While the Fourteenth Amendment required equal protection under the law, the court could find nothing to support that notion that equal protection should be interpreted in terms of the educational *needs* of students. Moreover, even if it were true that the Fourteenth Amendment could be interpreted in such a manner, the court found the whole notion of educational needs to be so vague and nebulous as to be nonjusticiable, that is, beyond the ability of the court to define and manage.

---

[101] Advocates for public education funding equity stayed away from state courts because those courts had a history of being unwilling to interpret suits about public education funding as anything more than an issue of taxpayer equity. Typical of those state court cases (Salmon and Alexander (1990)) was the 1912 Maine Supreme Court case *Sawyer v. Gilmore* in which the plaintiffs complained that the proceeds of a statewide property tax used to help fund local public schools were not distributed to school districts in proportion to the source of the revenues. The Maine Supreme Court in that case found that such issues were within the purview of the state legislature and not the courts, and it therefore refused to act. Such deferral was common in the pre-*Serrano* period even when issues raises were based on constitutional equal protection or due process arguments, or on state constitutional "thorough and efficient" education clauses. See Salmon and Alexander (1990) for more details.

[102] See also *Burruss v. Wilkerson* (1969).

2.   *SERRANO* AND THE EQUALIZATION MOVEMENT

The frustrations with the slowness with which *Brown* was improving educational opportunity in the public schools, the recognition that the issue of equal educational opportunity cut across racial lines, and the unwillingness of the courts to enter into the issue in the absence of explicit racial content led to an effort by advocates, most notably Arthur Wise and the team of John Coons, William Clune, and Stephen Sugarman, to develop a set of legal and economic arguments that they hoped the courts would find persuasive and that would provide the courts with a roadmap for developing a clear, judicially manageable remedy that keep the courts from becoming entangled in the continual oversight of the public education funding process.

2.1   Development of a Justiciable Remedy

Early work on the development of legal arguments and a judicially manageable remedy to persuade the courts to intervene in the public education funding process came in the form of Wise's book *Rich Schools, Poor Schools* (Wise (1968)).[103] Wise argued, both from a moral perspective as well as a legal one based on the Fourteenth Amendment and the right to equal protection under the law, that society had an obligation to assure that the education that a child receives in public school not be based on parental wealth or geographical location. He argued further that education is legally a state responsibility and that regardless of the structure used to raise revenues for public education and regardless of the structure used to deliver public education, all such structures were ultimately within the control of the state government. Thus, for example, state legislatures could, if they saw fit, decide to reallocate locally raised property tax revenues associated with the public education funding in anyway they saw fit, so long as such reallocations were consistent with the Fourteenth Amendment and the principle of equal protection. Likewise, local school boards were simply administrative units of the state and could, therefore, be regulated, eliminated, or redistricted as the state legislature saw fit. Having said this, however, Wise concluded that because of the history of resistance to public school desegregation and to the implementation of the one-person-one-vote principle, this obligation as a practical matter fell primarily to the federal courts.

---

[103] Wise's book was itself based on his doctoral dissertation that he had completed the previous year in the Department of Education at the University of Chicago.

Table 5-4. Wise's Alternative Definitions of Equal Educational Opportunity

	Based on Student Abilities & Needs
• Full-Opportunity	All students should leave school having attained the maximum level of education commensurate with their abilities.[104]
• Classification	Students should be classified according to ability and interest, with all students within a class treated equally.
• Competition	Resources should be allocated in proportion to student ability.
• Leveling	Resources should be allocated in inverse proportion to student ability.
• Minimum Attainment	All students should attain some defined minimum level of attainment.
	Based on Resources Provided to Students
• Equal-Dollars-per-Pupil	All students should have access to the same resources.
• Maximum-Variance-Ratio	Student access to resources should differ by no more than some defined ratio.
• Non-Discrimination	A child's educational opportunity should not depend on his parents' economic circumstances or location.
• Foundation	All students should have access to some defined minimum level of resources.[105]

Of course, as the *McInnis* case had shown, the real issue centered on the justiciability of the issue, which depended in turn on the characterization of equal educational opportunity and the nature of any proposed remedy. Wise offered nine possible definitions (See *Table 5-4* for details) that were based either on student needs (as was the litigants' claim in *McInnis*) or simply on

---

[104] This definition is reminiscent of the view of the Paideia movement (perhaps most closely associated with the philosopher Mortimer Adler known for his association with the Great Books movement) that all children should leave school with their glasses full, regardless of the size of the glass. For a general description of the rationale for the the Paideia philosophy and how it can be implemented, see Adler (1982, 1983, 1984). For current information on the Paideia movement in practice, visit the website of the National Paideia Center (www.paideia.org).

[105] This definition is reminiscent of the Strayer and Haig (1923) notion of equal educational opportunity described in earlier in this chapter.

the level of resources provided to students.[106] The needs based definitions ranged all the way from defining equal educational opportunity in terms of maximum individual attainment to simply requiring some minimum level of attainment. Likewise, the resource-based definitions ranged from strict equality across all students to defining equal educational opportunity simply in terms of what it should not be (what Wise called a non-discrimination definition). In the end, however, Wise never argued for any particular definition, but instead simply suggested that the argument that was most likely to find favor with the courts was the notion that a child's education should not depend on his parents' economic circumstances or geographic location. He then concluded with an exploration of funding mechanisms, ranging from mandated class sizes to eliminating all locally raised revenue, and suggested that the most likely solution would be some sort of hybrid grant structure composed of a foundation grant and a a grant dependent on the local school district's willingness to tax itself.

While Wise made important contributions to developing a justiciable remedy, his unwillingness to argue for the merits of a particular legal theory and associated remedy left his work too vague to be used directly in the courts. That task was left to the team of Coons, Clune, and Sugarman who, targeting California as a state ripe for court action, developed a detailed legal and economic brief (Coons, Clune, and Sugarman (1969, 1970)). Eschewing the needs-based definition of equal educational opportunity used in *McInnis*, they chose instead to work with Wise's non-discrimination definition of equal educational opportunity that Wise had suggested was the one most likely to be acceptable to the courts. However, instead of defining equal education opportunity as requiring the prohibition of the distribution of public education resources based on student location or *parental* status, they argued that equal education opportunity should require a prohibition against providing public education resources based on student location or *community* status (particularly wealth).

While such a characterization was a vast improvement from a justiciability perspective over the needs-based definition used in *McInnis*, it still allowed more discretion for state legislatures than Coons, Clune, and Sugarman thought desirable. Moreover, as they recognized, any proposal would, for political reasons, have to continue to allow for local control of spending. The result was they decided to argue that non-discrimination in the provision of public education resources should be interpreted as

---

[106] Berne and Stiefel (1999) provide an extended discussion of these alternative definitions in which they characterize the input-output dichotomy in terms of *ex post* versus *ex ante* wealth neutrality.

requiring equal taxable wealth per student across all public school districts.[107]

This definition had the virtue of continuing to allow for local decision making, and could easily be enacted through the use of a pure district-power-equalization (DPE) funding mechanism.[108] Their belief was that most of the differences in the levels of education provided across school districts were due to differences in access to a taxable tax base and not to differences in preferences. As a result, they believed that the use of local control would in the end not be important to the level of public education provided. School districts, offered the same per-student tax base through a DPE grant structure would choose much the same level of education for their children.

Thus, paradoxically, Coons, Clune, and Sugarman, who were intent on eliminating disparities in per-pupil educational expenditures across rich and poor school districts like Strayer and Haig, ended up proposing an educational grant structure similar in structure to the one proposed by Cubberley who emphasized adequacy some six decades before. Unlike Strayer and Haig, they saw no virtue in a foundation grant structure which they saw as a device for maintaining, if not exacerbating, inequalities in the provision of public education. The DPE educational grant if adopted would, they believed, greatly reduce disparities in education opportunities across rich and poor school districts.[109]

Using the approach advocated by Coons, Clune, and Sugarman, Los Angeles County public school children and their parents brought a class action lawsuit in the California court system. Defining the injured class to be all public school children in California and their taxpaying parents except for those in the school district providing the greatest level of educational opportunity, they claimed that students belonging to the injured class received an inferior education (both in terms of quality and availability of educational opportunities) compared to students not in the class, and that this disparity violated the equal protection clause of the Fourteenth Amendment of the US Constitution. Moreover, plaintiffs argued, because this disparity was itself the result of the state's financing scheme, the financing system for

---

[107] Coons, Clune, and Sugarman were critical of the requirement that local control be maintained, but saw no practical solution that did not maintain such control. Ideally, they would have preferred that the state provide all children with equal access to resources through what is now called a voucher system.

[108] The label "district-power equalization" seems to have originated with them.

[109] They also expressed the belief that such equality of local school district tax bases through the use of a DPE educational grant structure, by eliminating differences in the quality of public education across local school districts, would also significantly reduce the incentives for people to segregate according to income and class into homogeneous communities.

California public education should be declared to be unconstitutional, an order should be issued directing the state to reallocate funds, and the court should maintain jurisdiction to assure compliance. The case eventually reached the California Supreme Court (*Serrano v. Priest* (1971)) where the Court found that there was in fact discrimination by district wealth, that education was a fundamental interest, that there was no compelling interest in the current structure, and that this discrimination violated the Fourteenth Amendment of the US Constitution.[110]

2.2   *Rodriguez* and the Shift to State Constitutional Law

Within a year of the *Serrano* case, the nation was awash in litigation and state legislative activity concerning the funding of public education. Eleven state legislatures reformed their public education financing structures, federal and state courts (not necessarily state supreme courts) declared the public education financing structures in five states (Kansas, New Jersey, Michigan, Minnesota, and Texas) unconstitutional, and thirty-one states had litigation pending (Bosworth (2001)). Because of the confusion over this activity and especially the lack of clear direction for the federal courts (the *Serrano* case had, after all, been decided using federal law but adjudicated by a state and not a federal court), the US Supreme Court decided to take up the issue and chose a Texas case *San Antonio School District v. Rodriguez* (1973) to do so.

The *Rodriguez* case was remarkably similar to the *Serrano* one. On behalf of school children who were members of minorities or who were poor and resided in school districts with low per-student property tax bases, a class action suite was filed that claimed that education was a fundamental right protected by the US Constitution, that Texas's reliance on local property taxation for the funding of public education favored students from higher income families, and that this result violated the equal protection clause of the Fourteenth Amendment.

However, unlike the *Serrano* case, the US Supreme Court in a 5-4 decision concluded that education was not a fundamental right guaranteed by the US Constitution, that there were sufficient income and minority heterogeneity in the populations of students residing in local school districts to assure that any funding discrimination against school districts with low property tax bases does not constitute discrimination against the constitutionally protected classes of minorities or the poor, that the Texas

---

[110] The influence of Coon, Clune, and Sugarman on the outcome of the case can be seen in the numerous citations of Coons, Clune, and Sugarman (1969) in the California Supreme Court's opinion as well as by the fact that Coons served as one of several *amicus curiae*.

Table 5-5. After *Rodriguez:* State Supreme Court Equalization Litigation from 1971 to 1989

State	Year	Outcome	Legal Rationale
Arizona	1973	upheld	equal protection
Arkansas	1983	unconstitutional	equal protection
California	1971	unconstitutional	equal protection
	1976	unconstitutional	equal protection
Colorado	1982	upheld	equal protection & education clause *qua* equality
Connecticut	1977	unconstitutional	equal protection
Georgia	1981	upheld	equal protection & education clause *qua* equality
Idaho	1975	upheld	equal protection & education clause *qua* equality
Illinois	1973	upheld	equal protection
Maryland	1983	upheld	equal protection & education clause *qua* equality
New Jersey	1973	unconstitutional	equal protection
New York	1982	upheld	equal protection & education clause *qua* equality
North Carolina	1987	upheld	education clause
Ohio	1979	upheld	equal protection & education clause *qua* equality
Oklahoma	1987	upheld	equal protection & education clause *qua* equality
Oregon	1976	upheld	equal protection & education clause *qua* equality
Pennsylvania	1979	upheld	education clause
South Carolina	1988	upheld	equal protection
Washington	1974	upheld	equal protection
	1978	unconstitutional	education clause
West Virginia	1979	unconstitutional	education clause
	1982	unconstitutional	equal protection
Wisconsin	1989	upheld	equal protection & education clause *qua* equality
Wyoming	1980	unconstitutional	equal protection

Sources: Bosworth (2001) and Underwood (1994)

funding structure, as flawed as it might be, did bear a rational relationship to a legitimate state purpose, and that therefore the Texas funding structure did not violate the Fourteenth Amendment of the US Constitution.

The *Rodriguez* case was clearly a setback for advocates of equalization. While it did not stop their efforts, it did force them to furcate their efforts into fifty separate efforts based on *state* and not *federal* constitutional law. Advocates could still win in court as the rehearing of the *Serrano* case demonstrated (*Serrano II* (1976)). In this rehearing of the *Serrano* case, the process was quite simple – the California Supreme Court simply replaced the federal guarantee of equal protection with a similar guarantee that they found in the California Constitution. In fact, though each state's constitution is a little different with its own legal tradition of interpretation, the cases following *Rodriguez* generally continued to be based on equal protection arguments.[111]   Because public education is mandated in all state

---

[111] Only eighteen states (Alaska, California, Connecticut, Georgia, Hawaii, Idaho, Illinois, Kansas, Louisiana, Maine, Michigan, Montana, New Mexico, New York, North Carolina, Ohio, South Carolina, and Utah) have explicit equal protection clauses in their

constitutions,[112] an alternative legal path might have been possible. However, even when such education clauses were invoked, state supreme courts typically relied on the presumption that there was a correlation between the quality of education and the quantity of money provided (Sparkman (1990)), and as a result the argument remained one of equal protection with the remedy being the equalization of per-student spending. In the end (see *Table 5-5*), however, despite the "moral" force of California's original *Serrano* case and the heavy publicity which surrounded it, only seven of the twenty-one states where legal action reached the state supreme court witnessed a ruling that declared the public education funding mechanism to be unconstitutional.[113]

2.3   Effect of the Equalization Movement on Public Education Funding

Though the impact of the equalization movement varied state by state, there are some general conclusions that can be made on the basis of empirical research. For states in which there was no court intervention, there was in general, as the model in *Chapter 3* would predict, no change in either the distribution of per-pupil spending across school districts or the overall level of support statewide for public education. Interestingly, some analysts at the time argued that these states, nonetheless, had engaged in significant reform of their public education funding structures in order to pre-empt court action.[114] However, while there may well have been changes in the public education funding structures in such states, empirical research by Gregory Weiher (1988) using Texas data, and William Evans, Sheila Murray, and Robert Schwab (1997) using a national data base covering the years 1972 to 1992 found that disparities in per-student spending across school districts did not change in states where the courts did not intervene.

For states in which the courts did intervene, Evans, Murray, and Schwab (1997)[115] found, as *Figure 5-5* illustrates by the arrow emanating from point A, that intervention reduced overall disparities in per-student expenditures across school districts and resulted in increases in overall statewide per-pupil expenditures due to a rise in the lowest spending school districts, little if any

---

constitutions. For the remaining states, other clauses in their state constitutions are generally have been used to confer state guarantees of equal protection (Sparkman (1990).

[112] See Bosworth (2001) and Odden and Picus (1992) for extended discussions of the nature of these requirements and their historical origins.

[113] For a fuller examination of the state equal protection arguments and the state education clause arguments that have been used, see Underwood (1994).

[114] See Bosworth (2001) for a review of that literature.

[115] See also Murray, Evans, and Schwab (1998).

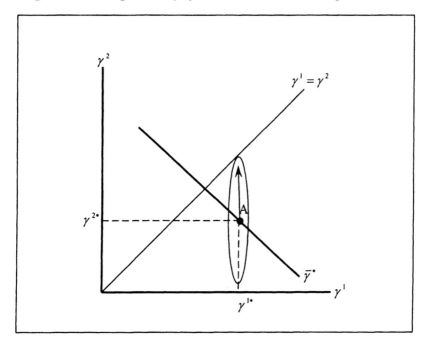

Figure 5-5. Leveling Up as a Result of Forced Equalization

fall in the spending of the highest spending districts, and an increase in the share of public education funding provided by the state legislature.

However, as Thomas Downes (1992), Raquel Fernández and Richard Rogerson (1999), Paul Minorini and Stephen Sugarman (1999b), and Fabio Silva and Jon Sonstellie (1995) document in their examination of California's experience, this experience was not universal. As a result of *Serrano II*, the California legislature adopted the DPE grant structure advocated by Coons, Clune, and Sugarman (1969, 1970). But before that DPE grant structure could be implemented, the California state constitutional amendment known as Proposition 13 passed in a statewide referendum.[116]

This state constitutional amendment put a 1% cap on local property tax rates of assessed value, prohibited any statewide property tax, and required that any state tax increase be passed with a two-thirds super majority of the state legislature.

The local property tax rate cap, in particular, because it was so low eliminated all local discretion in the funding of public education and

---

[116] A number of analysts argue that Proposition 13 was a direct result of the California legislature's adoption of a comprehensive DPE public education grant structure. See Leyden (1988) and Fischel (1989, 1996).

destroyed the ability of the recently adopted DPE grant structure to work as designed.   Disparities in per-pupil public education expenditures across school districts were virtually eliminated, but this elimination came at a high price.   Higher spending school districts saw large decreases in the level of per-pupil spending while lower spending school districts saw only small increases in the per-pupil spending.   Overall, according to Silva and Sonstelie's estimates, overall state support for public education fell between 1970 and 1990 by 23% (in per-pupil terms) with approximately half that decline directly attributable to the interactions between *Serrano* case and the passage of Proposition 13.

The reason for California's different experience lies in the political changes wrought by the adoption of the DPE grant structure and the ensuing adoption of Proposition 13.   In most cases, a state's legislature is dominated by the wealthier, typically higher spending, local jurisdictions.   Thus, as represented in *Figure 5-5* by the presence of the elliptical legislative indifference curve with a vertical long axis, these wealthier jurisdictions are politically more salient.   As a result, if the courts insist on reducing per-pupil expenditure disparities across higher- and lower-spending local school districts, these politically more salient school districts will insist on a reform that maintains the status quo for them as much as possible.   Thus, the reform will result in relatively large increases in the per-pupil expenditures in the lower-spending school districts and relatively small decreases in the per-pupil expenditures in the higher-spending school districts.   In short, these politically more salient school districts will insist on a reform that levels up.

But for California, circumstances were different.   The effective prohibition against using the local property tax to increase local school district expenditures, the implied redistribution embodied in the DPE educational grant structure, and the requirement of a super-majority to raise taxes at the state level effectively made the lower-spending school districts more salient than the higher-spending school districts.   Thus, as *Figure 5-6* illustrates, the indifference curves of the California state legislature, while elliptical, were oriented horizontally.   Faced then with a court order to equalize per-pupil spending across school districts, the California state legislature chose to eliminate disparities in per-pupil expenditures across school districts by imposing large cuts in per-pupil spending in higher spending school districts and imposing small increases in per-pupil spending in lower spending school districts.   This then resulted in an overall decrease in the level of support for public education, that is, the California state legislature chose to level down in an attempt to protect the politically more salient lower-spending school districts.   In California's case, as is illustrated by the move from point A to point B in *Figure 5-6*, this in fact resulted in near complete equalization of per-pupil expenditures across all school

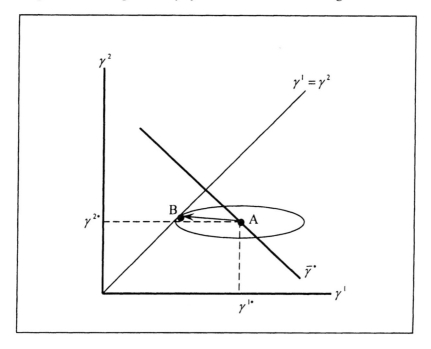

Figure 5-6. Leveling Down as a Result of Forced Equalization: the California Case

districts after more than a decade of litigation and several successful referenda restricting local property taxes and the state's ability to increase taxes, and mandating that at least 39 percent of the state's budget be spent on education.

Whether California's situation is unique can be debated. However, Robert Manwaring and Steven Sheffrin (1997) argue that California's situation is, in fact, not unique. Using a national data base covering the years 1970 to 1990, they conclude that whether a state levels up or levels down depends on the complex combination of a number of factors – the degree to which fiscal responsibility is located at the state versus the local level, the nature of the intergovernmental grant structure used to fund public education, and the relative distribution of income across the state. What does seem to be unique is California's virtual full compliance with the court's order and the near complete elimination of per-pupil expenditure disparities across all its school districts. In all other states, the necessity of maintaining some degree of local political control (something deeply embedded both legally and politically in these states) and the sometimes strong unwillingness of the legislature to increase spending because of the political repercussions, typically led to less than full compliance with court orders and only partial success in reducing disparities in per-pupil

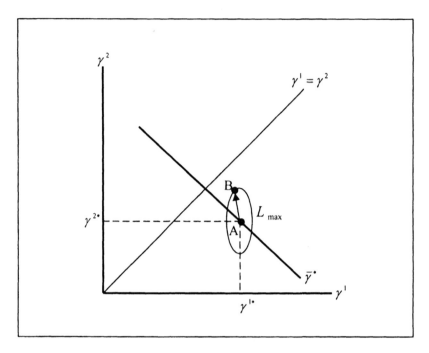

Figure5-7. A Refusal to Fully Comply: the New Jersey Case

expenditures across school districts. As Frederick Wirt and Michael Kirst (1997) observed, some states such as New Jersey were still engaged well into the 1990s in litigation that had its roots in the cases of the 1970s and that was all about the unwillingness of the state legislatures to fully comply with the original court orders to equalize per-pupil expenditures. Interestingly, Michael Mintrom (1993) in his empirical examination of the New Jersey legislature's reaction to various court orders found that the unwillingness to comply with the courts was primarily the result of lobbying by parents in the higher-spending, politically more salient school districts and the fear of a taxpayer revolt if state taxes were raised. In short, as *Figure 5-7* illustrates, the political strength of the politically more salient higher-spending local school districts was sufficiently strong to create a maximum political loss (represented in *Figure 5-7* by the indifference curve labeled L_{max}) beyond which the New Jersey legislature refused to go.

3. ***ROSE* AND THE TENTATIVE SHIFT TOWARD ADEQUACY AND ACCOUNTABILITY**

Although there were some successes, the two decades following *Serrano* were more often than not characterized by frustrations with the legal process and the responses of state legislatures. Even when the legal and legislative processes went smoothly, advocates were generally unhappy with the lack of significant improvement in reducing per-pupil spending variations (Evans, Murray, and Schwab findings notwithstanding) and the lack of perceived significant improvements in the quality of education for lower-spending local school districts. While initially the reaction to such frustrations was simply to redouble the effort to achieve equalization, by the late 1980s these frustrations gave way to a fundamental questioning of that strategic objective. Through academic advocacy, court cases, and legislative debates, the notion of equalization was gradually replaced by the notions of adequacy and accountability. However, while these objectives now have a remarkable amount of currency with state legislators, there have been difficulties developing working definitions of these objectives and putting policies into practice that allow these objectives to be pursued. The result has thus been a continued frustration with the reform process and a continued tendency to fall back on the discredited notion of equalization.

3.1 Frustrations with the Equalization Movement ...

As discussed above, there were a number of frustrations with the progress of public education finance reform in the wake of the *Serrano* decision. In many states, the courts refused to intervene, thus resulting in at best only cosmetic reforms of state public education funding mechanisms. In states where the courts did intervene, compliance was typically only partial because of political pressures on state legislators, and every reform effort ran the risk that the legislature would decide to comply by leveling down the overall level of support for public education.

Even when the equalization process worked relatively smoothly, however, other problems arose that added to the frustration with the process. One such problem, as Minorini and Sugarman (1999a) note, centered on the fact that the cost of running a local school system can vary, sometimes significantly, from system to system even within the same state. Urban school districts, in particular, found themselves at the time caught in a Catch 22. On the one hand, their per-pupil costs were higher than average because of the need to pay the higher wage rates associated with competitive urban labor markets and because of the greater number and proportion of special needs students. On the other hand, their levels of per-pupil property wealth were generally greater than average. Thus, any equalization reform would not typically provide urban school districts with additional financial support. Unfortunately, the higher per-pupil wealth levels were not sufficient to compensate for the higher per-pupil costs, in part because of the greater competition for local public dollars that characterizes urban communities. Thus, urban school districts often found themselves no better off after equalization reforms.

Another problem that contributed to the frustration with the equalization movement centered on the disappointingly small amount of spending equalization that was generated as a result of using the DPE educational grant structure. Implicit in Coons, Clune, and Sugarman's argument that the use of a DPE grant structure would naturally result in the equalization of per-pupil expenditure levels was the assumption that all school districts had a similar interest in educating their children but for the availability of funds for education. As a result, the disappointing results of using the DPE grant structure called into question whether in fact there was a difference between rich and poor school districts in the value placed on educating children. However, the failure to achieve large degrees of equalization can more easily be explained by the fact that the DPE grant structure, while giving all school districts an equal ability to provide a given level of education with the same tax rate, does not equalize total wealth across school districts. As a result, poor school districts while perhaps better off under a DPE grant structure, were still not on par with wealthier school districts.

To understand why this is so, consider two school districts one of which has a high per-pupil tax base and one of which as a low per-pupil tax base. As *Figure 5-8* illustrates using the graphical techniques developed in *Chapter 3*, in the absence of any state support for local public education, the median voter in the richer school district will have a budget line RS that is greater than the budget line PQ of the median voter in the poorer school district (C^i represents the level of all-other consumption for that median voter). As a result, the richer school district will typically have a level of per-pupil expenditures γ^i (represented by point C) that is greater than the level of per-pupil expenditures chosen in the poorer school district (represented by point A). If the richer school district has average property wealth $\bar{V}^*$, the poorer school district has local property tax wealth $\bar{V}^P$, and (using the DPE grant structure described in *Equation 3-3* in *Chapter 3*) the guaranteed per-pupil tax base is equal to the average property wealth in the richer school district, then we get a simple DPE structure that only provides aid for the poorer school district, and which does so according to the formula:

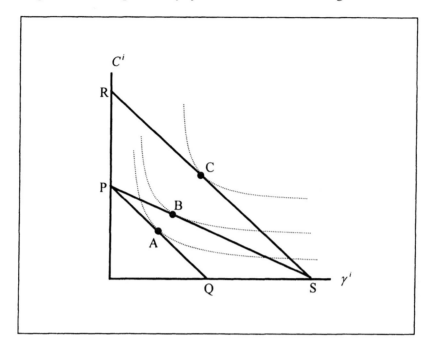

Figure 5-8. Poor School Districts are Still Poor Under DPE

$$G^P = (\overline{V}^* - \overline{V}^P)t^P \qquad\qquad (5\text{-}1)$$

where G^P is the per-pupil grant to the poorer school district and where t^P is that school district's local property tax rate. The result is that for any given tax rate, both school districts will provide the same level of per-pupil expenditure, that is, the median voter in the poorer school district will now have the budget line PS. But despite this equality of opportunity, the circumstances of the two school districts remain quite different. Even if preferences were the same in all school districts, it would be remarkable, given that both education and other consumption are normal goods, if the poorer school district did choose the same level of education as the richer district. What is more likely, is that the poorer school district, while increasing its level of per-pupil expenditure from point A to point B, will still prefer a lower level of such spending than the richer school district does at point C. In short, poor school districts are still poor under a DPE grant structure, and so will make decisions based on that lower wealth.

Despite these difficulties, many states continued even into the 1990s trying to make equalization work, and some experimented with a return to

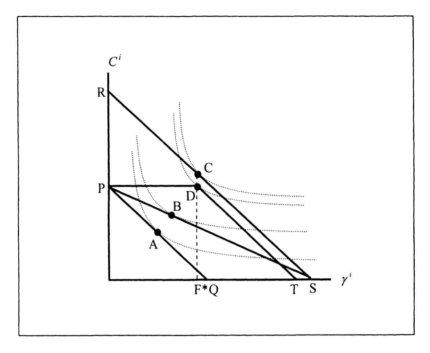

Figure 5-9. Replacing a DPE Structure with a Foundation Grant Structure

the use of foundation grants.   One state that tried to equalize expenditures with a foundation grant structure (reminiscent of Strayer and Haig work in the 1920s) was Michigan.   As Paul Courant and Susanna Loeb (1997), and Robert Wassmer and Ronald Fisher (1996) describe in their empirical studies of the Michigan experience, Michigan attempted in 1994 to equalize per-pupil expenditures by replacing most of its local property tax with a statewide sales tax, replacing its DPE grant structure with a foundation grant program that favored small, rural districts,[117] and putting a cap on the ability of local school districts ability to raise revenues above their foundation grant level.   The result was once again a disappointingly small diminution in spending disparities and an increase in the average level of spending state wide.   The problem was not so much in the structure of the foundation plan as in its overall size.   A foundation grant structure can equalize per-pupil expenditures across all school districts.   However, if local preferences are such as were illustrated in *Figure 5-8*, the size of the per-pupil foundation grant may have to equal the desired level of spending.   *Figure 5-9* represents such a case with the foundation grant necessary to induce the poorer school

---

[117] This bias against urban school districts is in addition to the cost problems noted previously.

district median voter to choose the same level of per-pupil expenditures as the richer school district equaling F* and the new budget constraint for that same median voter being the kinked line PDT. Of course such a foundation grant structure has its own problems both because of the expense and because of the destruction of local control that such a structure implies.

3.2   ... But Does It Matter Anyway?

Beyond the question of whether equalization could be achieved through some combination of court mandates, legislative compliance, and the right mix of educational grant structures, a more profound issue began to take shape in the late 1980s as to whether money in fact mattered at all. That is, even if equalization could be achieved, would it make a difference in the educational quality that children in poorer school districts receive and in the educational attainment of those children? Particularly because of the high costs that analysts were beginning to conclude would be necessary to equalize spending across school districts and because of the seemingly unending growth in real expenditures since the 1960s (as *Table 1-4* in *Chapter 1* documents, the annual growth rate in real per-pupil spending averaged roughly four percent from 1960 to 1990), many began to question whether in fact all this additional expense was producing any benefit.

What the education production function looks like and the connection between costs and the achievement of students is, of course, an old question with a large literature. The *Coleman Report* (Coleman et al. (1966)) had raised the issue much earlier in its conclusion that public school resources were not terribly important to student performance, and there had been a number of efforts to examine this issue in more detail. Anita Summers and Barbara Wolfe (1977), for example, in their analysis of the Philadelphia school district during the 1970-1 school year concluded that individual student data, and not the aggregated statistics used by the *Coleman Report*, were needed to accurately measure the impact of additional school resources, but that when such data were available the conclusion was clear – money does in fact matter and that many supposed effects of family background are (especially for disadvantaged students) actually the result of school inputs.

Other studies looked at the issue of whether equalization led to overall improvements in the level of student achievement, but results here also differed. Frederick Sebold and William Dato (1981) found a statistically significant, though quantitatively small, positive effect of equalization on performance. But others, such as Thomas Downes (1992) who used examined California data in the aftermath of the *Serrano* case, found that equalization did not result in any observable improvement.[118]

The result was that by the 1980s there was a plethora of studies with no consensus on whether in fact money mattered. Into that confusion stepped Eric Hanushek who, in a set of increasingly sophisticated meta-analyses of as many as 300 empirical studies (Hanushek (1981, 1986, 1991, 1994a, 1996b, 2002)) concluded that there was no compelling evidence that greater school expenditures or resources (in the form of lower student/teacher ratios, higher levels of teacher education, or greater teacher experience) had a consistent effect on student achievement. The reason for such a conclusion, he argued, was not that there weren't some teachers and schools that achieved more than others, but that public education as a whole tended to be highly inefficient with any additional dollars being dissipated on things that didn't improve student achievement. Thus, as *Figure 5-10* illustrates (the arrows indicating the deviations from the efficient outcome), when analysts went to estimate the relationship between school inputs and student achievement, the result was ambiguous.

Additional support for the view that money did not matter came from Allan Odden and William Clune (1995) who argued that public schools were generally inefficient because of their bureaucratic organization and their proclivity for focusing on inputs and services rather than outputs such as student achievement. Moreover, they argued, the *ex ante* pattern of expenditure in public schools tended to remain the same after public education finance reform with additional dollars spent unproductively on such things as smaller class sizes and the provision of non-classroom services. As a result, they concluded, it should not be surprising that money doesn't matter.

---

[118] Based on anecdotal evidence, Downes argued that part of the explanation, at least in California, was that the reduction in spending disparities was not quite as large as it seemed because richer school districts were able to compensate for the reduction in funds through such devices as increased volunteer time, the establishment of foundations, and the increased use of fees. All this, he suggested, raises the question whether it is in fact even possible to ever equalize the resources available to children in rich and poor school districts. But the debate continues. In 2002, David Card and Abigail Payne (Card and Payne (2002)) published an empirical study using a national data base that concluded that, at least for states where the courts intervened, public education finance reform was associated with a small reduction in student achievement across school districts.

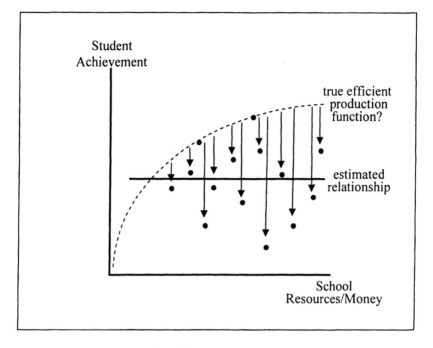

Figure 5-10. Estimating the Effect of Resources on Student Achievement with Generally Inefficient Schools

In response to these arguments, Rob Greenwald, Larry Hedges, and Richard Laine (Hedges, Laine, and Greenwald (1994a, 1994b), Greenwald, Hedges, and Laine (1996a, 1996b)) argued that Hanushek's statistical methods were faulty and that there was in fact strong evidence using more sophisticated statistical methods for the conclusion that resources did often matter, though perhaps not always and in all circumstances. Hanushek (1994c, 1996a) in response, though disputing the statistical argument, argued that at its base the debate was one of focus. Greenwald, Hedges, and Laine, he argued, had missed the point. He had never argued that students were *never* helped by additional resources. Rather, he had argued that public schools were *generally* inefficient, and that simply giving them additional funds would not result in a general improvement in student achievement. Greenwald, Hedges, and Laine, for their part, saw in Hanushek's response a shift in emphasis, if not direction, that boded well for future research.[119]

---

[119] For additional research on whether money matters using, see, for example, Ronald Ferguson and Helen Ladd's (1996) work using Alabama data that, they argue, provides strong support for the view that money matters.

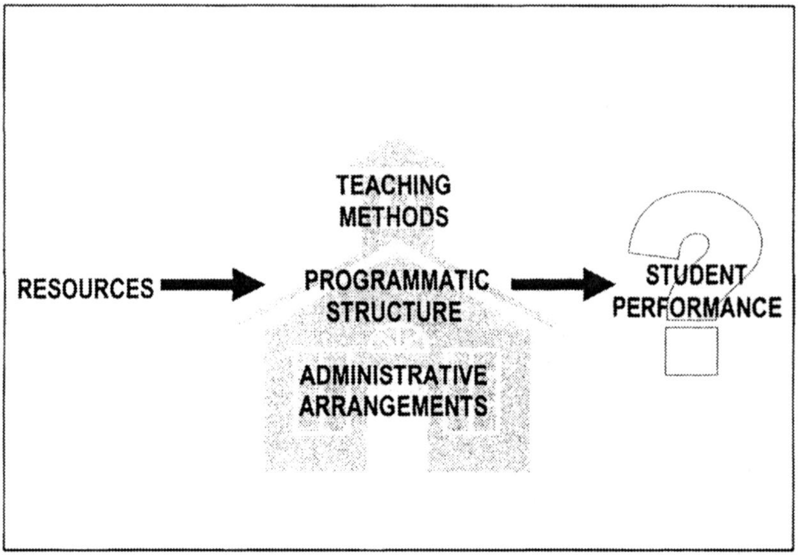

Figure 5-11. Uncertainty About the Production Process Makes Designing Education Policy to Pursue Adequacy Goals Difficult

3.3   Groping Toward an Alternative Strategy

The debate over whether money mattered and, more importantly, what ought to be the focus of future research efforts, was useful for exposing the fundamental problem – more resources did not seem to make much of difference for many schools, but for some schools it did, and we did not have an ability to explain why that was (see *Figure 5-11*). As Richard Murnane (1991) argued, the issue was not in discovering whether money mattered in some statistical sense. Indeed, he argued, because public schools had been given the task of providing a number of services not directly associated with student achievement, the whole search for the general connection between resources and student achievement was a chimera. Rather the focus should be on developing better methods of measuring output (that is, on the issue of assessment) and the link between those better measures, the level of specific inputs, and how those inputs are used in the classroom.

Advocates for public education finance reform quickly latched onto this argument. William Clune (1994), long famous for his advocacy of equalization as part of the team of Coon, Clune, and Sugarman, broke rank with his colleagues to argue that states had an obligation to establish high minimum education goals that focused on educational outcomes rather than inputs and to assure that sufficient resources were devoted to achieving these goals even if (because of differences in the cost of providing an adequate education to different populations) that meant providing different levels of aid to different school districts.   As Minorini and Sugarman (1999a) document, many advocates joined with Clune in abandoning the notion of equalization as wrongly focused (the fundamental problem was not that some students got a better education than other students, but rather that some students got an education that inadequately prepared them to be fully functioning citizens and workers) and impractical (richer school districts were likely to get around any restriction in their spending behavior).[120]

The problem of course was how to implement such general notions in a workable and politically feasible way.   That the establishment of minimum outcome performance goals was to be part of the process of tackling this problem was not at issue, and indeed many such as Laura Resnick (1993), co-director of the New Standards Project,[121] and Helen Ladd (1996) advocated strongly for the establishment of objective national standards that would, it was hoped, allow all children to achieve a minimum level of higher-order thinking, reasoning and problem solving skills.

However, setting outcome performance goals, as difficult as that might be, was one thing; knowing how to improve performance when the results fell below the desired goals was quite another.   Here, the view was less optimistic.   As Henry Levin (1994b) and Gary Orfield (1994) argued, our knowledge of the educational production function was in fact quite poor.   As a result, many, as Ladd and Hansen (1999) recognized, preferred to focus on relative, rather than absolute standards of performance.   Ultimately, this period, as Minorini and Sugarman (1999a) document, was often characterized by a continued focus on inputs (as had been the case during the efforts to equalize educational expenditures across school districts) in the hope that such inputs might proxy for the desired outcomes.   In short, it would appear that many advocates for school reform, in their haste to do

---

[120] Interestingly, the notion of educational adequacy, despite the sense of novelty that surrounded these arguments, was not new.   As noted earlier in this chapter, Strayer and Haig had some sixty years before criticized Cubberley for his argument that states ought to focus on assuring that local school districts have some minimum level of funds rather than trying to equalize spending across those same school districts.   And more recently, as Helen Ladd and Janet Hansen (1999) observed, the philosopher John Rawls (1971) had argued that the primary goods for individuals in society were rights and liberties, powers and opportunities, income and wealth, and self respect; that society had an obligation to assure that these goods were provided; and that to attain these primary goods some minimum level of education was necessary

[121] The New Standards Project was a project involving seventeen states and several metropolitan school districts that together comprised nearly half of all public school children in the US and was funded in part by grants from the Pew Charitable Trusts and the John D. and Catherine T. MacArthur Foundation.

something, and despite the criticisms of analysts such as Levin and Orfield, fell back on a modified version of the arguments used during the equalization period, now simply clothed in the language of performance and adequacy.

3.4   Back to the Courts

Parallel with the efforts among analysts to reframe the public education reform movement in terms of educational adequacy rather than expenditure equity was a similar development in the courts. Early experience with the use of adequacy arguments, as the 1968 Illinois case *McInnis v. Shapiro* bears witness, had not been successful. However, increasing frustration with the perceived lack of progress in the equity movement led a number of legal advocates to revisit the issue of educational adequacy. The problem was where to find the constitutional authority on which to base such a notion. Given the failure of the *McInnis* case, it was unlikely that such a legal hook was to be found in state equal protection clauses. However, many state constitutions also had education clauses, not a few of which required the establishment and maintenance of a "thorough and efficient" system of public education. The original intent of such clauses, as Allen Odden and Lawrence Picus (1992) note, varied from state to state with some states simply intending to create a public education statewide while others intending something closer to the modern notion of equal opportunity. However, original intent is not the only standard by which the courts interpret constitutional issues, and particularly with "thorough and efficient" education clauses, the courts seemed willing to entertain interpretations tied to modern perceptions regarding the need for education. As a result, legal advocates began bringing suites in the late 1970s claiming that states had failed to fulfill the obligation under such clauses to provide a public education system that adequately prepared *all* its students to be fully functioning citizens and workers. In three states (New Jersey, Washington State, and West Virginia), advocates were successful.[122] Though in the end, the remedies for these cases fell back on the notion of equalization and thus did not result in the development of a justiciable definition of adequacy, these cases did establish that state constitution education clauses could provide the legal hook on which to hang adequacy arguments (Minorini and Sugarman (1999a)).

Further developments in the 1980s increased the pressure to drop the notion of fiscal equalization that had become the law in so many states and

---

[122] The three cases were *Robinson v. Cahill* 1976 (New Jersey), *Seattle v. State of Washington* 1978 (Washington State), and *Pauley v. Kelly* 1979 (West Virginia).

adopt instead educational adequacy as a guiding principle. Particularly influential was the publication of *A Nation at Risk* in 1983 (National Commission on Excellence in Education (1983)). Commissioned by US Secretary of Education Terrel Bell and chaired by David Gardner (then president of the University of Utah and later president of the University of California system), the study concluded that the entire US system was doing a poor job of educating its students and that the fundamental problem had little to do with issues of spending equality and everything to do with a poorly structured and poorly delivered public education system attributable to poorly focused content, low and misdirected expectations, inadequate time on task both in and out of the classroom, and poorly trained and rewarded teachers.

Such arguments were increasingly viewed sympathetically by the courts who were experiencing their own frustrations with issues of equity. As Minorini and Sugarman (1999a) describe in more detail, by the 1980s, the *Brown* decision was nearly thirty years old. While much had been accomplished, the past decade had witnessed large amounts of white flight that left many school districts predominantly black. Though the courts had attempted to get around such behavior through the use of extensive busing, the results were disappointing, frustrating for the courts who had to maintain an almost administrative role in such situations (much to their dismay), and fraught with public controversy and animosity. The result was that by the 1980s, the courts had begun to wonder if the *Brown* case had essentially run its course, and the future lay not so much in desegregating school systems (or even desegregating collections of school systems) but rather in focusing on improving the quality of education.

Thus, in 1989 the Kentucky Supreme Court in *Rose v Council for Better Education* declared the state's entire public education in violation of the state constitution's guarantee of an adequate education inherent in its education clause. Rather than returning to fiscal equality remedies, the Court ordered a radical redesign of Kentucky's entire public education system (Mandelker et al. (1990), p. 673):

> Lest there be any doubt, the result of our decision is that Kentucky's entire system of common schools is unconstitutional.... This decision applies to the statutes creating, implementing and financing the system and to all regulations, etc., pertaining thereto. This decision covers the creation of local school districts, school boards, and the Kentucky Department of Education to the Minimum Foundation Program and Power Equalization Program. It covers school construction and maintenance, teacher certification -- the whole gamut of the common school system in Kentucky.

The result was that the Court ordered the state legislature to provide all students with a minimum level of education in oral and written communication; in economic, social, and political systems; in governmental processes, in physical and mental self knowledge, in cultural and historical heritage, and in work training so that students upon reaching adulthood are able to compete in the region with other workers and for acceptance at institutions of higher education.

The impact the ruling was substantial. Here for the first time was a state supreme court accepting not just the argument that state constitutional education clauses imposed obligations on state governments, but more importantly that the remedy for failures to provide adequate educations for its students was not in further attempts at equalization, but rather in structural redesigns focusing on improving student outcomes. In short, the key was not equalization but adequacy and accountability. Kentucky's legislature in response passed the Kentucky Education Reform Act which established a new foundation grant program that required increased minimum per-pupil expenditures in all school districts and created an outcome-based assessment system with incentives to encourage pursuit of the desired outcomes. The act had a clear impact on spending levels with educational spending statewide rising in real terms by nearly a fifth by 1993 (Ladd and Hansen (1999)). The degree to which the reform has resulted in improved student performance is less clear (Minorini and Sugarman (1999a). Following *Rose,* as *Table 5-6* documents, many state supreme courts have found their states' public education systems in violation of adequacy standards implicit in their state constitutions' education clauses. However, as Minorini and Sugarman (1999a) and Andrew Reschovsky and Jennifer Imazeki (2001) document, few state supreme courts have been willing to go as far as Kentucky's supreme court in declaring the entire public education system to be unconstitutional and requiring a comprehensive reform. In most states the courts, even if finding their public education systems unconstitutional under an adequacy standard, have continued to rely on some form of equalization remedy in the spirit of *Serrano.* Where the courts have been more ambitious and have pushed for a system off accountability based on adequacy norms, they have typically deferred to state legislatures in the design and implementation of such remedies.

The difficulty, of course, is that imposing an accountability requirement based on adequacy norms for judging the performance and constitutionality of a state's public education system requires (1) the creation of outcome standards, (2) the periodic assessment of outcomes to determine compliance with those standards, (3) the understanding of education production process from start to finish, and (4) the political will to provide the funds and to make the changes in teaching methods, programmatic structure, and

Table 5-6. Working Toward an Adequacy Standard: State Supreme Court Rulings from 1989 to 2003

State	Year	Outcome	Legal Rationale
Alabama	1993	unconstitutional	education clause *qua* adequacy
	1997	unconstitutional	education clause *qua* adequacy
	2002	reversed prior decisions	education clause *qua* adequacy
Alaska	1997	unconstitutional*	education clause *qua* adequacy
Arizona	1994	unconstitutional	education clause *qua* adequacy
Arkansas	2002	unconstitutional	education clause *qua* adequacy
Connecticut	1996	unconstitutional	education clause *qua* adequacy
Florida	1996	upheld	education clause *qua* adequacy
Idaho	1998	unconstitutional	education clause *qua* adequacy
Illinois	1996	upheld	education clause *qua* adequacy
	1999	upheld	education clause *qua* adequacy
Kansas	2003	unconstitutional	education clause *qua* adequacy
Kentucky	1989	unconstitutional	education clause *qua* adequacy
Louisiana	1998	upheld	education clause *qua* adequacy
Maine	1995	upheld	equal protection
Maryland	1996	unconstitutional	education clause *qua* adequacy
Massachusetts	1993	unconstitutional	education clause *qua* adequacy
Minnesota	1993	upheld	equal protection
	2000	settled	equal prot. & educ. clause *qua* adequacy
Missouri	1993	unconstitutional*	equal prot. & educ. clause *qua* adequacy
Montana	1989	unconstitutional	education clause *qua* adequacy
Nebraska	1990	upheld	equal protection
N. Hampshire	1993	unconstitutional	education clause *qua* adequacy
	1997	unconstitutional	equal protection
	2002	unconstitutional	education clause *qua* adequacy
New Jersey	1990	unconstitutional	education clause *qua* adequacy
	1994	unconstitutional	education clause *qua* adequacy
	1997	unconstitutional	education clause *qua* adequacy
	1998	unconstitutional	education clause *qua* adequacy
	2000	unconstitutional	education clause *qua* adequacy
	2002	unconstitutional	education clause *qua* adequacy
New Mexico	1999	unconstitutional*	equal protection
New York	1991	upheld	education clause *qua* adequacy
	1995	unconstitutional	education clause *qua* adequacy
	2003	unconstitutional	education clause *qua* adequacy
North Carolina	1997	unconstitutional	education clause *qua* adequacy
North Dakota	1994	upheld	education clause *qua* adequacy
Ohio	1997	unconstitutional	education clause *qua* adequacy
	2000	unconstitutional	education clause *qua* adequacy
	2001	unconstitutional	education clause *qua* adequacy
	2002	unconstitutional	education clause *qua* adequacy

continued next page

Table 5-6. Working Toward an Adequacy Standard: State Supreme Court Rulings from 1989 to 2003

State	Year	Outcome	Legal Rationale
		continued from previous page	
Oregon	1991	upheld	education clause *qua* adequacy
Pennsylvania	1998	upheld*	equal prot. & educ. clause *qua* adequacy
Rhode Island	1995	upheld	education clause *qua* adequacy
South Carolina	1999	unconstitutional	education clause *qua* adequacy
South Dakota	1994	upheld*	education clause *qua* adequacy
Tennessee	1993	unconstitutional	equal prot. & educ. clause *qua* adequacy
	1995	unconstitutional	equal prot. & educ. clause *qua* adequacy
	2002	unconstitutional	equal prot. & educ. clause *qua* adequacy
Texas	1989	unconstitutional	equal prot. & educ. clause *qua* adequacy
	1991	unconstitutional	equal prot. & educ. clause *qua* adequacy
	1992	unconstitutional	equal prot. & educ. clause *qua* adequacy
	1995	upheld new	equal prot. & educ. clause *qua* adequacy
	1997	unconstitutional	equal prot. & educ. clause *qua* adequacy
Vermont	1997	unconstitutional	equal prot. & educ. clause *qua* adequacy
Virginia	1994	upheld	education clause *qua* adequacy
West Virginia	1996	unconstitutional*	education clause *qua* adequacy
	2003	upheld new	education clause *qua* adequacy
Wisconsin	1989	upheld	equal prot. & educ. clause *qua* adequacy
	2000	upheld	equal protection
Wyoming	1995	unconstitutional	equal prot. & educ. clause *qua* adequacy
	2001	upheld new	education clause *qua* adequacy

Sources: Advocacy Center for Children's Educational Success with Standards (2003),
 Bosworth (2001) Ladd and Hansen 1999 and Underwood (1994)
* lower court ruling

administrative arrangements that are necessary to improve the state's compliance with its education standards

Given the history of past equalization efforts, the incomplete knowledge of the education production process, and the unavoidable need to consider funding even in an adequacy based system, it is not surprising that state legislatures more often than not have fallen back on what William Clune (1994) calls "equity plus" remedies. These remedies essentially use equity arguments in the *Serrano* tradition in conjunction with a greater willingness to use a high foundation aid programs, ignore wealthy districts, and put in place some form of output-based policies, often vaguely defined, with the expectation (hope?) that the schools will in some way find ways to meet the outcome goals. As *Figure 5-12* illustrates, the effect of such changes on the finances of local school districts has been to increase the overall level of funding statewide for public education with the effect on individual school

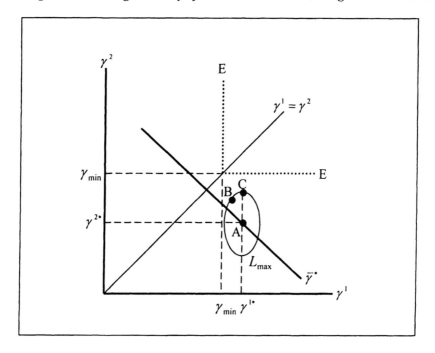

Figure 5-12. The Effect of Adequacy-Based Reform in the Wake of the *Rose* Decision

districts depending on the particular public education funding mechanism in place before these changes. For those states that had been unaffected by the *Serrano*-based funding reforms, the effect of these equity-plus remedies has been a shift from point A to point C, that is, an increase in per-pupil spending for school districts at the bottom of the spending distribution but little effect on school districts at the top of the distribution. For those states that had engaged in some *Serrano* based equity funding reforms, the effect of this new set of equity-plus remedies has been a more subtle shift from point B (recall a similar point B in *Figure 5-7*) to point C, that is, an increase in the per-pupil spending of all school districts but with spending in school districts at the bottom of the spending distribution rising more than those at the top of the spending distribution. On average, then, these equity-plus reforms have resulted in relatively small increases in total financial support for public education with real per-pupil expenditures only rising by an annual rate of 2.1% during the 1990s, the smallest annual rate of increase over the past half century.[123] Interestingly, although total support for public education by 1999-2000 was 4.0% of GDP, it was still below the peak of 4.1% in 1969-70. The effect of these adequacy reforms on reducing per-

---

[123] See *Table 1-4* in *Chapter 1*.

pupil expenditure disparities across school districts was also small though they did reduce disparities somewhat (Moser and Rubenstein (2002)).[124]

The effect on student performance, either in the aggregate or in distributional terms, is much less clear. To the extent to which additional funding translates into improved performance, one might expect a similar pattern of changes in performance to what occurred in spending. However, given the general uncertainty among policy makers and administrators over what improves performances, it perhaps should not be surprising that Hanushek's critique continues to be valid. While some performance improvements have occurred, the overall pattern of student performances does not suggest that these modest improvements in funding have generated improvements in performance.

4.   CONCLUSIONS

The past half century has witnessed a remarkable transformation of the public education funding landscape. Though academics and commissions weighed in from time to time (most notably Cubberley and the team of Strayer and Haig), public education funding was essentially a state legislative affair with little substantive court intervention prior to the 1970s. With the California *Serrano* case, however, state courts (federal courts being barred from acting after the *Rodriguez* case in 1973) became increasing willing to intervene in the public education funding decisions of state legislatures. Initially, such interventions focused on attempts to redress disparities in per-pupil expenditures across school districts, often using DPE structures advocated by Coons, Clune, and Sugarman. The outcome of these reforms was mixed with states dominated by higher-spending school districts tending to level up, states dominated by lower-spending districts tending to level down, and full compliance more the exception than the rule. In the end, while there was some success in reducing spending disparities across school districts, public education reform advocates were disappointed

---

[124] Note that, unlike the case of *Serrano* based reforms, the issue of leveling up versus leveling down is not germane. Because of the structure of foundation grant programs, in all cases, we would expect aggregate spending statewide to rise. Note also that *Figure 5-12* is drawn for the case where the higher spending school districts dominate the state legislature (the more common case). In the case where lower spending school districts dominate the state legislature, the effect of switching from a *Serrano* based funding mechanism to a *Rose* based funding mechanism, the shift would still be from some point B to point C. However, the increase in per-pupil spending in the higher spending school districts relative to the increase in per-pupil spending in the lower spending school districts would be greater.

with these reductions and even more disappointed in the lack of growth in the quality of public education in lower-spending school districts.

With these frustrations came efforts to redirect public education reform efforts toward the objective of educational adequacy rather than equality of funding. State courts in reaction to this shift began haltingly to move away from equality based reforms and toward adequacy based reforms. Finally, in 1989 a state court (the Kentucky Supreme Court in its *Rose* decision) for the first time embraced the notion that a state should be held accountable for its system of public education based on adequacy norms. While generally heralded as a landmark case in the history of public education reform litigation, the impact of the *Rose* decision has been mixed. Nearly a decade and a half later, state courts more often than not continue to fall back on equity remedies even when the justification of the case is one of adequacy. Where courts have been more insistent on an adequacy based remedy, they have typically deferred to their state legislatures on both the design and evaluation of the remedy. The result is that to date there is still no clear legal and workable definition of adequacy.

Such a deference is not surprising given the history of tension between the courts in issues of desegregation (particularly concerning busing) and the general lack of full compliance during the equity period of public education finance reform. The *Rose* decision is thus all the more remarkable both for the comprehensiveness of the Kentucky Supreme Court's order and for the willingness of the Kentucky legislature to attempt to comply in good faith. But it has not provided a working model for other states to follow. Indeed, given the mixed results that Kentucky's reforms have had on student performance, there are real questions whether it ever will.

Chapter 6

THE FUTURE OF PUBLIC EDUCATION FUNDING

"Before I draw nearer to that stone to which you point," said Scrooge, "answer me one question. Are these the shadows of the things that Will be, or are they shadows of the things that May be, only?"
— Charles Dickens, *A Christmas Carol*[125]

The past half century has witnessed a remarkable transformation of the public education funding landscape. Beginning with the California *Serrano* case, state courts have increasingly intervened in the public education funding decisions of state legislatures. However, because of frustrations associated with attempts to eliminate spending disparities across school districts and the lack of substantive improvement in the quality of public education, recent years have seen a shift in reform efforts away from a focus on reducing funding disparities and toward explicit accountability structures based on adequacy norms. While the 1989 *Rose* decision by the Kentucky Supreme Court was heralded at the time as a landmark case in this regard, the past decade and a half have not resulted in significant, widespread benefits, and state legislatures seem especially chary today about engaging in any reforms that would entail significant increases in funding.

As *Figure 6-1* illustrates, any reforms worth considering in the future will have to address three issues – the presence of political forces that constrain state legislatures from fully complying with current court spending and student-outcome mandates; the failure so far to develop a set of measurable student outcome standards that have the general support of the public (particularly parents), policy makers (particularly legislatures and administrators), and teachers; and the lack of detailed knowledge about the public education production function, that is, about what works and for which students. Each of these issues comes with its own special need – the need to devise reforms that can be implemented using existing resources, the need to achieve a consensus between legislatures, teachers, and parents, and

---

[125] Dickens (1966).

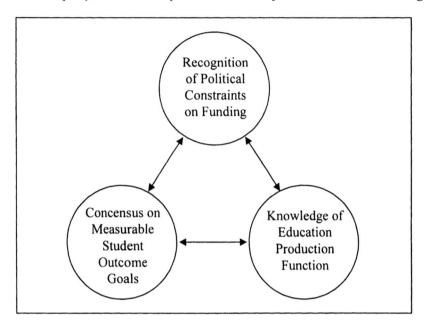

Figure 6-1. Needs for Effective Public Education Reform

the need to engage in increased and more careful empirical research to discover what works in the classroom and with which students. Successful reform, therefore, will require a delicate balancing of various interests, a willingness to make hard choices about both what to do and what to eliminate, and an increased knowledge of the public education production process than can inform the resolution of the first two problems.

This chapter examines these issues in order to get a better sense of what is likely to occur to the support for public education in the future. In brief, the answer depends upon what choices are made in the future. As a result, this chapter begins by laying out the current state of the reform process and what is likely to occur if things don't change. That future is rather bleak. The chapter then turns to the alternatives that the advocates of public education reform might employ if they wish for a brighter future. The chapter then closes with an examination of the role that structural reforms of public education, such as decentralization and the use of markets, might play in public education reform. These structural reforms are an increasing part of the public education landscape and a significant part of what reformers debate. In fact, though reformers tend to view such structural changes as either good or as bad, it turns out that such changes are a double edged sword and thus require special handling. On the one hand, they can be used to target particular, though perhaps limited, sets of students and thus provide a potential, additional instrument for improving public education for those in particular need. On the other hand, it is certainly true that many of these structural changes have been championed by those who have little faith in the general public education system that most children participate in. As a result, they are perceived as a potential threat to the general public education system by diverting attention and resources away from that system.

1. A BLEAK FUTURE?

Despite the promise that the *Rose* case and the shift from equalization to accountability and adequacy generated more than a decade ago, results to date have been less than hoped for at the time. Such disappointment is due not so much to the lack of effort by public education reform advocates or even the lack of good will on the part of legislators and judges. Rather it is due to limitations inherent in the legal and political processes that govern public education. If public education reform efforts in the future continue to focus simply on finance reform and persuading state legislatures through the carrot of lobbying and the stick of court action to enact such funding reforms based on adequacy norms, the future is likely to be rather bleak for those who had held high hopes that the shift to adequacy norms would result in a substantive improvement in the quality of public education. State legislatures are unlikely for the foreseeable future to accede to such pressures with or without pressure from the courts. Moreover, even were state legislatures to accede to such pressures, it would likely have little effect on the more substantive and difficult issue of raising student performance, particularly for those students currently at the bottom of the performance distribution.

Adoption of funding adequacy norms implies a need to increase the expenditures in the lowest spending local school districts. Ostensibly, this could be funded by reducing the level of spending in the higher spending school districts and transferring those funds to the lower spending local school districts. However, the political reality is that the higher spending local school districts are generally more salient in state legislatures. As a result, these legislatures will have a strong preference for preserving the existing levels of education spending in those higher spending school districts even if that means a higher budget. *Figure 6-2* illustrates this situation for the case of a state with two school districts, one of which spends less per pupil than some court-ordered minimum γ_{min} (the spending level of school district 1 being γ^{1*} and the spending level of school district 2 being γ^{2*}). As explained originally in *Chapter 3*, point *A* represents the state legislature's ideal mix of spending levels in local school district *1* and

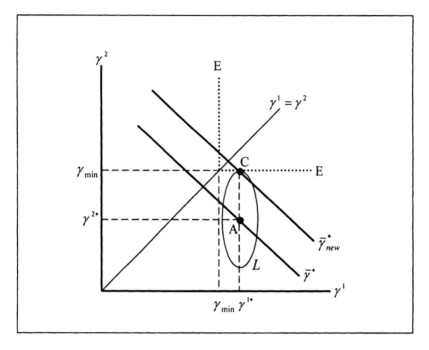

Figure 6-2. The Effect of Adequacy-Based Reform in the Wake of the *Rose* Decision

2, with ellipses centered around point *A* representing political indifference curves, that is, the set of combinations of spending in those two school districts that would result in the same political loss associated with deviating from the legislature's ideal at point *A*. Ellipse *L* thus represents the particular state legislature's political indifference curve which satisfies the court's order (represented by the constraint *EE*) with minimum political loss. Because the higher spending school district is the politically more salient school district, the ellipse *L* is vertically oriented. As a result, the state legislature will prefer moving in the direction of point C in the diagram, that is, in preserving the level of per-pupil spending in the higher spending school district.[126] Thus, one would expect (as represented by the movement from the line $\bar{\gamma}^*$ to the line $\bar{\gamma}^*_{new}$) that any attempt to redress spending inadequacies would have to be accompanied by an increase in the total level of resources provided to the state's public education system.

---

[126] In fact, this result is more general. Even if the state is dominated by lower spending school districts (which would imply horizontally oriented political indifference curves), the state legislature will still prefer to maintain the level of spending in the higher spending districts.

Despite the occasional allure of a new, painless revenue source such as revenue from state lotteries or revenue from fines levied on illegal drugs, such novel sources have not become a significant source of revenue (Webb (1990), Wood (1990)), and there is no prospect of their becoming so. As a result, funding to redress educational inadequacies will continue to depend on traditional revenue sources – the state sales tax, the state income tax, and the local property tax – for the foreseeable future.

This, in turn, suggests that there are likely to be real political limits on the willingness to increase public education spending, whether it be through increased taxes, a reduction in the resources provided to other state governmental programs, or some combination of the two (Carr and Fuhrman (1999)). Theoretically, it is certainly possible that this political limitation might not be binding. However, experience suggests that legislative full compliance with court orders is more the exception than the rule.[127] Though not always a political majority, all state legislatures have a strong anti-tax constituency, and the recent reappearance of federal government deficits suggest that states will not be able to depend on federal aid to help fund increases in public education funding. Finally, the experience with public education funding equalization is now part of the political memory in many states, and as a result voters have become more insistent (in part driven by the anti-tax constituency) that any reforms have demonstrated benefits beyond simply increasing funding.

Interestingly, an examination of public education funding levels over the past century suggests much the same conclusion. As *Table 1-1* revealed in *Chapter 1*, a remarkably constant share of GDP (in the neighborhood of four percent) has been devoted to public education nationwide since the late 1960s. In addition, an examination of real GDP and real aggregate public education revenues nationwide from 1929 to 2000 reveals a strong correlation (0.9891) between those two variables, and a simple univariate linear regression of real aggregate public education revenues on real GDP reveals (with an R^2 statistic of 0.9784) that over the period from 1929 to 2000 real aggregate public education revenues rose by just over forty million

---

[127] Perhaps the best known example is New Jersey where the legal process continued through several decades. California is an interesting exception, though it took many years to arrive at that outcome. After 17 years of litigation and several successful referenda restricting local property taxes, restricting the state's ability to increase taxes, and mandating that at least 39 percent of the state's budget be spent on education, the state appears to be in compliance. However, the changes have been dramatic with the state's share of education funding rising from 35% to 85% (Mandelker et al. (1990; pp. 649-654)).

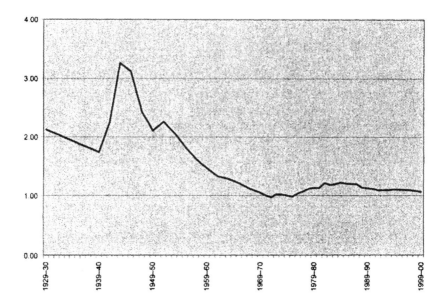

Figure 6-3. Elasticity of real public education revenues with respect to real GDP, 1929-2000

dollars for every billion dollar increase in real GDP.[128]

To get a better sense of the connection between these variables, the elasticity of real aggregate public education revenues with respect to real GDP was calculated using the estimated regression equation. The results (see Figure 6-3) reveal that recent decades have seen a convergence in this elasticity to a value just above one. Such a value suggests that the resources available for public education are unlikely to rise in the future except to the extent the size of the general economy grows, and then only at about the same rate. This in turn suggests that if reformers continue the tactic of lobbying state legislatures to increase spending in the lower-spending local school districts they are likely to fail.

Legal history since the *Rose* case also suggests that using the courts as a device to force state legislative to increase funding in the future is also likely to fail. Despite the *Rose* case and its progeny, state legislatures are simply unwilling to increase spending on public education. As *Figure 6-4*

[128] More specifically, the estimated equation was:

$$X = -28,769,976 + 42,777\ Y$$
$$(5.54)\qquad (45.15)$$

where Y represents real GDP, X represents real public education revenues, and t-statistics for the two coefficients are reported beneath the estimated coefficients inside parentheses (see *Table 1-1* for data sources).

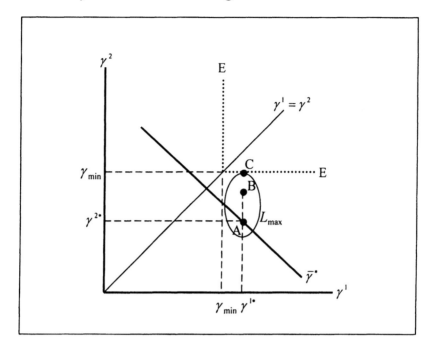

Figure 6-4. The Effect of Adequacy-Based Reform in the Wake of the *Rose* Decision

illustrates, state legislatures that have been pushed by the courts to reform their public education funding using adequacy norms seem to have reached the maximum political loss they are willing to incur (point B on the political indifference curve L_{max} in the figure), and are unwilling to move closer to point C where the court's wishes are fully satisfied.

That the courts would be expected to acquiesce in such an outcome shouldn't be surprising. As Robert Williams (1990) notes, and recent history confirms, the courts are generally hesitant to mandate specific legislation even in issues of constitutionality.[129] Thus, during the 1970s and 1980s, the courts generally were willing to accept less than full equalization of per-pupil spending levels across school districts. Indeed, the Kentucky *Rose* decision is all the more remarkable (but consequently less indicative of future court behavior in other states) for its comprehensiveness and for the

---

[129] See also Mandelker et al. (1990). Perhaps the most noteworthy example of the courts backing down in the face of recalcitrant political forces centers on the courts' involvement with desegregation through the use of busing (see Wilkerson (1979)). Such reaction is not, however, universal. See, for example, *Commonwealth ex rel. Carroll v. Tate* (1971), a Pennsylvania case in which the court ordered the government to increase an appropriation to fund the courts themselves.

willingness of the Kentucky legislature to comply in good faith. In part, the success of the *Rose* case was due to the existence of complementary political forces. But it was also due to the Kentucky Supreme Court being willing to take the risky strategy of declaring the entire public education institutional framework unconstitutional.

It is doubtful that other states (and indeed even Kentucky today) have similarly receptive state legislatures and supreme courts willing to force matters in such a dramatic fashion.[130]   But in the end, even if states were willing to provide the additional resources, there is little hope that such resources would alone result in the improvements in student performance that presumably underlie the argument for additional resources. As noted in *Chapter 5* (recall the debate between Hanushek and the team of Greenwald, Hedges, and Laine over the question of whether money matters), while new programs clearly require resources, there is no persuasive evidence that an increase in local school district resources *untied to specific changes in classroom programs, incentives, or administrative structures* results in reliable and predictable improvements in performance. As a result, even if state legislatures were willing in the future to provide increased resources, there is little hope that such increases in resources by themselves would result in greater student performance for those school districts.

2.   SOURCE OF THE PROBLEM

The decision to lobby state legislatures (with or without the help of court pressure) to increase funding for lower-spending, poorer-performing local school districts and thereby improve the quality of education for needy students was based on the implicit assumption that the objectives of public education were clear and that those delivering public education knew what needed to be done to achieve those objectives. As a result, all that was thought to be needed was to give needy local school districts the resources necessary to achieve such improvements and the incentives to encourage such improvements. But the reality is quite different. Despite Henry Levin's (1994b) and Stanley Pogrow's (1994) warnings a decade ago, there is today neither a consensus on what the objectives of public education should be nor the knowledge necessary to attain those objectives, and both these factors have resulted in a general inability to improve student

---

[130] See Minorini and Sugarman (1999a; 204-5) and Mintrom (1993). Raquel Fernández and Richard Rogerson (1999) argue, using California data, that in fact the shift to increased state funding may result in a general fall in the level of support statewide for public education even if the distribution of that support becomes more equal.

performance reliably and consistently through increases in public education expenditures.[131]

The lack of consensus concerning the purpose of public education can be seen in the reaction to legislative efforts since the early 1990s to implement accountability requirements through the promulgation of assessment standards and procedures. The impetus for formal assessment standards and procedures came from two forces present at the time – the desire to reform public education in line with the new adequacy norms that underlay various public education funding reform cases (again, most notably Kentucky's *Rose* case) and the desire to improve the public schools more generally as a result of the perception that the United States was at a competitive disadvantage relative to other nations because of its poor system of public education. By the turn of the twenty-first century, a number of states had adopted mandatory systems of assessment based on adequacy norms and the general view that all of public education should become more productive. While state efforts continue, much of the impetus for state specific assessment systems has been preempted by the US Congress's passage in 2001of the *No Child Left Behind Law* (US 107th Congress (2002a)). The law envisions a twelve year implementation period with its primary effects being the imposition of teacher training requirements and the requirement that all states: [132]

> implement statewide accountability systems covering all public schools and students. These systems must be based on challenging State standards in reading and mathematics, annual testing for all students in grades 3-8, and annual statewide progress objectives ensuring that all groups of students reach proficiency within 12 years. Assessment results and State progress objectives must be broken out by poverty, race, ethnicity, disability, and limited English proficiency to ensure that no group is left behind (US Department of Education (2004)).

For states that do not meet federal requirements, the law specifies a set of penalties including the requirement that students be allowed to switch

---

[131] That is not to say that resources and incentives are unimportant. Particularly with regard to incentives, as Helen Ladd and Janet Hansen (1999; Chapter 6) notes, there are a variety of incentive schemes that have been, or should be, used to assure that teachers and administrators are more receptive to pursing adequacy goals. However, funding and incentives are of secondary importance if the purpose of public education is vague and if teachers and administrators don't know what works.

[132] The *No Child Left Behind Law* is formally an amendment to the *Elementary and Secondary Education Act* of 1965. For the federal government's view of the law, its value, and its implementation, see the US Department of Education's websites http://www.ed.gov/nclb and http://www.ed.gov/policy.

schools if the school they currently attend chronically fails to meet federal requirements.

Unfortunately, the development of such assessment structures, and particularly the federal law, have been based in large part on a principal-agent model of decision making in which the problem is how best to ensure that teachers (the agents) fulfill the wishes of the legislature (the principal) through the imposition of various rewards and penalties. The result of this minimization of teacher input has been a general alienation of teachers.[133] While proponents of existing assessment requirements sometimes attribute this lack of support to the unwillingness of teachers to recognize the changing needs of society and teacher anxiety over job security, such attribution misses the point – legislators and the public more generally have a different opinion than teachers do as to what the purpose of public education should be. For many in the general public, the purpose of public education is to instill in children some given amount of knowledge in a set of well defined subject areas and to teach them a fixed set of skills whose attainment can be measured through standardized proficiency tests. Hence, state and federal assessment standards tend to focus on student demonstrations of knowledge in a finite set of defined areas and the acquisition of a fixed set of skills (most commonly reading and mathematics) based typically (though not entirely) on standardized testing. Many teachers and other critics argue, however, that while the above is certainly part of what education should be about, it should also inculcate intellectual, job, and life skills that go beyond what can be measured by existing standardized testing.[134] Because success along these dimensions is ultimately manifest in the satisfaction adults have long-term in their personal lives, in their lives as citizens, and in their ability to be employable and adapt to changing job markets, success is difficult to measure, particularly if one wishes to measure the degree of success while students are still in school. In such cases, only indirect indicators can be used, and the list of these indicators remains ill-defined, though centering on such notions as the integration of knowledge across subject areas, the ability to problem solve,

---

[133] An additional problem, beyond the issue of assessment standards definition and process is that the federal law represents in practice another example of an unfunded mandate. Though state legislators have complained about this problem, it should be noted that local government officials have long complained of similar impositions by their state legislatures.

[134] Beyond the general concern that existing standardized tests cannot fully measure the benefits of a public education (Ladd and Hansen (1999; pp. 113-4), there are also more specific concerns about the process of implementing the *No Child Left Behind Law* including such mundane issues as the accurate tabulation of test results (Galley (2003), Olson (2003)).

the ability to reflect on oneself in the act of intellectual activity (namely, critical thinking), and (perhaps most importantly) the ability to continue to learn on one's own.

One may agree or disagree with this criticism of current assessment standards and the implicit values that underlie this criticism. However, what is important is that there is a significant gap between legislatures and teachers, and that such differences lead to a bifurcation of public education's efforts in educating children, as teachers attempt to meet the constraints imposed on them by mandated assessment standards while also attempting to deliver what they believe in good faith to be a proper education.

Compounding this problem of a lack of focus is a lack of knowledge about what works and what doesn't work. As the Institute of Education Sciences notes in its survey of education policymakers ranging from federal government officials down to school district superintendents and other local officials (US Department of Education, Institute of Education Sciences (2003b)), there is a decided lack of knowledge about the education process from what happens in the classroom all the way up to what state and federal government funding and assessment policies are most effective, and little current research that can be expected to rectify the situation. As a result, there is currently no agreement on what teaching methods, reward structures, and administrative arrangements reliably and consistently result in improved student performance and whether such methods, structures, and arrangements work with all students or only with particular subpopulations of students. In the absence of such knowledge, decisions about teaching methods, rewards, and administrative structures are often made on the basis of anecdotal evidence, personal experience, and instinct. The result is a rather confused and conflicting set of claims about what works and what does not.

Either of these problems alone might explain the lack of connection between increased expenditures and increased student performance. But together, the lack of focused effort and the lack of knowledge about how to increase student performance *whatever the objective* generates a disconnect between increased expenditures and increased student performance that currently cannot be overcome, especially for poorer performing school districts and disadvantaged students.

3. REQUIREMENTS FOR A BRIGHTER FUTURE

If all students are to have a chance of receiving an adequate education, reforms must be premised on the fact that for the foreseeable future there will be no significant increase in aggregate public education funding. As

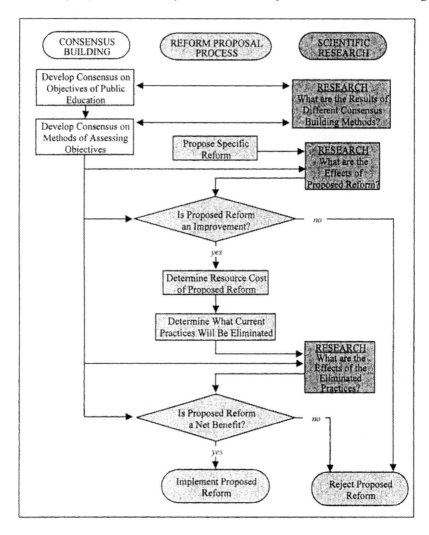

Figure 6-5. An Alternative Strategy for Public Education Reform

Allan Odden and Carolyn Busch (1998) observe in the preface to their study of school-based financing, any successful reform, which necessarily must involve resources, can only succeed by redirecting existing resources in more productive ways. Add to this the need to develop a consensus among the general public, policy makers, and teachers about what the objectives of public education should be, and the need for scientific research on the nature of the public education production process, and you have the outline of a workable strategy for public education reform. *Figure 6-5* illustrates such a process in which consensus building and scientific research are used to guide and assess an accountability reform process constrained by no increase in resources.

3.1   Developing a Consensus

The lack of agreement over the appropriate goals of public education and therefore the best means of assessing the success of teachers, school, and school systems has resulted in considerable anxiety among teachers, frustration for both policy makers and teachers, and an inability to sufficiently improve public education both as a general proposition and certainly for those disadvantaged students who have been the focus of so much attention by public education reform advocates over the past half century.

While the development of an agreement about such goals will not by itself achieve public education reform, it clearly is a necessary condition.[135] Without agreement about what the purpose of public education should be, it will be impossible to discriminate between productive and unproductive reforms, and public education will run the risk of a future in which reforms conflict, resources are misdirected, and teacher morale (and hence productivity) is threatened.[136]   Indeed, even if it were possible to only promulgate productive reforms, the lack of consensus would lead to poor implementation due to a lack of teacher buy-in, thus threatening the ability of any reform to effect improvements. Clearly, then, a critical component of any reform process if it is to be successful is agreement about what direction public education should take.

How that agreement should be reached is still an open question. However, some insight can be gleaned from Judith Innes and David Booher's (1999a, 1999b) efforts to construct a theory of consensus building. While sometimes viewed as a reaction to a failure to resolve conflict using other strategies, Innes and Booher (1999a; p. 412) argue that consensus building is better seen as a rational reaction to "changing conditions in increasingly networked societies, where power and information are widely distributed, where differences in knowledge and values among individuals and communities are growing, and where accomplishing anything significant

---

[135] See Jessica Portner's (1999) article on the need for consensus building in science education, and Geraint Johnes's (1993) chapter on performance indicators in his economics of education text.

[136] An additional complication to developing a consensus, as Mark Blaug (1972; pp. 266-7) notes, is that "education services multiple objectives" that requires that we essentially "resort to an 'objective function' or 'social welfare function' that orders the different objectives in terms of priorities."

or innovative requires creating flexible linkages among many players." In contrast to other decision making mechanisms, consensus building offers the potential for higher quality, more stable outcomes because participant knowledge is used more efficiently and because the process assures that outcomes are more closely connected to the interests of the entire group. Finally, they argue that consensus building, because it results in the challenging of assumptions and the status quo more than other mechanisms do, typically results in greater innovation.

This consensus building process would appear to have great potential value in public education. Teachers to a large degree have not been part of past efforts to define the goals of public education or the standards by which progress toward those goals are to be measured, and this lack of participation has reduced morale and raised the specter of even poorer teacher retention in the future. By using a consensus building process to reach an agreement about public education's goals and assessment standards, valuable teacher knowledge, as well as their views about what public education should be about, could be exploited to the benefit of public education in general as well as resulting in greater teacher commitment to the assessment process and greater innovative activity.

Stating that agreement should be reached through consensus, and actually engaging in a consensus building are, of course, two separate matters. While the work of Innes and Booher is valuable in going from one to the other,[137] much is still unknown about the consensus building process and how, institutionally, such a process can be fostered and nurtured. Within the context of public education, among the interesting questions that remain to be answered are:

- Are some forms of school, district, and even state administration governance more conducive to developing such a consensus?
- What role do compensation schemes, teacher evaluation processes, and management techniques play in this process?[138]
- What role does teacher training play in the same process?
- To what extent should assessment be used to evaluate programs, schools, districts, or states versus individual student and individual teacher success?

Whether some sort of consensus building process will take place is a more difficult question to answer. As Frederick Wirt and Michael Kirst (1997; 302-3) and Andrew Reschovsky and Jennifer Imazeki (2001)

---

[137] See also Innes's (1996) application to the problem of city planning, and Jodie Altice and William Dugger's (1998) description of consensus building in the area of technology education.

[138] For a critique of the literature on investments in teacher quality and student performance, see Plecki (2000).

observe, while there is a broad agreement among politicians at all levels of government and among a broad array of private-sector public interest organizations in support of a standards-based approach to public education reform, other interest groups see such change as a threat. As a result of such conflict and the general reticence of politicians to engage in policy changes when there is conflict (not to mention fiscal stress), the prospect of reaching a consensus would seem less than assured.

Assuming that an agreement on objectives can be reached, the consensus building process could then turn to the development of methods of assessment. Even more than the problem of reaching consensus on the purpose of public education, the issue of how to assess public education has been a difficult one for teachers because of its direct impact on the classroom and the amount of discretion that teachers have there. Exacerbating this difficulty (beyond the fact that there is no agreement about the purpose of public education) is the lack of knowledge about the optimal design of assessment processes and the impact of differing assessment methods on student behavior/achievement, teacher morale, and the cost of such methods.

Performance measures are more likely to be accepted if they are connected to the school's production process and system of rewards, if they reflect the multidimensional nature of public education's goals, and if they allow meaningful comparisons across schools such that pursuit of better performance measures results in improved educational quality and success (Belfield (2000; p. 177-8), Hanushek (1996b), Ladd and Hansen (1999; p. 134-8). However, despite the seeming simplicity of these desirable traits and despite early work by individuals such as Allan Odden and Lawrence Picus (1992; Chapter 3), developing specific measures that embody these desirable traits is a difficult process that is far from complete. In part, this difficulty can be traced to the fact that the fundamental objectives of public education are long-term (for example, increased earnings and increased employment) but the only performance measures that are typically available for assessing specific programs are short-term in nature. Robert Meyer (1996), for example, argues that the common use of average test scores as assessment measures is weak and counterproductive and ought to be replaced by value-added indicators of academic performance. Meyer may indeed be correct, but, as James Heckman, Anne Layne-Farrar, and Petra Todd (1995) demonstrate in their analysis of school quality and increased earnings, the connection between near-term performance measures and long-term goals is not clear. Again, more research would help assure that efforts to develop effective measures of performance are consistent with the long-term goals we assign to public education.

3.2   Evaluating and Implementing Reform Proposals

Given a set of agreed upon educational objectives and methods of assessment, a successful reform proposal process would require the development of particular reform proposals and the evaluation of those proposals to assure that the implementation of such proposals would result in improvements. In keeping with the fact that there is today no exploitable relationship between simple changes in funding and improved performance, such reform proposals could not consist simply of reformulating existing state funding mechanisms. Rather, they would have to consist of more substantive proposals to change the public education production process including curriculum (at the school, district, or state level), teacher recruitment and retention, school and district management, etc, in conjunction with changes in funding mechanisms to allow and encourage such proposals to be implemented.[139]

In assessing the value of these proposed reforms, two steps would be required, the first being an evaluation of the educational impact of the reform through careful scientific research and using the accepted assessment standards, the second being an evaluation of the economic and political feasibility of the proposed reform. Assuming that this first evaluation resulted in a positive result and that the proposed reform did in fact result in improved student performance for the targeted student population (as defined by accepted assessment standards),[140] the process could then turn to evaluating the proposed reform's economic and political feasibility.

While some of the evaluation of the economic and political feasibility of the proposed reform would deal with determining the resource cost of the reform,[141] much of the effort would center on the more difficult problem of assessing programmatic and political tradeoffs. Because the aggregate level of financial support for public education is unlikely to change in the foreseeable future, any proposed reform that would be implemented, to the extent it requires resources (time or money), would require that it take those resources away from some current practice. As a result, implementing any

---

[139] Indeed, even the issue of the level of government involvement ought to be open to investigation. While education has decided public good aspects that private markets cannot deliver efficiently and that therefore warrant government involvement, government involvement raises the potential for inefficiencies of its own. See Clive Belfield's (2000) Chapter 8 for an extended treatment of the issue.

[140] See section 3.3 below on the role of scientific research for details on this first step in the assessment process.

[141] This problem of identifying reforms that are productively efficient is not a trivial problem. For an appreciation of some of the problems with measuring productive efficiency, see Rubenstein, Schwartz, and Stiefel (1999).

reform would require deciding what current practices would be given up to make room for the reform. In some cases, this "displacement" cost might be minimal. Thus, for example, one can envisage a proposed change in which the evaluation of the performance of teachers by a principal would simply involve replacing the existing rubric with an alternative one. However, many reforms are not likely to be so straightforward and would require significant shifts of resources away from other practices. If, for example, the reform required additional class time, teacher preparation time, and/or administrative time, what class, teacher, and/or administrative activities would have less time devoted to them? And what would be the cost of such reductions in terms of the quality of education? Such an evaluation process would clearly require careful research into the educational cost of such changes.[142] Given such research, the net benefit of the proposed reform would then be equal to the direct educational benefits of the proposed reform minus the lost educational benefits associated with cutting back elsewhere.

If the displacement cost were along the same dimensions as the touted benefits of the proposed reform (for example, both focus on the same measure of reading ability), then the calculation of the net benefit would be relatively straightforward. However, if the displacement cost were along different dimensions, the problem of calculating the net benefit would become more difficult. Take, for example, a proposal to improve mathematical skills that would require additional time on task in the classroom, and that the decision is made to take that time away from efforts currently devoted to reading. In such a situation, it is possible that the outcome of this reform would be to improve student abilities in terms of mathematics but reduce student abilities in terms of reading. The fundamental problem then becomes one of deciding the relative value of mathematical skills versus reading skills. It is here that the value of having a consensus on what public education should achieve and how such achievement should be measured becomes crucial. In the absence of a pre-existing consensus, it is unlikely such a conflict could be resolved.

---

[142] David Monk and Jennifer Rice (1999) provide a preliminary sketch of how such a cost evaluation process might take place. Most cost evaluations in the economics literature, unlike Monk and Rice's work, focus on an overall assessment of the additional cost that would be required to provide an adequate education to all students (see, for example, Imazeki and Reschovsky (1999)). While such estimates are fraught with the problems of not having a clear notion of what an adequate education is and not having a full understanding of the education production function, they do serve the useful purpose of providing policy makers with at least a rough estimate of the overall size of the problem from a resource perspective. But see Levin (1992) for a fuller critique of the usefulness of such studies.

An even more difficult tradeoff, both for its political as well as its ethical dimensions, is one involving different populations of students. What is to be done, for example, if a proposed reform would help one group of students but would (by the associated shift in resources) harm other students? While the identity of those two groups of students and the agreed upon objectives of public education would be important in resolving this issue, there is a political complication. The belief in the right to the status quo is a strongly held value in the US, particularly in local politics,[143] and policies that violate this right are much more difficult (though not always impossible) to adopt. Moreover, the public has over the past several decades become jaded (some might say, become more sophisticated) with respect to the efficacy of government actions and as a result requires greater demonstrations of proof that government programs will achieve what advocates claim they will achieve, particularly with regard to programs that affect the public directly or that cost a great deal.

The result is that the success of reforms may in some cases, particularly in those cases associated with improving the quality of education for students at the bottom of the performance distribution, require a juggling of reforms to assure that they are not perceived as hurting other students. Key in this regard would be the development of a financing structure that is flexible enough to allow such juggling while still assuring that the balance swings in favor of those programs that benefit the most needy students. As William Clune (1994) and Margaret Goertz and Gary Natriello (1999) note, this requires a linkage between education reform and finance reform that historically has not been there. The difficulty, of course, as James Guthrie and Richard Rothstein (1999) and as William Duncombe and John Yinger (1999) note in their research on developing such funding structures, is that providing funding to assure an adequate education for all students depends both on taking into account local circumstances and on creating incentives for teachers and administrators to assure that they work to achieve the particular adequacy standards in place.

One way of assuring a sufficiently flexible funding structure would be to centralize the administration, like the state of Hawaii, into a single, unified school district for the entire state with local superintendents under the direct control of the state government. This would allow funds to be distributed

---

[143] See Zajac (1995) for a general introduction to the role of equity in economic analysis. Edward Zajac argues that there is a strong consensus in modern developed economies that people have a right to the status quo, along with a right to necessities (such as food, clothing, education, and health care), a right to insurance for risks that are not one's fault (such as natural disasters and unemployment due to recessions), a right to competitive markets (both to buy and to sell in), and a right to be treated with horizontal and vertical equity.

through a more flexible, internal administrative process similar to the flexibility that local school district superintendents' have with regard to the funding of individual schools and would eliminate the formulaic funding method common with current state foundation or district power equalization systems. The difficulty with such an option, of course, is that it would also eliminate much of the current political power of locally elected school boards. As a result, given that the system of locally elected school boards and locally chosen superintendents is so entrenched politically, the change to a statewide unified school district would appear to be politically infeasible.

A more likely method for assuring a sufficiently flexible funding structure would be to fund new reforms centrally through categorical grants. This would allow the state to have significant control over the terms of the funding and still allow local school boards to function. The state could then assure that funds are provided on the basis of program efficacy and local school district need. To the extent that an increasing share of state funding were distributed through such categorical grants, the overall funding structure of public education would become more complex. However, my analysis of intergovernmental grants (Leyden (1992b)) suggests that such complexity is, from a political perspective, a natural part of the political funding process. Legislatures prefer complex grant structure precisely because it allows them to better target benefits to various political constituencies and thereby increase the political utility they get from the funding process.

3.3   Role of Scientific Research

The reform process depends critically on being able to conduct scientific research, both to inform the consensus building process as well as to provide needed feedback on the effectiveness of various reform proposals.[144] While the particulars of the research process will depend on the specific reform proposal being investigated, in broad terms good scientific education research involves three distinct steps.

First, because resources will be scarce (including resources for research), the research process should begin with an evaluation of the proposed reform using the existing literature and data, the latter most likely being (at least

---

[144] The call for more and better research is a near universal cry in both the education and the economics literatures. For examples, see Monk (1992), Hanushek (1994b, 1996b), Ladd (1996), Smith, Scoll, and Link (1996), Wirt and Kirst (1997; Chapter 15), and Evers, Izumi, and Riley (2001). Of course, research is only valuable if it ends up informing the behavior of practitioners. For an example of an effort to improve the connection between researchers and practitioners, see US Department of Education, Institute of Education Sciences (2003a).

initially) in aggregated form. While such evaluations should not be viewed as conclusive,[145] they do provide a useful way to decide which proposals are worth further empirical evaluation and to design further empirical evaluations.

Next, should be an evaluation of the impact of the proposed reform on performance through controlled experimental trials.[146] One of the difficulties with much of the current empirical education research is that it tends to use cross-sectional survey data (either micro-level or aggregated). While econometric methods have become increasingly sophisticated, students tend to enroll in programs that they (or their parents) believe will be effective, thus making inferences about the effect of expanding a program to students not currently participating in the program difficult. Experimental trials, though not a panacea for solving these selectivity problems, go a long way to getting results that are more reliable. The creation of laboratory schools would, in this context, be quite useful. While not all proposed reforms are amenable to examination in laboratory schools, certainly many proposals (especially those that focus on what occurs in the classroom) would be.

While such efforts might be viewed as redundant when the results from a related (though not identical), existing literature are available, one ought to be suspicious of such cost savings. The education research literature is rife with results that can not be replicated. The reason for such problems stems at least in part from the complicated education production process. A student's ability to learn is a function of several factors – what occurs in the classroom, the student's personal and family background, the backgrounds and behaviors of the student's peers, etc. Most of these factors are outside the control of the school and only imperfectly accounted for in empirical research. As a result, the behavioral parameters estimated in one study do not always remain the same across different experiments. While such a problem is not insurmountable, it is sufficiently important to justify as a general proposition the view that controlled experimentation is beneficial.

Of course, experiments are not without their pitfalls. One potential problem is that the experiment may be conducted in such specialized circumstances that it has no value beyond the experiment. Another potential problem is the possibility of Hawthorne effects in which the subjects of an experiment respond not because of the particular stimulus applied but simply because they are being studied. Such effects were originally noted by Elton Mayo in his industrial psychology study of Western Electric's Hawthorne

---

[145] See Summers and Wolfe (1977) for evidence on the limitations of using aggregated rather than micro-level (that is, individual student) data.

[146] This discussion of controlled experiments draws upon Clive Belfield's (2000; pp. 12-14) review of the empirical economics literature of education. The reader is encouraged to refer to Belfield for additional references and a more technical treatment.

Works in Chicago (Roethlisberger and Dickson (1939)). In the context of public education policy reform, the potential exists that a positive assessment of a proposed reform is not the result of the intrinsic qualities of the proposed reform, but simply because there was an experiment. In such circumstances, the changes in behavior and outcome are simply the result of the attention paid to the experiment's subjects, be they students, teachers, or administrators.

As a result, the final step in the research process requires the empirical examination of the proposed reform in field tests. As Frederick Mosteller, Richard Light, and Jason Sachs (1996) recognize in the conclusion to their review of research on the effects of skill grouping and class size, controlled experimentation, while crucial and necessary, is often not sufficient to determine the efficacy of a proposed reform. The general environment of public education is confronted by a variety of forces coming both from inside and outside the school, and such forces cannot typically be controlled. As a result, any proposed reform, if it is to be successful, must be able to survive despite such influences. Hence, the need for field tests to assure as best as can be determined that the success of the proposed reform is robust in the face of such forces and that these forces do not end up canceling out the positive effects already documented in controlled experiments. Indeed, it is this third step of the research process that is likely to be most persuasive for the general public, higher level administrators, and legislators.

Finally, it should be noted that in addition to formal field test research, it is also possible to engage in what might be termed "virtual" field test research. Strictly speaking, such research is not field test research at all. Rather, it is opportunistic research that simply looks at the effects of changes in policy that have taken place. While the data for such virtual field tests may be more difficult to come by and may be of lower quality due to the opportunistic nature of the research, such analyses have the virtue of allowing for the investigation of a broader set of policies than are likely to be tested formally.[147]

3.4 How Likely Is This Future?

It is not at all clear at this juncture whether the brighter future described above will in fact occur, though recent changes suggest that the nation may have begun to move in the right direction. Perhaps the most obvious sign of a shift away from the old reform efforts based almost exclusively on finance

---

[147] For an example of this type of virtual field testing applied to the question of whether tax and expenditure limits have an effect on the quality of teachers, see Downes and Figlio (1999), and Imazeki (2001).

reform is the advent of state and federal efforts to put in place assessment mechanisms, most notably the *No Child Left Behind Law*. The difficulty with such efforts, again most notably with the federal effort, is the failure to date to get significant teacher buy-in on the law. But whether Congress or the various state legislatures will be willing to revise their laws is yet to be determined.

There is certainly precedent in the past for failure. In 1994 (Jorgenson (1996)), Congress reauthorized the *Elementary and Secondary Education Act* with a $60 billion allocation and passed *Goals 2000* legislation during the Clinton administration that called for the fulfilling of eight national education goals first established in 1990 by President Bush the elder and the nation's governors:

- All children should be ready to learn when they start school.
- High school graduation rates should be 90% or higher.
- Grades 4, 8, and 12 should be competency gateways in several specific subjects.
- US students should be first in the world in math and science achievement.
- Every American adult should be literate.
- Every US school should be free of drugs and violence.
- Teachers should have access to the continuing education necessary to achieve the other objectives.
- Every school should promote partnerships to increase parental involvement in promoting social, emotional, and academic growth.

Reaction at the time was mixed with some, like Massachusetts Senator Kennedy, thinking the effort impressive while others, such as New York Senator Moynihan, thinking the effort unrealistic and therefore harmful. Since 1994, these goals appear to have been permanently shelved. In hindsight, the reason for this failure seems clear. While many of the goals may appear to be laudable, they are as a whole a rather specific and limited wish-list unaccompanied by the creation of a process that would allow the teaching profession to have input and eventually buy into the process. Moreover, no provision was made for creating a process to refine these goals (and the implied assessment measures) in the light of changing circumstances and new knowledge. Finally, no provision was made for creating a single, or better yet, double loop assessment process whereby progress toward goals could be measured and used to revise the process by which public education is delivered, both in the classroom and administratively.[148]

---

[148] A single loop assessment process is one in which, given a set of outcome measures, assessment results are used to adjust how public education is delivered. A double loop

The current federal effort in the form of the *No Child Left Behind Law*, while doing much better at creating a single loop assessment process, still fails to allow for teacher buy-in in a meaningful manner or create a double loop assessment process to allow educational goals and assessment measures to be refined in the light of changing circumstances and new knowledge. Whether that law will adjust to these needs or, like the 1994 effort, eventually be permanently shelved is not clear.

In many ways, the key to the entire reform process is research, and here again there is reason for hope though much still needs to be done. As has been noted before, research is needed to take stock of current practices, to evaluate proposed reforms, and to help develop and refine both the goal setting process as well as the process by which assessment instruments are chosen and used. While some solid, scientific research is occurring, much of what passes for research is the sharing of anecdotes and case studies.

Federal government efforts in support of research present a hope that the situation may improve. The Federal government currently funds 10 regional educational laboratories. Originally created as part of the 1964 *Elementary and Secondary Education Act* (*ESEA*), these laboratories received refocused attention as part of the reauthorization of the *ESEA* to focus on the promotion of knowledge-based school improvements (Spencer and Stonehill (1999)). Then in 2002, Congress passed the *Education Sciences Reform Act* that calls on the Department of Education's Institute of Education Sciences to support (including the possibility of creating) at least eight national education R&D centers that will engage in R&D activity in a wide variety of areas required by the law (US 107th Congress (2002b)):

- Adult literacy.
- Assessment, standards, and accountability research.
- Early childhood development and education.
- English language learners research.
- Improving low achieving schools.
- Innovation in education reform.
- State and local policy.
- Postsecondary education and training.
- Rural education.
- Teacher quality.
- Reading and literacy.

---

assessment process is one in which the single loop assessment process is itself assessed and modified as desired and in the light of new information. Single loop assessment processes tend to focus on short term measures of outcome (for example, reading ability, graduation rates, etc.); double loop assessment processes tend to focus on longer-term objectives (lifetime earnings, employability, etc). For background on single versus double loop assessment processes, see Innes and Booher (1999b).

What results these efforts eventually generate has yet to be determined, but certainly these efforts are in the right direction. But more is needed than can possibly be done by a relatively small set of federal labs. Unfortunately, while state government supported research would seem a natural addition to the work done at federal laboratories, the current *No Child Left Behind* legislation requires a uniformity across states that makes experimentation more difficult than it might be. Indeed, the classic argument that states are the civic laboratories for the US holds for education as it does for other policy issues.   It would seem prudent, then, to relax some of the requirements in the *No Child Left Behind Law* to make it easier for individual state governments to try out alternative policies, perhaps in collaboration with colleges and universities interested in engaging in public-education focused research.

Finally, one should not ignore the critical role that the courts are likely to play in this future. The spate of standards legislation passed recently and based on adequacy norms leaves many issues both substantively and legally in dispute. In broad terms, these issues center on the fundamental questions of what it means to be educated, and what are reasonable performance standards that we can and should hold states and their local school districts accountable to.   In addition, although standards legislation such as the federal *No Child Left Behind Law* does focus in part on requiring that a wide array of student subgroups benefit from public education reform, many in the general public are less aware of such distributional requirements and tend to think only in terms of their own children, regardless of whether they are at the bottom, the middle, or the top of the performance distribution. Because poorer educated children typically come from families and communities that wield relatively less political power, this suggests that in the absence of pressure from the courts, there will be a gradual drift away from an emphasis on assuring that public education reforms help those at the bottom. As a result, there is a real need for the courts to continue to serve guarantors of the equity requirements embodied in recent standards legislation (Carr and Fuhrman (1999)).[149]

The success of the courts in this regard will depend critically on their ability to learn more about the nature of the education production process and adapt their judgments as such knowledge increases over time. As has been emphasized above in the discussion of the importance of scientific research, the courts along with society in general have only a poor

---

[149] That is not to say that policies that benefit all students should be ignored. Indeed, policies that improve the education of all students can serve two functions, the first being to help students at the bottom of the distribution directly, the second being to create the necessary political good will among those associated with better performing students to be able to redirect resources into programs that only benefit those at the low end.

understanding of the education production process, what would work to improve student performance, and therefore what would be reasonable standards to hold states and their local school districts to. To the extent scientific research reveals a better understanding of the education production process, the courts can refine their judgments and thereby assure that legal standards fit with the best understanding possible. In the absence of increased understanding of the education production process, it is likely that the courts will fall back on the same mix of equity funding remedies with a façade of adequacy rhetoric that characterized their decisions in the 1990s. Interestingly in this regard, and despite the advent of federal government legislation, an argument can be made that such court flexibility is greater at the state, rather than the federal level. As Matthew Bosworth (2001) notes in the conclusion to his book *Courts as Catalysts: State Supreme Courts and Public School Finance Equity*, preliminary research suggests that despite the greater clout of federal courts, state courts are generally more willing to work with state legislatures and that such willingness may be able to achieve more than aloof directives that are more typical with federal courts. In short, in matters of defining fundamental principles, the federal courts may be more effective, but in developing and refining policies to bring these principles into practice, state courts may be the more effective.[150]

4. THE ROLE OF STRUCTURAL CHANGES IN PUBLIC EDUCATION

Though not intended to be restrictive, the above analysis has implicitly focused on curricular and teaching-method reforms. While such a focus is natural (indeed, in the end, the very success of public education reform will depend on what happens in the classroom), there is a broader class of possible reforms that center on the general structure of public education, how it is managed, and how it is delivered. While these reforms may not directly effect what occurs in the classroom, they have the potential to significantly change the environment in which teachers and administrators work (and thereby what occurs in the classroom), and are often associated with passionate advocates.[151]

---

[150] Paul Minorini and Stephen Sugarman (1999a; pp. 191-2) describe a variety of methods the courts can use to adapt their conception of adequacy to new knowledge. Among these are the use of expert opinion, case studies of successful school districts, and the results of statistical research that connects inputs and performance.

[151] Clune (1994), for example, argues that structural changes (by which he means site-based management, school choice, and school restructuring or reorganization) are imperative to achieve truly adequate levels of education for all students.

Table 6-1. Plank and Boyd's Taxonomy of Structural Reforms in Public Education

• Centralization	Decision-making authority is shifted to a higher level of government. Examples include giving mayors control of school systems or increasing the level of control by state or federal governments.
• Decentralization	Decision-making authority is shifted to a lower level. Examples include school-based management, giving parents greater control of curriculum and management, or allowing private-sector groups to run schools.
• Installation of Experts	Decision-making authority is given to outside professional authorities. Examples include the use of outside consultants and putting failing school districts into receivership.
• Market Decision Making	Decision-making authority is diffused so as to create competition among schools by allowing students a choice as to where to go to school. Examples include magnet schools, charter schools, and voucher systems.

The class of structural reforms that have been proposed in recent decades is quite broad (Education Commission of the States (1999a, 1999b)). However, what they share in common is what David Plank and William Boyd (1994) call a flight from democracy, that is, the replacement of local school districts as the primary locus of decision-making authority. Following Plank and Boyd's taxonomy (see *Table 6-1*), these structural reforms can be divided into four general types – concentration of decision making at a higher, more centralized level of authority, decentralization of decision making at a lower level of authority, installation of experts as primary decision makers, and replacement of government control with markets.[152]

4.1   Centralization

Concentration of decision-making authority at a higher, more centralized level of government could take a variety of forms. In fact, some of this proposed method of reform has, to mixed reviews, already taken place in the form of the shift over the past half century from local school boards to state

---

[152] Following Ladd (1996), an alternative taxonomy is to group reforms according to whether they involve internal or external accountability. Internal accountability, which involves reforms within the existing governmental administrative structure, would include Plank and Boyd's centralization and installation-of-experts categories; external accountability, which involves turning responsibility over to parents or other private groups, would include Plank and Boyd's decentralization and market-decision-making categories.

legislatures as the dominant player in determining public education policy and financing.[153] Thus, as discussed in previous chapters, state legislatures in the 1970s began to use public education grant structures to actively attempt to manipulate local school district spending levels. More recently, state legislatures have imposed, or tightened up existing, curriculum requirements, promulgated higher standards for teachers, and imposed various types of performance standards. Finally, we have witnessed most recently an additional shift in authority to the federal government, particularly with the passage of the *No Child Left Behind Law.*

There are, however, other possible forms of centralization. One intriguing proposal is to place the public schools within the control of the local mayor. Though only possible in cities that use a strong-mayor form of municipal government, this proposal has received strong support in some circles. Several cities (Boston, Chicago, Cleveland, and Detroit) now have mayoral control of the public schools, and many other city mayors either have considerable influence over the public schools or are contemplating gaining such control (Kirst and Bulkley (2000)).

While advocates of centralization point to the elimination of parochial control and the protection of minority interests as arguments in favor of centralization, in practice it is sometimes difficult to determine how much that drives the desire for centralization and how much the desire is simply an attempt to find a government more sympathetic to the advocates' particular point of view.[154]

Clearly, centralization would seem to be a necessary factor in reforming public education to assure accountability and an adequate education for all students. The difficulty is that with increased centralization can also potentially come an inability to be flexible to particular local needs. Thus, I have argued earlier in this chapter for the federal government playing a general role in supporting research and in assuring accountability through the establishment of a system of standards and assessments, but in giving state governments the discretion to adapt that general approach to their needs and to engage in research and other forms of experimentation. Within that context, the argument for mayoral control of public schools would seem to be weaker because of the inability of mayoral control to address inter-district problems with public education.[155] To the extent intra-district problems

---

[153] See, for example, Paul Courant and Susanna Loeb's (1997) and Robert Wassmer and Ronald Fisher's (1996) contrasting evaluations of Michigan's 1994 radical centralization of public education financing.

[154] This behavior is quite common in the legal arena where lawyers will often engage in "court shopping" to find a judge who is more likely to be sympathetic to their position.

[155] For a fuller description of the movement to shift control to mayors and the concerns about such a shift, see Kirst and Bulkley (2000).

exist,[156] however, it might be of some value by providing a balance to the narrower perspective of school boards that are typically elected by district. However, there are potential risks with such centralization (recall the shifts in the method of electing school board members over the past century as described in *Chapter 5*). Moreover, local school district superintendents already have a district-wide perspective, thus raising the question what the effect of having an elected mayor rather than an appointed superintendent would make.

4.2   Decentralization

Like centralization, decentralization of decision-making authority can take place in a variety of ways. Paradoxically, the concentration of authority at the state and federal level of government and the use of the school as the primary unit of analysis in recent performance legislation has resulted in a simultaneous shift in some decision-making authority down to the school level. Though this authority is not without constraints and continued supervision by the school district's board and superintendent, school principals have in recent years been given additional discretion and responsibility for what happens in their schools, along with a commensurate increase in the risk of losing their job for failing to achieve assigned objectives. But decentralization can also take place in a variety of other ways. In addition to allowing private-sector groups or organizations to run individual schools (see the section on market decision making below), school districts can give more control and authority to the teachers within an individual school, or school districts can solicit the input (and resources) of parents and the local community through the delegation of school functions to parent-teacher associations and the creation of appointed boards of directors for individual schools. It is even possible for school districts to be divided into smaller districts each with its own board and superintendent (Ladd and Hansen (1999; p. 228). In some cases, the decentralization may be inadvertent, as when the solicitation of donations from local businesses results in those businesses having input into the management of the school.[157]

The impact of such devolution of power on the ability of public education to provide an adequate education for all students is not clear. Marshall Smith, Brett Scoll, and Jeffrey Link (1996) and Anita Summers and Amy Johnson (1996) conclude in their assessments of the empirical

---

[156] William Camp, David Thompson, and John Crain (1990) provide a review of the legal and economic literature on intra-district inequities and call for further research on the issue.

[157] See Chapters 11 and 12 of Odden and Picus (1992) for greater detail on these various ways of decentralizing the decision-making process.

literature on school-based management reforms that the value of such reforms is in its potential for allowing programmatic changes in the classroom, but that there is no evidence that changes in the management structure of a school by itself results in improved student performance. Eric Hanushek (1996b), a strong advocate of decentralization, observes in support that the key is not just decentralization, but decentralization coupled with incentives to improve what happens in the classroom by linking teacher and administrator rewards to student performance. Leaving aside those forms of decentralization associated with introducing market decision making (such as charter schools), decentralization provides the *potential* for allowing schools to adapt more fully to the particular needs of its students, but that potential will only be reached if it is linked to what occurs in the classroom. In the absence of such a link, there is little reason to believe decentralization will result in improvements; indeed, it may result instead in narrower, more parochial interests that actually harm the quality of education that students receive. Moreover, such reforms by their nature cannot address inter-district problems of inadequate education. To the extent problems with inadequate education are traced to a lack of resources, decentralization is unlikely in general to help those schools most in need. It is certainly true that decentralization can energize parents and the local community. But such increased interest and donation of time and resources is more likely to occur in schools with students in the middle or the top of the student performance distribution, not those at the bottom. But, as with all these proposals, our understanding of the dynamics of decentralization is poor at best and would profit from future empirical research.

4.3   Installation of Experts

Those who argue for giving experts primary decision-making authority generally do so in the belief that management of public education is more or less a technical task and would profit from eliminating political input. Interestingly, this modern push for increased use of experts mirrors the efforts during the Progressive Era around the turn of the 20th century to eliminate politics from the management of public education through the creation of professional, appointed local school district superintendents. Today the range of available experts is broader and includes government agencies, academics, business executives, and other private-sector entities. What all these experts share is, in the view of advocates for this approach, a higher level of technical training in the issues that are important for the management of public education either at the district or the school level.

While the ostensible motivation for such a transfer of decision-making authority is that public education requires more technically skilled decision makers who are divorced from the political arena, in practice, the motivation may also (or even primarily) reflect a desire to insulate current authorities from political risk, that is, to simply outsource decision making to others.[158] Thus, local school districts and superintendents increasingly turn to outside consultants and often employ citizen taskforces when making decisions on controversial issues.   At the state level, many states have provisions for putting local school districts that fail to meet minimal state standards under a form of expert receivership, whether it be an agency of the state government or some other independent expert authority (Feuerstein (2002)).

The value of using experts to help redress inadequacies in public education would seem to be mixed, though as always, there is little in the way of careful empirical studies to make definitive conclusions.   Certainly, experts, if in fact they have increased knowledge about public education, would seem to be able to make valuable contributions to the running and reform of public education.   However, many public education issues are fundamentally political.   Thus, for example, how much do we as a society value equity versus adequacy as norms for running public schools?   Turning decision making over to experts runs the risk of either ignoring these fundamental political issues or simply hiding political agendae beneath the façade of apolitical expert decision making.

4.4   Market Decision Making[159]

Advocates for the use of market decision making in public education are typically inspired by a desire to garner the same efficiencies associated with perfectly competitive markets and/or to avoid the coercion associated with governmental decision making.   Though such advocacy could go as far as to argue for the removal of compulsory attendance laws and the elimination of all forms of government from the provision and production of education, in practice advocates tend to argue for some hybrid form of education with both market and governmental decision making.[160]

---

[158] For a more general analysis of risk shifting as a motivation for the privatization of governmental functions, see Leyden and Link (1993).

[159] Market decision making in education, which focuses on the use of markets to decide which students go to which schools, is part of a larger issue of public education privatization, which also includes the use of markets on the production side.   For an interesting attempt to look at the issue of public education privatization in non-polemical terms, see Levin (2001a) which contains papers from a conference at Columbia University's Teachers College to establish a research agenda for the newly created National Center for the Study of Privatization in Education.

[160] For a background analysis of the political, social, economic, and educational forces that underlie the rise in support for market decision making, see Murphy (1999).

As with the other forms of structural reform, a variety of proposals are possible here. However, the proposals that get the most attention and that are considered most seriously are magnet schools, charter schools, and voucher systems that give students (and their parents) the ability to choose which school to attend.[161] Though advocates argue that such ability to choose would result in cost efficiencies and better student performance, others often argue strongly against such proposals.[162] The objections vary according to the specific proposal and the context in which the proposal is put forth, but in general center on the argument that such proposals are a diversion of attention and resources from the main task of assuring that all students receive an adequate education and that ultimately this diversion harms society in general.

4.4.1 Magnet Schools

A magnet school is a public school that students voluntarily chose to attend and whose curriculum is distinguished by some particular subject matter (for example, the arts, Spanish immersion, or global studies) and/or some particular method of instruction (for example, year-round instruction, Montessori methods, or open-classroom). Though originally promulgated in the 1970s as an alternative to busing that would be a less controversial way of desegregating public schools,[163] by the 1990s, magnet schools were being used more generally as a way to target specific populations of students for special forms of instruction.

The specific target population that the magnet school is designed to attract can vary considerably from school to school but at a minimum is

---

[161] An additional alternative that has not receive much attention from researchers is home schooling. Though numbers are difficult to come by, it appears that a little over one percent of all students are schooled at home. See Houston and Toma (2003) for initial empirical work that seeks to explain when children will be schooled at home.

[162] There is little literature that directly and empirically assesses the impact of choice on student performance within the context of the three non-traditional delivery structures that are examined here. More typically, empirical analyses tend to be based either on studies finding superior private education performance (see, for example, Chubb and Moe (1994)) or on studies of student performance in a Tiebout world, that is, in a world in which school choices are made through one's choice of where to live (see, for example, Grosskopf, Hayes, Taylor, and Weber (1999) and Hoxby (2000)).

[163] For background from the courts' perspective on the controversy surrounding the use of busing as a mechanism for desegregating the public schools, see Wilkerson (1979). The potential ability of magnet schools to achieve desegregation can be debated, but recent commentary on the legacy of the *Brown* decision fifty years later would seem to indicate that in practice magnet schools, while less controversial than busing, have also been less effective or used too little to achieve significant amounts of desegregation.

defined geographically and by grade. Thus, for example, a school district might offer a science magnet school for elementary school students who reside in the school zones associated with five specific elementary schools. Beyond that, the target population is generally those students (or their parents) who find the particular focus of the magnet school attractive. However, in some cases (schools of the performing arts come to mind) the target population may be students with both an interest in the magnet schools focus area and a defined proficiency in that area.

Admission to a magnet school is based on whether the number of qualified applicants exceeds the number of seats in the school. If the number of applicants who meet the qualifications for admission is less than the number of available seats, then all those qualified applicants will be admitted. However, if the number of applicants that meet the admission qualifications exceeds the number of available seats, some sort of lottery, possibly based on specific diversity objectives, is typically used. The diversity objectives will depend on the particular desires of the school district (particularly in the arts, for example, there may be a need for so many violinists, so many cellists, etc.), but often the diversity criteria are based on race, ethnicity, and/or gender.

From the perspective of public education reform based on adequacy norms, the issue is whether magnet schools can serve as a useful tool. No empirical evidence of significant contributions in that regard exists at this point, but clearly, whatever benefits magnet schools might provide, those benefits will only apply within particular school districts and therefore cannot address the broader problem of educational inadequacies across different school districts. To be sure, there are statewide magnet programs that potentially could be used to address such inter-district inequities.[164] But these programs are few in number and there are no plans for states to create large statewide magnet programs in the future.

Their ability to contribute to redressing intra-district inadequacies would also appear to be limited. While magnet schools may be associated with specific themes or methods of teaching, there is nothing necessarily unique to magnet schools in that respect. Any public school could employ the same focus that a magnet school employs if the district so chose. Moreover, there is no evidence to date that magnet schools are in general any more effective in educating children than regular schools in public education. As has been noted before, there is a woeful lack of knowledge about the public education production process, and there is no reason to believe that magnet schools are

---

[164] North Carolina's School of Science and Mathematics comes to mind (North Carolina School of Science and Mathematics (2004)).

a secret font of knowledge in that regard.[165] What magnet schools do have that differentiates them from regular public schools is that they serve populations of students who have chosen (or whose parents have chosen) to be there. What is not clear (and is thus a topic of needed scientific research) is to what extent having a population of students who have elected to attend the school makes a difference in the educational success of those students. If it does, it presumably does so through increased interest and commitment by students and increased parental involvement.[166] If such effects turn out to occur, magnet schools would seem to have a potential role in addressing intra-district problems if these schools target students currently receiving inadequate educations.

The difficulty is that they are not likely to reach all, and perhaps even a significant number, of the most needy students. Magnet schools, to the extent they are a superior form of education would seem to work because students elect to be there. But clearly, not all students (and, perhaps just as importantly, their parents) will take an interest in such schools. If, as Mary Raywid (1985) and Charles Clotfelter (1993) argue, parents with lower economic and social status are less likely to take an active interest in their children's education, the children of such parents will not benefit from the existence of magnet schools. While the notion of a complete system of magnet schools where every student is *forced* to choose their school is intriguing (essentially a form of open enrollment district-wide), such a system is fundamentally different from a smaller system of magnet schools where students only choose the school if they are interested.

In short, while magnet schools have the potential for redressing some intra-district inadequacies in education, they cannot redress those inadequacies that are inter-district in nature, and even within the narrower area of intra-district problems, they are not likely to reach all the students who need help. In practice, there is little evidence that magnet schools are serving this purpose now. Instead, their primary value seems to be to provide a more varied menu of public education options that give all students and their parents (especially students from middle and upper socio-economic families) greater satisfaction, not so much with the *outcome*, but with *process* of public education (what economists call the consumption

---

[165] It should be noted, however, that magnet schools provide a potentially attractive mechanism for research and experimentation as laboratory schools or as sites for field tests.

[166] See Raywid (1985) for evidence of increased satisfaction among students, parents, and teachers when some method of school choice is used.

value of education).[167]   Whether this also provides them with improved educational outcomes is less clear (recall again the lack of knowledge about the education production process), but if it does, it does not particularly focus its efforts or benefits on those students most in need from an adequacy perspective of a better education.

Interestingly, while it may be that magnet schools have only limited potential for improving public education along the lines examined in this book, it may in an indirect way provide local school districts with an ability to address problems by providing local school districts with the necessary political capital, and thereby administrative flexibility, to put into place other programs that do directly help students at the low end of the distribution. To the extent magnet schools provide greater consumption value (and perhaps greater outcomes), parents are more likely to look favorably on the policies of the local school district and therefore to provide political support to that local school board and its superintendent.   That is, magnet schools may be part of a larger logrolling process that has the potential for benefiting all. To be sure, potential is one thing; actually occurring is another.   Add to this the possibility that magnet schools could also serve as useful laboratories and field test sites for scientific research, and the conclusion would seem to be that magnet schools may be a useful, though neither a necessary nor a sufficient, component for dealing with improving public education in general and especially for students caught at the bottom.

4.4.2   Charter Schools

Another alternative mechanism for delivering public education that has received considerable attention in recent decades is the charter school.   The vast majority of states have authorized charter schools (Cobb and Glass (1999), Levin (2001b)), and, like magnet schools, charter schools are public schools that students voluntarily chose to attend and whose curriculum is distinguished by some particular curricular focus and/or some particular method of instruction.   The target population for the charter school is typically all students within the school district in which the charter school is located who are in a particular set of grades.   Admission is then based on whether the number of qualified applicants exceeds the number of seats in the school.   If the number of applicants who meet the qualifications for admission is less than the number of available seats, then all those qualified applicants will be admitted.   However, if the number of applicants that meet

---

[167] Raywid (1985) in her review of the history of education choice options argues that such options have arisen in part because of a sense of impotence and alienation among parents and disaffection and estrangement among students.

the admission qualifications exceeds the number of available seats, some sort of lottery, possibly based on specific diversity objectives, is typically used. The diversity objectives can differ from one charter school to another (even within a single school district) but often are based on ensuring that the student population reflects the general diversity of the population of students in the district as a whole.

Unlike magnet schools, charter schools are not subject to the same set of laws, regulations, and requirements that regular public schools (and indeed magnet schools) are subject to. While basic state curriculum and testing requirements typically still hold, they are not subject to their district's curriculum requirements. Although funding comes from the district with charter schools typically receiving "tuition" from the school district that is equal to the average per-pupil current operating cost for schools in the school district of equivalent grade, charter schools are not governed by the local school board nor are they under the local superintendent. Instead, the school is run independently by either a private for-profit corporation or some other non-profit organization. Unlike for-profit corporations which are often regional or national in scope, the non-profit organizations that run charter schools are often locally based and specifically created to manage the charter school. Thus, for example, a group of concerned and like-minded parents may form a governing board, define the mission of the charter school, and hire an administrator to run the school. Charter schools do not receive a share of district and state funds allocated for such things as capital expenditures, transportation, and school lunches. However, because charter schools are typically not required to provide many of the auxiliary services that a regular public school is required to provide, their costs are typically lower than those of a regular public school.

Like magnet schools, charter schools as currently employed are incapable of addressing problems with educational inadequacies that are associated with disparities in resources across different local school districts. They are typically district based and only available in practice, if not law, to students within the district.[168] Moreover, charter schools, again like magnet schools, are tied to the available resources of the local school district. As a result, any value they might have in eliminating educational inadequacies must be within the context of a single local school district.

While little empirical evidence exists to be able to judge whether charter schools alleviate educational inadequacies relative to other schools within

---

[168] Most charter schools do not provide transportation. Citing research using California and Scotland experiences, Casey Cobb and Gene Glass (1999) conclude in their study of Arizona charter schools that transportation is an even more critical issue in the choice of school than curriculum is and that, as a result, most students who attend charter schools do not travel far from their homes.

the same local school district, their ability to do so would seem to be tied to two characteristics – the fact that they serve populations of students (and their parents) who have chosen to attend that school, and they are free of many of the curricular requirements and management structures that regular public schools (including magnet schools) are subject to.

The fact that they serve a voluntary population of students suggests that they, like magnet schools, might (though again confirming empirical evidence is lacking) be able to perform better because of increased student interest and commitment and because of increased parental involvement.

The other asset that charter schools have, and that distinguishes them from magnet schools, is flexibility in curriculum and management. Except for funding and basic state and federal requirements, they can use whatever curricula, teaching methods, and administrative structures they choose. In this respect, they have an advantage over magnet schools. There is little evidence to date that such flexibility is associated with superior performance (Ladd and Hansen (1999; pp. 186-8)). However, an intriguing econometric study by Eugenia Toma (1996) of private versus public school productivity using data from five countries (Belgium, Canada, France, New Zealand, and the US) with different institutional arrangements concludes that private schools generally outperform public schools, that public funding of private schools does not change that result, but that public control of private schools does. Because Toma's analysis does not identify what characteristics of public control in particular result in private schools losing their productivity advantage, it is difficult to know whether her results can be used to conclude that US charter schools are likely to be more productive than private schools.[169] Moreover, given our general lack of knowledge about the education production process, it is intriguing why private schools (and by extension possibly charter schools) should be more productive in the first place. Clearly, such results beg for careful research to learn more, and in this regard charter schools, like magnet schools, have the potential for serving as important laboratory schools and field testing sites in future research.

---

[169] Bruno Manno, Chester Finn, and Gregg Vanourek (2000) argue in their advocacy for an alternative form of charter school regulation that current accountability standards in the US assure that charter schools will be no different than regular public schools. From a public policy perspective, the issue of whether, and if so how, to regulate alternative public schools, not to mention private schools, is, of course, more than simply which policy results in greater educational performance. To understand this last point, suppose for the sake of argument that private schools are more productive because they use corporal punishment, but that society as a whole believes that corporal punishment violates basic civil rights. In such a case, society may wish to forbid the use of corporal punishment by private schools even if it results in poorer performance by students in those schools.

While charter schools may harbor educational advantages, the difficulty with them is that, even more than magnet schools, they are unlikely to reach the students most in need of better education. No public school can long operate with inefficiently low enrollments. However, within that constraint, local school districts have a considerable amount of flexibility to offer relatively small programs through choice of location (for example, a small magnet school can be run out of a larger facility that also houses a regular public school) and a willingness to provide some subsidies not justified by enrollment numbers. Charter schools, however, do not have the same flexibility. They must attract sufficient students to generate the necessary tuition revenues to cover their costs. As a result, charter schools must provide programs that are attractive to students who are relatively inexpensive to educate and whose parents are willing to send (and often transport) them to a charter school.[170] Both those factors suggest that charter schools are more likely to try to attract students who are relatively inexpensive to educate and whose parents participate actively in their children's education. As a result, charter schools may not be a significant factor in redressing intra-district inadequacies in education among those who need it the most.[171]

Finally, it is not likely that a successful charter school would generate the same level of political support for the local school board and its superintendent as a successful magnet school might. Charter schools are managed independently of the local school board and its superintendent, and there is little reason to believe that any success that a charter school might have would be attributed to the local school board and its superintendent. As a result, charter schools would not seem to have the potential for creating the same political good will that might be used to create other programs directly of benefit to poorer schools and lower performing students.

---

[170] An additional argument in favor of charter schools is that they operate at lower per-pupil cost because they are forced to pay more attention to costs. Certainly there are greater pressures on a charter school to keep its costs down. But the effect of those pressures on the quality of education is less clear. To the extent parents focus on education as a consumption good rather than an investment, charter schools may actually have less of an incentive to pay attention to educational quality than regular public schools do. Again, careful research here would be valuable to making more informed policy decisions.

[171] Empirical evidence is sparse. While there is mixed evidence whether charter schools attract students from higher income families (Ladd and Hansen (1999; 187), Fiske and Ladd (2000)), I know of no evidence that looks at charter versus regular public schools in terms of parental involvement.

4.4.3   Vouchers

Still a third alternative mechanism for delivering public education that has received considerable attention over recent decades is a voucher system. Though not common, voucher systems have been used in a number of locations including Cleveland, Milwaukee, and Florida (Rouse (1998), Witte (2000), and Levin (2001b)). Under such a system, parents who choose to send their children to a public or private schools different from the one assigned by the local school district would be able to have some amount of the tuition cost (up to some maximum) paid for by the government.[172] Though the details of such a system may vary (choice may be restricted to accredited schools or the size of the voucher may be an inverse function of household income), the touted benefits of such a system are much the same as for charter schools. By allowing students and their parents to have greater choice over which school to attend, private and public schools alike will be more cost efficient and will tailor their programs more toward what those students and parents want.   From the perspective of redressing historic inadequacies in the provision of public education, however, the question is whether such a system would result in improved educational performance and whether students at the bottom of the performance distribution would be assured of participating in such a system.

As with all the other alternative forms of delivering public education, there is little empirical evidence to answer the question whether such a system would result in a more effective education system, that is, a system where students would perform better (Ladd and Hansen (1999; pp. 192-4). Moreover, while in theory a voucher system would allow students to enroll in schools outside their home school district and thereby potentially help address the problem of educational inadequacies across different local school districts due to differences in available resources, in practice such enrollment activity is unlikely to occur in significant numbers especially for students most in need of a better education. As a result, if a voucher system is to help redress educational inadequacies, it will only be able to do so

---

[172] The modern origin of voucher systems can be traced to Wiseman (1959) and Friedman (1962) and was originally conceptualized as a comprehensive replacement for an entire public education system. While attendance would still be mandatory, the parent could choose to send their children to any school that their children could gain admission to. All public and private schools would charge tuition, and parents would be obliged to pay that tuition, subsidized, of course, by the voucher. Most proposals for a voucher system call for the voucher to be an add-on to an existing system, rather than as a comprehensive replacement for an existing system.   Mark Blaug (1972) argues that the intellectual foundations of the proposal lie in the works of John Stuart Mill and Tom Paine. Finally, see Ladd and Hansen (1999; pp. 229-30) for background surrounding the controversy about whether religious schools can take part in a voucher system.

relative to other schools in the same local school district. Whether, in fact, it can do even that will depend, in turn, on whether the increased choice associated with the voucher system results in a better matching of student interests and abilities with specific programs, a greater enthusiasm by the student, and/or greater involvement by parents. As with magnet schools and charter schools, there is to date little empirical evidence based on scientific study that would allow a confident answer.

If a voucher system does in fact result in students receiving a better education and performing better, there is still the issue of whether the students most in need of a better education would choose to use such vouchers. This issue of whether vouchers would be an effective tool in addressing (intra-district) disparities and inadequacies in the quality of education depends ultimately on who and how many would participate. Although Helen Ladd (1996) argues that the weight of current research suggests that any voucher system should be biased in favor of students from economically disadvantaged backgrounds, there is little empirical evidence to determine whether such a system would generate sufficient participation by such students to make it worthwhile. Indeed, research by Caroline Hoxby (1996) finds that a universal private-education voucher system would only increase the proportion of all children receiving a private education by four percentage points. Clearly, additional research on the relationship between vouchers, and particularly the size of vouchers, and participation rates by different student populations would be needed to make an informed policy decision.

4.4.4 Are Markets a Threat?

The lack of scientific empirical evidence to support the view that magnet schools, charter schools, or voucher systems result in better student performance suggests that popular support for such mechanisms may be connected to their consumption value. Beyond any educational value, many public schools, as William Fischel (2002) notes, provide considerable social benefit for the general community, and not just for students. However, over the past several decades, public school have witnessed dramatic changes in the demographic diversity of students (due to desegregation and to demographic changes in the general population) and in the range of social mores and behaviors. While for some, such changes may be refreshing and exciting, for others they are disquieting. Magnet schools, charter schools, and voucher programs because of their voluntary nature offer the chance for students and (perhaps especially) their parents to select a group that shares the same preferences. Such shared preferences may focus on academics (for example, a magnet school that uses the great books philosophy as the foundation for its curriculum), student behavior (for example, a charter school that focuses its curriculum around conservative moral behavior), or simply assuring that students share some common ethnic, religious, or socio-economic status.[173]

The political advantage of such programs, from the perspective of state legislatures, school boards, and superintendents is clear – it gives the appearance (real or otherwise) that something is being done to improve education,[174] and thereby creates greater satisfaction and hence greater political support among those who are connected to, or who value such schools. Despite such benefits, however, some argue that these programs (perhaps excluding magnet schools) are corrosive because they siphon off students from regular public schools (Raywid (1985), Cobb and Glass (1999), Fiske and Ladd (2000)). Such siphoning, they argue, results in less general support for public education that eventually translates to reduced funding and poorer quality education for all students but especially for the most needy. In the end, they argue, this frays the social fabric that holds us together, and results in a more divided society, and, as Roland Bénabou (1996) argues, eventually results in slower economic growth.

Whether this is an imminent threat is not clear, though private school enrollment data (see *Table 1-2* in *Chapter 1*) suggest, however indirectly, that there has been no growth in the general public's desire to eliminate regular public schools. A reading of Downes and Schoeman (1998) and Husted and Kenny (2002) suggests that the demand for private schools (which I use here as a proxy for a demand for alternative forms of education in general) increases when states attempt to equalize per-pupil expenditures across school districts and decreases when they increase the overall level of support for public schools. Though this issue clearly warrants further research, these results suggest that the steady proportion of students in private education over the past half century is the result of these two forces

---

[173] Cobb and Glass (1999) note, for example, that Arizona charter schools were more segregated by ethnic group than nearby, regular public schools and that these charter schools were for the most part dominated by whites. Edward Fiske and Helen Ladd (2000), in their study of New Zealand's national shift to universal school choice, note that after five years under the public education choice regime, students had sorted by ethnic group and, to a lesser degree, by socio-economic status to a greater extent than changes in housing patterns would indicate. See Ladd and Hansen (1999; p. 194) for additional evidence of social stratification. Even with such segregation, such market-based school options may not hold much public interest. William Fischel (2002) argues that vouchers are generally unattractive to voters because they destroy the adult social capital that is typically created by regular public schools. As a result, political support for such options may be low except in larger, more urban school districts.

[174] Kenneth Wong and Francis Shen (2002) find, for example, that states are more likely to adopt charter school legislation if student performance is declining.

balancing over time. Given that support for public education is not likely to grow in the foreseeable future, these results also suggest that the shift in public education reform efforts away from equality-based norms and toward adequacy-based norms may have been a fortuitous shift for those who hope to see a prosperous and vibrant public education sector.

As Henry Levin (1994a, 2001b), notes, however, there is an additional risk with moving public education toward market-based structures. Education generates both public and private benefits with many of the public benefits of education associated with the development of "a common language, heritage, values, knowledge of institutions, and modes of legitimate behavior" (Levin (2001b, p. 7)). The move toward market models of education and its associated increase in school choices results, Levin argues, in a move away from those common educational experiences and therefore a reduction in the social benefits of education.

In the end, of course, whether such mechanisms are beneficial devices for improving public education, benign devices for increasing the consumption value of education, or corrosive devices that threaten all of society is an empirical issue. Unfortunately, as noted in the concluding summary to a compilation of various recent structure reform efforts that was commissioned by the National Commission on Governing America's Schools:

> There is very little research specific to public education on how or to what extent governance affects organizational outcomes, especially student achievement (Education Commission of the States (1999b; p. 28).

As with many other issues in public education, careful research is needed here to understand better the dynamics and the tradeoffs of employing such mechanisms (Meier (2002)). However, to the extent there is no underlying desire by the general public to downsize or eliminate public education (Cambron-McCabe (1990)), magnet schools, charter schools, and even voucher systems will most likely serve as political relief valves that allow states and their school districts to satisfy constituency desires in ways that don't threaten the public education as a whole.[175] Indeed, political and

---

[175] In terms of the spatial voting model first developed in *Chapter 3*, the use of such alternative mechanisms for delivering public education would result in a reduction in the political saliency of regular public education for upper-income school districts. This reduction in political saliency would then have two effects on the shape of the elliptical political indifference curves, one that results in the ellipses expanding in size (that is, the preference map of the legislature becomes flatter), the other that results in the ellipses becoming less vertical and more rounded in their orientation. The first of these effects would allow the legislature to engage in greater redistribution (that is, it would provide political cover); the second of these effects would result in a greater chance that the

bureaucratic self interest suggests that legislators and administrators would usually prefer to maintain the public education system rather than eliminate it. From the general perspective of public education reform, the issue then is not how to eliminate such mechanisms but rather how to use them effectively. In that regard, the most obvious uses are as devices for scientific experimentation and as devices for targeting particular forms of education to special populations of students who need it the most.

5.   CONCLUSIONS

A sluggish economy and the fiscal demands on legislatures since 9/11 have combined with an underlying limit on the willingness of the public to fund public education to assure that for the foreseeable future public education will have to live with the level of resources it is currently receiving. As a result, any attempt to simply continue the historic efforts at persuading legislatures through lobbying and court action to increase the overall funding of public education and to redistribute funds away from richer school districts and toward poorer school districts is likely, despite the sound and fury that may accompany such efforts, to be frustrated. As recent history and a reading of current political realities reveal, Congress and the various state legislatures simply have no stomach for the increased taxes (or funding reallocations) necessary to increase public education funding to any significant degree, nor have they the stomach for further efforts at redistributing public education resources.

The difficulty, of course is that providing an adequate education for all students will require both a more productive public education system and a redistribution of resources in favor of students currently receiving an inadequate education. These two requirements are not alternative policies based on different readings of the public education landscape. They are, in fact, two sides of the same policy coin. Unfortunately, much of the debate in the past couple of decades has focused on whether the coin has a head or tail. Contrast, for example, Michael Armacost's observation that despite many education reform proposals having the:

> potential for improving student outcomes, they should not be viewed as a substitute for additional resources or increased capacity to deliver educational services, especially in schools serving disadvantaged

---

legislature would level down in its effort to redistribute resources from wealthier to poorer jurisdictions. The argument above essentially claims that the first of these effects is likely to be the larger, but of course in the end this is an empirical one.

students[.] ... [E]ducational inputs ... do affect learning, especially of students who are performing poorly (Armacost (1996; p. viii).

with Eric Hanushek's observation that:

The current inefficiencies of schools, with too much money spent for the student performance obtained, indicate that schools can generally improve their performance at no additional cost. They simply need to use existing resources in more effective ways (Hanushek (1996b; p. 40).

Hence, the more promising strategy for providing all students with an adequate education would be to shift the focus away from lobbying and court action (though some of those efforts may be useful to keep legislatures honest) and toward a focus on careful scientific empirical research to learn more about what works to improve student performance. To the extent such research allows us to understand more fully and in a more useful way what the public education production function looks like, such a strategy would allow for greater productivity in public education that would benefit all students and would allow the public schools to gradually shift the emphasis toward students most in need of attention, all within the existing levels of support.

The difficulty with such a strategy is that it is likely to be slower than what one might wish for. Reforms would be implemented incrementally so that at any given time there may be little sense of improvement. However, over time, such efforts are more likely to bear fruit, hence the importance of tying this research-and-implementation process to an accountability framework that would allow such improvements to be measured over time.

Key also to this process of research and implementation is a willingness to experiment. In that context, efforts to use alternative forms for delivering public education like magnet schools, charter schools, and even voucher systems have the potential for playing a useful role as well as their historic role of providing a political relief valve for state legislatures and local school boards. In fact, and perhaps remarkably, state legislatures have shown some interest and a willingness to experiment and to fund initiatives so long as the total bill for public education does not change and so as key constituency groups, particularly those in higher performing and higher spending school districts, are not hurt.

Chapter 7

CONCLUSION

Doctr. Franklin looking towards the Presidents Chair, at the back of which a rising sun happened to be painted, observed to a few members near him, that Painters had found it difficult to distinguish in their art a rising from a setting sun. I have, said he, often and often in the course of the Session, and the vicissitudes of my hopes and fears as to the issue, looked at that behind the President without being able to tell whether it was rising or setting: But now at length ...
— James Madison, *Journal of the Constitutional Convention*[176]

The impetus for today's public education reforms can be traced to the confluence of three forces – a general movement to improve the efficiency of government, an increased concern over the nation's international competitiveness, and an interest in remedying inequities in the provision of public education. While the first two forces have been important to giving public education reforms the necessary energy to help keep the issue on the front burner, the primary impetus for public education reforms and its continual presence on the US political stage over the past half century has been the desire and effort to redress inequities in the provision of public education. While the roots of this effort to redress inequities can be traced at least back to the early 20th century, the crystallizing events that have come to define the current effort to reform public education are the 1954 *Brown* decision by the US Supreme Court that called for the end to racial discrimination in public education and the 1971 *Serrano* decision by the California Supreme Court that called for the end to discrimination based on the wealth of students' communities.

Despite these cases, by the 1990s advocates for public education reform had become frustrated with the lack of progress, and the question became one of what, if anything, was to become of a movement that, at best, had only been partially successful and seemed to be bogged down in endless litigation. The solution was both to synthesize and to reformulate the goals of the two court cases in even broader terms. Instead of two related efforts insisting separately on ending racial and geographic/wealth discrimination in the provision of public education, the focus shifted to insisting that students

---

[176] Farrand (1911).

of all races, ethnic backgrounds, abilities, community wealth, and geographic location receive an education sufficient to assure them an ability to compete in the workplace, to function effectively as citizens, and to pursue a life of personal satisfaction; in short, educational adequacy.

This notion of an adequate education was not, of course, a new idea, and early advocates were at pains to distinguish this egalitarian notion of adequacy from the discriminatory one associated with the Jim Crow era and the legacy of the US Supreme Court's 1896 *Plessy v.Ferguson* decision. What made this new insistence on an adequate education different from both earlier notions of adequacy and from the earlier push for funding equalization was that, thanks in part to the contributions by those interested in government efficiency and increased US competitiveness in the world economy, it was linked to student performance outcomes and an insistence that such outcomes be documented and used to further inform the reform process; in short, accountability.

Previous chapters have documented this process of public education reform and reformulation, examined the links between this process and the funding of public education, and attempted to predict the likely shape of public education funding in the foreseeable future. Predicting the future is a difficult endeavor at best, and the reader may be disappointed to find that future of public education funding is even murkier.

The history of public education funding is, of course, much simpler and clearer. Following the *Serrano* case, public education reform focused almost exclusively on public education funding and the need both to increase the overall level of financial support for public schools and to equalize the ability to access such support regardless of the wealth of the school district. Such simplicity, however, came at the cost of an inability to achieve reform objectives. In retrospect, this reduction of public education reform to a mechanical funding problem seems naïve with its focus on inputs rather than outputs and its implicit belief that the primary (or even the only) limitation on helping children learn was the availability of resources.

What we know today is that the links between public education reform and public education funding are much more nuanced and circumscribed. Crucial to understanding this more complicated relationship is recognizing the importance of our current lack of knowledge about the education production process. As has been documented in detail in earlier chapters, we currently don't know what we need to know to effectively use resources to achieve the level of adequacy that we wish to have. As a result, public education funding policy, if it is to be effective, must step back from the general funding and redistribution that has been the hallmark of past public education funding reform. In its place, public education funding needs to focus on the goal of increasing the quantity and quality of scientific research on the public education production process and on the goal of assuring that the results of such careful research are used constructively to improve current teaching methods, curricula, management techniques, administrative arrangements, and, indeed, the public education reform process itself so that progress is made toward the adequacy goals that we have set for ourselves.

This nuanced relationship between the funding of public education and the pursuit of adequacy goals also suggests that the federal structure of public education funding itself should become more nuanced as well. For the federal government, the primary roles would be as guarantor of adequacy norms and accountability, and as the main supporter of basic research on education. For state governments, the focus would be more applied. Funding for research would concentrate on learning how to put the lessons from basic research into practice, and operational funding would gradually shift away from general funding support and toward support tied to the refinement of current assessment systems and the adoption of practices with a proven ability to make progress toward adequacy goals. Finally, local school district contributions to funding would be tied to implementation of refined assessment systems and improved practices, all with an eye to making progress toward adequacy goals.

Such a funding structure would clearly be much more difficult to characterize, track, and assess compared to the relatively simple school aid formulae that developed as a result of *Serrano*. Indeed, because the responsibility for success would be distributed throughout the federal governmental structure, it suggests that new accounting structures that allow one to see the contributions and performance of each level of government would be useful.[177]

Such an accounting structure would also be of value because, as noted above, public education funding is much more circumscribed that previously believed. In particular, it is constrained by economic and political realities that make it highly improbably that public education in the foreseeable future will receive much more support in real terms than it is receiving now. As a result, the above process of funding will have to take place in a world in which any new expense is likely to have to be balanced by a reduction in expenditures elsewhere. That doesn't make reform impossible, but it certainly makes it more difficult and makes the development of a coherent system of public education accounting all the more important.

---

[177] Such an accounting structure would be complex and probably resemble the accounting structure associated with national income and product accounts produced by the Bureau of Economic Analysis (US Department of Commerce, Bureau of Economic Analysis (2004)) and that have been so important in the development of intelligent macroeconomic research and policy.

Much of the above, particularly the arguments for a systematic system of differentiated roles, for increased research, and for a unified system of accounting, is, of course, proscriptive in nature and deals with what *should* occur to make progress toward achieving adequacy goals, not with what *will* occur. It seems clear that what will occur is that there will be little more money for public education than there is now, but beyond that the future is much like the proverbial half-empty/half-full glass whose description says more about the spectator's general tendency toward optimism versus pessimism than it does about the glass itself.

Events of the past few years suggest that the nation is moving in the right direction. Accountability structures in the form of various state laws and the federal *No Child Left Behind Law* assure that public schools are now working toward achieving adequacy goals, assessing the degree to which they succeed, and holding accountable those schools, school districts, and states that do not make progress toward improving the level of adequacy. In addition there is increased emphasis on solid scientific research about the nature of the education production process so that we may discover what works and what doesn't work.

But the glass is also half empty. While the above structures are in place, they are imperfect, too rigid, and, many would argue, both misguided and misguiding in their specifics. While there is increased emphasis on research, there is little to show for such emphasis to date, and there are real questions whether such emphasis can be sustained. As a result, it is not at all clear that the current set of efforts signifies the beginning of a successful journey or simply one of many past failed attempts to make significant progress in improving the quality and the accessibility of public education for all students. In short, we stand at a crossroad, and what the future brings will, to a large extent, be up to us.

Acknowledgments

E poi che la sua mano a la mia puose con lieto volto, ond' io mi confortai, mi mise dentro a le segrete cose.

— Dante Alighieri, *La Divina Commedia*[178]

This book is the result of a long period of research that I have conducted off and on over the past two decades. Along the way, I have been helped and guided by a remarkable number of people who in one way or another have contributed to whatever merit this book contains.

I must begin with an expression of gratitude to Al Link, mentor and colleague here at UNCG, for his support and encouragement of this project. Indeed, his abiding support and guidance during my years at UNCG have been the *sine qua non* of my career as an economist, and I will be forever grateful for his efforts and his friendship. I also wish to offer a special thanks to Bruce Caldwell and Chris Ruhm, two other colleagues of mine at UNCG, for their support and willingness to serve as sounding boards, and to Marilea Fried, senior publishing editor at Kluwer, for her remarkable support and patience.

Thanks also go to Dennis Epple at Carnegie Mellon University, Bill Fischel at Dartmouth College, Abagail McWilliams at the University of Illinois at Chicago, Johnathan Silberman at Arizona State University West, and Don Siegal and Donald Vitaliano at Rensselaer Polytechnic Institute for their early support for this project and their useful suggestions.

At a more personal level, I am indebted to my wife Peggy for her patience, support, and critical eye as an editor, and to my children Ben and

---

[178] Alighieri (1979; Canto III (19-21)).

Sarah for putting up with a more than usually distracted father; to all my professors, too numerous to name, who in my graduate work at Carnegie Mellon University and my undergraduate work at the University of Virginia provided me with a liberal education and the technical skills that have been a source of personal and professional happiness and utility ever since; and to my parents Anne and Dennis for providing a home where the intellectual life was cherished and encouraged. If not for all of them, this book could not have been written.

References

Legal cases

Brown v. Board of Education 347 US 483 (1954).
Brown v. Board of Education 349 US 294 (1955).
Burruss v. Wilkerson 310 F. Supp. 572 (W. D. Va. 1969) affd., 397 US 44 (1970).
Commonwealth ex rel. Carroll v. Tate 442 Pa. 45, 274 A.2d 193 (1971) (Pennsylvania)
Horton v. Meskill (172 Conn. 615) (Connecticut)
Kovacs v. Cooper 336 US 77 (1949).
Lucas v. Colorado General Assembly 377 US 713 (1964).
McInnis v. Shapiro 293 F. Supp. 327 (N. D. Illinois 1968), affirmed sub nom. *McInnis v. Ogilvie*, 394 US 322 (1969).
McLaurin v. Oklahoma State Regents 339 US 637 (1950).
Minersville School District v. Gobitis 310 US 586 (1940).
Missouri ex rel. Gaines v. Canada 305 US 337 (1938).
Pauley v. Kelly, 255 S.E.2d 859 (1979) (West Virginia).
Plessy v. Ferguson 163 US 537 (1896).
Robinson v. Cahill, 355 A.2d 129 (1976) (New Jersey).
Rose v Council for Better Education 790 S.W.2d 186 (1989) (Kentucky).
San Antonio School District v. Rodriguez 411 US 1 (1973).
Sawyer v. Gilmore 109 Maine 169, 83 A. 673 (1912) (Maine).
Seattle v. State of Washington, 585 P.2d 71 (1978) (Washington).
Serrano v. Priest 5 Cal.3d 584 (1971) (*Serrano I*).
Serrano v. Priest 18 Cal.3d 728 (1976) (*Serrano II*).
Sweatt v. Painter 339 US 629 (1950).
US v. Carolene Products Company 304 US 144 (1938).

General references

Addonizio, M. F. (1991). Intergovernmental grants and the demand for local educational expenditures. *Public Finance Quarterly* 19(2): 209-232.

Adler, M. J., editor (1982). *The Paideia Proposal: An Educational Manifesto*. New York: Macmillan.

Adler, M. J., editor (1983). *Paideia Problems and Possibilities*. New York: Macmillan.

Adler, M. J., editor (1984). *The Paideia Program: An Educational Syllabus*. New York: Collier.

Advisory Commission on Intergovernmental Relations (1973). *Financing Schools and Property Tax Relief – A State Responsibility*, A-40. Washington, DC: US Government Printing Office.

Advisory Commission on Intergovernmental Relations (1994). *Characteristics of Federal Grant-in-Aid Programs to State and Local Governments: Grants Funded FY 1993*, M-188. Washington, DC: US Government Printing Office.

Advocacy Center for Children's Educational Success with Standards (2004). *Finance Litigation*. Internet (http://www.accessednetwork.org/litigationmain.html). January 29, 2004.

Alighieri, D. (1978). *La Divina Commedia: Vol. 1 – Inferno*. Firenze: La Nuova Italia Editrice,

Altice, J. L. and W. E. Dugger, Jr. (1998). Building consensus for technology ed. standards. *The Technology Teacher* 57(4): 25-8.

Armacost, M. H. (1996). Forward. In H. F. Ladd, editor. *Holding Schools Accountable: Performance –Based Reform in Education*. Washington, DC: Brookings Institution, vii-viii.

Barnett, W. S. (1994). Obstacles and opportunities: some simple economics of school finance reform. *Educational Policy* 8(4): 436-52.

Baumol, W. J. (1967). Macroeconomics of unbalanced growth: the anatomy of urban crisis. *American Economic Review* 57(3): 415-26.

Behrman, J. R. and N. Stacey, editors (1997). *The Social Benefits of Education*. Ann Arbor, Michigan: University of Michigan Press.

Belfield, C. R. (2000). *Economic Principles for Education: Theory and Evidence*. Cheltenham, UK: Edward Elgar.

Bénabou, R. (1996). Heterogeneity, stratification, and growth: macroeconomic implications of community structure and school finance. *American Economic Review* 86(3): 584-609.

Benson, C. S. (1961). *The Economics of Public Education*. Boston, Massachusetts: Houghton Mifflin.

Bergstrom, T. C., Rubinfeld, D. L., and Shapiro, P. (1982). Micro-based estimates of demand functions for local school expenditures. *Econometrica* 50(5): 1183-1205.

Berne, R. and L. Stiefel (1999). Concepts of school finance equity: 1970 to the present. In H. F. Ladd, R. Chalk, and J. S. Hansen, editors. *Equity and Adequacy in Education Finance: Issues and Perspectives*. Washington, DC: National Academy Press, 7-33.

Blaug, M. (1972). *An Introduction to the Economics of Education*. Harmondsworth, UK: Penguin Books.

Bosworth, M. H. (2001). *Courts as Catalysts: State Supreme Courts and Public School Finance Equity*. Albany, New York: State University of New York Press.

Brennan, G. and J. Pincus (1990). An implicit contract theory of intergovernmental grants. *Publius: Journal of Federalism* 20(4): 129-144.

Buchanan, J. M. and M. R. Flowers (1987). *The Public Finances: An Introductory Textbook*. Homewood, Illinois: Irwin.

Buchanan, J. M. and G. Tullock (1962). *The Calculus of Consent: Logical Foundations of Constitutional Democracy*. Ann Arbor, Michigan: University of Michigan Press, p. 13.

Buchanan, J. M. and G. Tullock (1975). Polluters' profits and political response: Direct controls versus taxes. *American Economic Review* 65(1): 139-147.

Cambron-McCabe, N. H. (1990). Governmental aid to individuals: parental choice in schooling. In J. K. Underwood, editor. *The Impacts of Litigation and Legislation on Public School Finance*. New York: Ballinger, 103-21.

Camp, W. E., D. C. Thompson, and J. A. Crain (1990). Within-district equity: desegregation and microeconomic analysis. In. J. K. Underwood and D. A. Verstegen, editors. *The Impacts of Litigation and Legislation on Public School Finance: Adequacy, Equity, and Excellence*. New York: Ballinger, 273-92.

Card, D. and A. A. Payne (2002). School finance reform, the distribution of school spending, and the distribution of student test scores. *Journal of Public Economics* 83(1): 49-82.

Carr, M. C. and S. H. Fuhrman (1999). The politics of school finance in the 1990s. In H. F. Ladd, R. Chalk, and J. S. Hansen, editors. *Equity and Adequacy in Education Finance: Issues and Perspectives*. Washington, DC: National Academy Press, 136-74.

Carroll, S. J. and R. E. Park (1983). *The Search for Equity in School Finance*. Cambridge, Massachusetts: Ballinger Publishing.

Chubb, J. E. and T. M. Moe (1994). Politics, markets, and the organization of schools. In E. Cohn and G. Johnes, editors. *Recent Developments in the Economics of Education*. Aldershot, England: Edward Elgar, 234-56.

Citrin, J. (1979). Do people want something for nothing: public opinion on taxes and government spending. *National Tax Journal* 32(2/Supplement): 113-29.

Clotfelter, C. T. (1993). The private life of public economics. *Southern Economic Journal* 59(4): 579-96

Clune, W. H. (1994). The shift from equity to adequacy in school finance. *Educational Policy 8(4): 376-94.*

Cobb, C. D. and G. V. Glass (1999). Ethnic separation in Arizona charter schools. *Education Policy Analysis Archives* 7(1). Internet (http://epaa.asu.edu/epaa/v7n1), May 27, 2004.

Cohen, D. K. (1996). Standards-based school reform: policy, practice, and performance. In H. F. Ladd, editor. *Holding Schools Accountable: Performance-Based Reform in Education*. Washington, DC: Brookings Institution, 99-127.

Cohn, E. (1979). *The Economics of Education*, revised edition. Cambridge, MA: Ballinger.

Coleman, J. S., E. Q. Campbell, C. J. Hobson, J. McPartland, A. M. Mead, F. D. Weinfeld, and R. L. York (1966). *Equality of Educational Opportunity*. Washington, DC: US Department of Health, Education, and Welfare.

Conlan, T. (1988). *New Federalism: Intergovernmental Reform from Nixon to Reagan*. Washington, D C: Brookings Institution.

Connecticut Office of Policy and Management (1980). *Equalized Grand Lists, 1980*. Hartford, Connecticut: Connecticut Office of Policy and Management, Intergovernmental Relations Division.

Connecticut Public Expenditure Council (1976). *Local Public School Expenses and State Aid in Connecticut: School Years 1970-71 through 1974-75*. Hartford, Connecticut: Connecticut Public Expenditure Council.

Connecticut Secretary of State (1980). *Register and Manual*. Hartford, Connecticut: State of Connecticut.

Connecticut State Board of Education (1979). *Equity and Excellence in Education: The Responsibilities and Opportunities Presented by Connecticut's New Educational Equity Legislation*. Hartford, Connecticut: Connecticut State Board of Education.

Connecticut State Board of Education (1981). *Equal Education Opportunity in Connecticut: Review and Recommendations for State School Finance Reform.* Hartford, Connecticut: Connecticut State Board of Education.

Coons, J. E., W. H. Clune, and S. D. Sugarman (1969). Educational opportunity: a workable constitutional test for state financial structures. *California Law Review* 57(2): 305-421.

Coons, J. E., W. H. Clune, and S. D. Sugarman (1970). *Private Wealth and Public Education.* Cambridge, Massachusetts: Harvard University Press.

Courant, P. N. and S. Loeb (1997). Centralization of school finance in Michigan. *Journal of Policy Analysis and Management* 16(1): 114-36.

Craig, S. and Inman, R. (1986). Education, welfare, and the 'new' federalism. In H Rosen, ed., *Studies in State and Local Public Finance.* Chicago, IL: University of Chicago Press, pp. 187-222.

Cubberley, E. P. (1905). *School Funds and Their Apportionment: A Consideration of the Subject with Reference to a More General Equalization of Both the Burdens and the Advantages of Education.* New York: Teachers College, Columbia University.

DeBoer, L., K. T. McNamara, J. Cranfield, and T. Graham (2000). Legislator influence and public school finance. *Review of Regional Studies* 30(2): 117-35.

Denzau, A. T. (1975). An empirical survey of studies on public school spending. *National Tax Journal* 28(2): 241-249.

Dickens, C. (1966). *A Christmas Carol in Prose: Being a Ghost Story of Christmas.* New York: Atheneum, p. 133.

Downes, T. A. (1992). Evaluating the impact of school finance reform on the provision of public education: the California case. *National Tax Journal* 45(4): 405-19.

Downes, T. A., R. F. Dye, and T. J. McGuire (1998). Do limits matter? Evidence on the effects of limitations on student performance. *Journal of Urban Economics* 43(3): 401-417.

Downes, T. A. and D. N. Figlio (1999). Do tax and expenditure limits provide a free lunch? Evidence on the link between limits and public sector service quality. *National Tax Journal* 52(1): 112-28.

Downes, T. A. and D. Schoeman (1998). School finance reform and private school enrollment: evidence from California. *Journal of Urban Economics* 43(3): 418-443.

Duncombe, W. D. and J. M. Yinger (1999). Performance standards and educational cost indexes: you can't have one without the other. In H. F. Ladd, R. Chalk, and J. S. Hansen, editors. *Equity and Adequacy in Education Finance: Issues and Perspectives.* Washington, DC: National Academy Press, 260-97.

Education Commission of the States (1999a). *Governing America's Schools: Changing the Rules.* Denver, Colorado: Education Commission of the States.

Education Commission of the States (1999b). *The Changing Landscape of Education Governance.* Denver, Colorado: Education Commission of the States.

Enelow, J. M. and M. J. Hinich (1984). *The Spatial Theory of Voting: An Introduction.* Cambridge, UK: Cambridge University Press.

Evans, W. N., S. E. Murray, and R. M. Schwab (1997). Schoolhouses, courthouses, and statehouses after *Serrano. Journal of Policy Analysis and Management* 16(1): 10-31.

Evers, W. M., L. T. Izumi, and P. A. Riley, editors (2001). School Reform: The Critical Issues. Stanford, California: Hoover Institution Press and San Francisco, California: Pacific Research Institute.

Farrand, M., editor (1911). *The Records of the Federal Convention of 1787, Volume II.* New Haven, Connecticut: Yale University Press, p. 648.

Feldstein, M. S. (1975). Wealth Neutrality and Local Choice in Public Education. *American Economic Review* 65(1): 75-89.

Feldstein, M. S. (1984). Public education: reply. *American Economic Review* 74(4): 820-821.

Ferguson, R. F. (1991). Paying for public education: new evidence on how and why money matters. *Harvard Journal on Legislation* 28(2): 465-98.

Ferguson, R. F., and H. F. Ladd (1996). How and why money matters: an analysis of Alabama schools. In H. F. Ladd, editor. *Holding Schools Accountable: Performance-Based Reform in Education.* Washington, DC: Brookings Institution, 265-298.

Fernández, R. and R. Rogerson (1999). Education finance reform and investment in human capital: lessons from California. *Journal of Public Economics* 74(3): 327-50.

Fernández, R., and R. Rogerson (2003). Equity and resources: an analysis of education finance systems. *Journal of Political Economy* 111(4): 858-97.

Feuerstein, A. (2002). Elections, voting, and democracy in local school district governance. *Educational Policy* 16(1): 15-36.

Filimon, R., Romer, T., and Rosenthal, H. (1982). Asymmetric information and agenda control: The bases of monopoly power in public spending. *Journal of Public Economics* 17(1): 51-70.

Fischel, W. A. (1989). Did *Serrano* cause Proposition 13? *National Tax Journal* 42(4): 465-73.

Fischel, W. A. (1996). How *Serrano* caused Proposition 13. *Journal of Law and Politics* 12(4): 607-36

Fischel, W. A. (2002). An economic case against vouchers: why local public schools are a local public good. Dartmouth Economics Department Working Paper 02-01 (October 20, 2004 draft). Internet (http://www.dartmouth.edu/~wfischel/WP.html).

Fisher, R. C. (1979). A theoretical view of revenue sharing grants. *National Tax Journal* 32(2): 173-184.

Fisher, R. C. (1982). Income and grant effects on local expenditure: the flypaper effect and other difficulties. *Journal of Urban Economics* 12(3): 324-345.

Fisher, R. C. (1996). *State and Local Public Finance,* second edition. Chicago, Illinois: Irwin.

Fiske, E. B. and H. F. Ladd (2000). *When Schools Compete: A Cautionary Tale.* Washington, DC: Brookings Institution.

Fort, R. D. (1988). The median voter, setters, and non-repeated construction bond issues. *Public Choice* 56(3): 213-31.

Fowler, W. J. Jr. and D. H. Monk (2001). *A Primer for Making Cost Adjustments in Education,* NCES 2001-323. Washington, DC: US Department of Education, National Center for Education Statistics.

Friedman, M. (1953). The methodology of positive economics. *Essays in Positive Economics.* Chicago, Illinois: University of Chicago Press, pages 3-43.

Friedman, M. (1962). *Capitalism and Freedom.* Chicago: University of Chicago Press.

Fusarelli, L. D. (2002). The political economy of gubernatorial elections: implications for education policy. *Educational Policy* 16(1): 139-60.

Galley, M. (2003). More errors are seen in the scoring of tests, Boston researchers say. *Education Week* 22(June 18): 10. Internet (http://www.edweek.org/ew), June 23, 2003.

Goertz, M. E. and G. Natriello (1999). Court-mandated school finance reform: what do the new dollars buy? In H. F. Ladd, R. Chalk, and J. S. Hansen, editors. *Equity and Adequacy in Education Finance: Issues and Perspectives.* Washington, DC: National Academy Press, 99-135.

Goldfeld, S. M., R. E. Quandt, and H. F. Trotter (1966). Maximization by quadratic hill-climbing. *Econometrica* 34(3): 541-551.

Goldfeld, S. M., Quandt, R. E., and Trotter, H. F. (1968). Maximization by improved quadratic hill-climbing and other methods. Research Memorandum No. 95, Econometric Research Program. Princeton, NJ: Princeton University.

Gordon, R. J. (1975). The demand for and supply of inflation. *Journal of Law and Economics* 18(3): 807-836.

Greenwald, R., L. V. Hedges, and R. D. Laine (1996a). The effect of school resources on student achievement. *Review of Educational Research* 66(3): 361-96.

Greenwald, R., L. V. Hedges, and R. D. Laine (1996b). Interpreting research on school resources and student achievement: a rejoinder to Hanushek. *Review of Educational Research* 66(3): 411-6.

Griliches, Z. (2000). *R&D, Education, and Productivity: A Retrospective.* Cambridge, Massachusetts: Harvard University Press.

Grosskopf, S., K. Hayes, L. L. Taylor, and W. L. Weber (1999). Allocative inefficiency and school competition. *Proceedings of the 91st Annual Conference on Taxation.* Washington, DC: National Tax Association, 282-290.

Grossman, P. J. (1990). The impact of federal and state grants on local government spending: a test of the fiscal illusion hypothesis. *Public Finance Quarterly* 18(3): 313-327.

Guthrie, J. W. and R. Rothstein (1999). Enabling "adequacy" to achieve reality: translating adequacy into school finance distribution arrangements. In H. F. Ladd, R. Chalk, and J. S. Hansen, editors. *Equity and Adequacy in Education Finance: Issues and Perspectives.* Washington, DC: National Academy Press, 209-59.

Hamilton, A., J. Jay, and J. Madison (1787). *The Federalist Papers.* Internet (http://memory.loc.gov/fed/fedpapers.html). October 6, 2003.

Hamilton, B. W. (1983). The flypaper effect and other anomalies. *Journal of Public Economics* 22(3): 347-361.

Hanushek, E. A. (1981). Throwing money at schools. *Journal of Policy Analysis and Management* 1(1): 19-40.

Hanushek, E. A. (1986). The economics of schooling: production and efficiency in public schools. *Journal of Economic Literature* 24(3):1141-77.

Hanushek, E. A. (1989). The impact of differential expenditures on school performance. *Educational Researcher* 18(4): 45-51, 62.

Hanushek, E. A. (1991). When school finance "reform" may not be good policy. *Harvard Journal on Legislation* 28(2): 423-56.

Hanushek, E. A. (1994a). A jaundiced view of "adequacy" in school finance reform. *Educational Policy* 8(4): 460-9.

Hanushek, E. A. (1994b). *Making Schools Work: Improving Performance and Controlling Costs.* Washington, DC: Brookings Institution.

Hanushek, E. A. (1994c). Money might matter somewhere: a response to Hedges, Laine, and Greenwald. *Educational Researcher* 23(4): 5-8.

Hanushek, E. A. (1996a). A more complete picture of school resource policies. *Review of Educational Research* 66(3): 397-409.

Hanushek, E. A. (1996b). Outcomes, costs, and incentives in schools. In E. A. Hanushek and D. W. Jorgenson, editors. *Improving America's Schools: The Role of Incentives.* Washington, DC: National Academy Press, 29-52.

Hanushek, E. A. (2002). Efficiency and equity in education. *NBER Reporter* (Spring): 15-19.

Heckman, J., A. Layne-Farrar, and P. Todd (1995). *Does measured school quality really matter? An examination of the earnings-quality relationship.* NBER Working Paper: 5274. Cambridge, Massachusetts: National Bureau of Economic Research.

Hedges, L. V., R. D. Laine, and R. Greenwald (1994a). Does money matter? A meta-analysis of studies of the effects of differential school inputs on student outcomes. *Educational Researcher* 23(3): 5-14.

Hedges, L. V., R. D. Laine, and R. Greenwald (1994b). Money does matter somewhere: a reply to Hanushek. *Educational Researcher* 23(4): 9-10.

Hettich, W. and S. L. Winer (1988). Economic and political foundations of tax structure. *American Economic Review* 78(4):701-712.

Holcombe, R. G. (1989). The median voter in public choice theory. *Public Choice* 61(2): 115-25

Houston, R. G. Jr. and E. F. Toma (2003). Home schooling: an alternative school choice. *Southern Economic Journal* 69(4): 920-35.

Hoxby, C. M. (1996). The effects of private school vouchers on schools and students. In H. F. Ladd, editor. *Holding Schools Accountable: Performance-Based Reform in Education.* Washington, DC: Brookings Institution, 177-208.

Hoxby, C. M. (1998a). The economics of school reform. *NBER Reporter* Spring: 6-12.

Hoxby, C. M. (1998b). How much does school spending depend on family income? The historical origins of the current school finance dilemma. *American Economic Review* 88(2): 309-314.

Hoxby, C. M. (2000). Does competition among public schools benefit students and taxpayers? *American Economic Review* 90(5): 1209-38.

Hoyt, W. H. and E. F. Toma (1993). Lobbying expenditures and government output: The NEA and public education. *Southern Economic Journal* 60(2): 405-417.

Husted, T. A. and L. W. Kenny (2002). The legacy of Serrano: the impact of mandated equal spending on private school enrollment. *Southern Economic Journal* 68(3): 566-83.

Iatarola, P. and L. Stiefel (2003). Intradistrict equity of public education resources and performance. *Economics of Education Review* 22(1): 69-78.

Imazeki, J. and A. Reschovsky (1999). Measuring the costs of providing an *adequate* public education in Texas. *Proceedings of the 91st Annual Conference on Taxation.* Washington, DC: National Tax Association, 275-81.

Inman, R. P. (1979). The fiscal performance of local governments: An interpretive review. In P. Mieszkowski and M. Straszheim, editors, *Current Issues in Urban Economics.* Baltimore, MD: Johns Hopkins University Press, 270-321.

Inman, R. P. (1988). Federal assistance and local services in the United States: the evolution of a new federalist fiscal order. In H. Rosen, editor. *Fiscal Federalism: Quantitative Studies.* Chicago: University of Chicago Press, 33-74.

Innes, J. E. (1996). Planning through consensus building: An new view of the comprehensive planning ideal. *Journal of the American Planning Association* 62(4): 460-72.

Innes, J. E. and D. E. Booher (1999a). Consensus building and complex adaptive systems: A framework for evaluating collaborative planning. *Journal of the American Planning Association* 65(4): 412-23.

Innes, J. E. and D. E. Booher (1999b). Consensus building as role playing and bricolage: Towards a theory of collaborative planning. *Journal of the American Planning Association* 65(1): 9-26.

Johnes, G. (1993). The Economics of Education. New York: St. Martin's Press.

Jorgenson, D. W. (1996). Introduction. In E. A. Hanushek and D. W. Jorgenson, editors. *Improving America's Schools: The Role of Incentives*. Washington, DC: National Academy Press, 1-8.

Kearns, D. T. (1991). Forward. In D. P. Doyle, B. S. Cooper, and R. Trachman, editors. *Taking Charge: State Action on School Reform in the 1980s*. Indianapolis, Indiana: Hudson Institute, v-ix.

Kettl, D. F. (1988). *Government by Proxy: (Mis?)Managing Federal Programs*. Washington, DC: Congressional Quarterly.

Kiesling, H. J. (1990). Economic and political foundations of tax structure: comment. *American Economic Review* 80(4): 931-934.

Kirst, M. and K. Bulkley (2000). 'New, improved' mayors take over city schools. *Phi Delta Kappan* 81(7): 538-46.

Krueger, A. B. and M. Lindahl (2001). Education for growth: why and for whom? *Journal of Economic Literature* 39(4): 1101-36.

Ladd, H. F. (1996). Introduction. In H. F. Ladd, editor. *Holding Schools Accountable: Performance-Based Reform in Education*. Washington, DC: Brookings Institution, 1-19.

Ladd, H. F. and J. S. Hansen, editors (1999). *Making Money Matter: Financing America's Schools*. Washington, DC: National Academy Press.

Ladd, H. F. and J. Yinger (1994). The case for equalizing aid. *National Tax Journal* 47(1): 211-224.

Lankford, H. and J. Wyckoff (1999). The allocation of resources to special education and regular instruction. In H. F. Ladd, editor. *Holding Schools Accountable: Performance-Based Reform in Education*. Washington, DC: Brookings Institution, 221-57.

Levin, H. M. (1992). Measuring efficiency in educational production. In M. Blaug, editor. *The Economic Value of Education: Studies in the Economics of Education*. Aldershot, England: Edward Elgar, 314-35.

Levin, H. M. (1994a). The economics of educational choice. In E. Cohn and G. Johnes, editors. *Recent Developments in the Economics of Education*. Aldershot, England: Edward Elgar, 137-58.

Levin, H. M. (1994b). Little things mean a lot. *Educational Policy* 8(4): 396-403.

Levin. H. M., editor (2001a). *Privatizing Education: Can the Marketplace Deliver Choice, Efficiency, Equity, and Social Cohesion?* Boulder, Colorado: Westview Press.

Levin. H. M. (2001b). Studying privatization in education. In H. M. Levin, editor. *Privatizing Education: Can the Marketplace Deliver Choice, Efficiency, Equity, and Social Cohesion?* Boulder, Colorado: Westview Press, 3-19.

Leyden, D. P. (1988). Intergovernmental grants and successful tax limitation referenda. *Public Choice* 57(2): 141-54.

Leyden, D. P. (1991). Modified quadratic hill-climbing with SAS/IML. *Computer Science in Economics and Management* 4: 15-31.

Leyden, D. P. (1992a). Court-mandated changes in educational grant structure. *Public Finance/Finances Publiques* 47(2): 229-247.

Leyden, D. P. (1992b). Donor-determined intergovernmental grants structure. *Public Finance Quarterly* 20(3): 321-337.

Leyden, D. P. and A. N. Link (1993). Privatization, bureaucracy, and risk aversion. *Public Choice* 76(3): 199-213.

Logan, R. R. (1986). Fiscal illusion and the grantor government. *Journal of Political Economy* 94(6): 1304-1318.

Lovell, M. C. (1978). Spending for education: The exercise of public choice. *Review of Economics and Statistics* 60(4): 487-495.

Mandelker, D. R., D. C. Netsch, P. W. Salsich Jr., and J. W. Wegner (1990). *State and Local Government in a Federal System: Cases and Materials*, third edition. Charlottesville, Virginia: Michie.

Manno, B. V., C. E. Finn Jr., and G. Vanourek (2000). Charter school accountability: problems and prospects. *Educational Policy* 14(4): 473-93.

Manwaring, R. L. and S. M. Sheffrin (1997). Litigation, school finance reform, and aggregate educational spending. *International Tax and Public Finance* 4(2): 107-27.

Marshall, L. (1991). New evidence on fiscal illusion: The 1986 tax "windfalls." *American Economic Review* 81(5): 1336-1344.

Martinez-Vazquez, J., and D. L. Sjoquist (1988). Property tax financing, renting, and the level of local expenditures. *Southern Economic Journal* 55(2): 424-431.

Megdal, S. B. (1987). The flypaper effect revisited: An econometric explanation. *Review of Economics and Statistics* 69(2): 347-351.

Meier, K. J. (2002). A research agenda on elections and education. *Educational Policy* 16(1): 219-30.

Meier, J. J. and J. Stewart, Jr. (1991). *The Politics of Hispanic Education: Un Paso Pa'lante Y Dos Pa'tras*. Albany, New York: State University of New York Press.

Meyer, R. H. (1996). Value-added indicators of school performance. In E. A. Hanushek and D. W. Jorgenson, editors. *Improving America's Schools: The Role of Incentives*. Washington, DC: National Academy Press, 197-223.

Minorini, P. A. and S. D. Sugarman (1999a). Educational adequacy and the courts: the promise and problems of moving to a new paradigm. In H. F. Ladd, R. Chalk, and J. S. Hansen, editors. *Equity and Adequacy in Education Finance: Issues and Perspectives*. Washington, DC: National Academy Press, 175-208.

Minorini, P. A. and S. D. Sugarman (1999b). School finance litigation in the name of educational equity: its evolution, impact, and future. In H. F. Ladd, R. Chalk, and J. S. Hansen, editors. *Equity and Adequacy in Education Finance: Issues and Perspectives*. Washington, DC: National Academy Press, 34-71.

Mintrom, M. (1993). Why efforts to equalize school funding have failed: towards a positive theory. *Political Research Quarterly* 46(4): 847-62.

Moffitt, R. A. (1984). The effects of grants-in-aid on state and local expenditures. *Journal of Public Economics* 23(3): 279-305.

Moffitt, R. A. (1986). The econometrics of piecewise-linear budget constraints: A survey and exposition of the maximum likelihood method. *Journal of Business and Economic Statistics* 4(3): 317-328.

Monk, D. H. (1992). Education productivity research: an update and assessment of its role in education finance reform. *Educational Evaluation and Policy Analysis* 14(4): 307-32.

Monk, D. H., and J. K. Rice (1999). Modern education productivity research: emerging implications for the financing of education. In W. J. Fowler, Jr., editor. *Selected Papers in School Finance, 1997*, NCES 1999-334. Washington, DC: National Center for Education Statistics, US Department of Education. Internet (http://nces.ed.gov/pubs99/1999334/text5.html), May 28, 2003.

Moser, M. and R. Rubenstein (2002). The equality of public school district funding in the United States: a national status report. *Public Administration Review* 62(1): 63-72.

Mosteller, F., R. J. Light, and J. A. Sachs (1996). Sustained inquiry in education: lessons from skill grouping and class size. *Harvard Educational Review* 66(4): 797-842.

Mueller, D. C. (2003). *Public Choice III*. New York: Cambridge University Press.

Munley, V. G. (1990). *The Structure of State Aid to Elementary and Secondary Education*, M-175. Washington, DC: US Advisory Commission on Intergovernmental Relations.

Munley, V. G. (1995). State aid programs for equalizing spending across local school districts: Does the structure of the program matter or only its size? Mimeo. Department of Economics, Lehigh University.

Murnane, R. J. (1985). An economist's look at federal and state education policies. In J. M. Quigley and D. L. Rubinfeld, editors., *American Domestic Priorities: An Economic Appraisal*. Berkeley: University of California Press, 118-47..

Murnane, R. J. (1985). An economist's look at federal and state education policies. In J. M. Quigley and D. L. Rubinfeld, editors. *American Domestic Priorities: An Economic Appraisal*. Berkeley, California: University of California Press, 118-47.

Murnane, R. J. (1991). Interpreting the evidence of "Does money matter?" *Harvard Journal on Legislation* 28(2): 457-64.

Murphy, J. (1999). New consumerism: evolving market dynamics in the institutional dimension of schooling. In J. Murphy and K. S. Louis, editors. *Handbook of Research on Educational Administration*. San Francisco: Jossey-Bass, 405-19.

Murray, S. E., W. N. Evans, and R. M. Schwab (1998). Education-finance reform and the distribution of education resources. *American Economic Review* 88(4): 789-812.

National Commission on Excellence in Education (1983). *A Nation at Risk: The Imperative for Educational Reform*. Washington, DC: US Government Printing Office.

Nechyba, T. (1996). A computable general equilibrium model of intergovernmental aid. *Journal of Public Economics* 62(3): 363-397.

Niskanen, W. A. Jr. (1972). *Bureaucracy and Representative Government*. Chicago: Aldine-Atherton.

North Carolina School of Science and Mathematics (2004). *The North Carolina School of Science and Mathematics*. Internet (http://www.ncssm.edu), May 14, 2004.

Oakland, W. H. (1994). Fiscal equalization: an empty box? *National Tax Journal* 47(1): 199-209.

Odden, A. and C. Busch (1998). *Financing Schools for High Performance: Strategies for Improving the Use of Educational Resources*. San Francisco, California: Jossey-Bass.

Odden, A. and W. Clune (1995). Improving educational productivity and school finance. *Educational Researcher* 24(9): 6-10, 22.

Odden, A. R. and L. O. Picus (1992). *School Finance: A Policy Perspective*. New York: McGraw-Hill.

Olson, L. (2003). All states get federal nod on key plans. *Education Week* 22(June 18): 1, 20-1. Internet (http://www.edweek.org/ew), June 23, 2003.

Opfer, V. D. (2002). Introduction: elections and education – a question of influence. *Educational Policy* 16(1): 5-14.

Orfield, G. (1994). Asking the right questions. *Educational Policy* 8(4): 404-13.

Organization for Economic Cooperation and Development (2003). *Education at a Glance 2002*. Internet (http://www.oecd.org/EN/statistics/0,,EN-statistics-4-nodirectorate-no-no-no-4,00.html), July 1, 2003.

Perkins, G. M. (1984). Public education: comment. *American Economic Review* 74(4): 814-819.

Peters, R. A. (1996). School finance reform's impact on New Jersey's state spending priorities. *Public Budgeting & Finance* 16(3): 74-89.

Plank, D. N. and W. L. Boyd (1994). Antipolitics, education, and institutional choice: the flight from democracy. *American Educational Research Journal* 31(2): 263-81.

Plecki, M. L. (2000). Economic perspectives on investments in teacher quality: lessons learned from research on productivity and human resource development. *Education*

Policy Analysis Archives 8(33). Internet (http://epaa.asu.edu/epaa/v8n33.html), May 28, 2003.

Pogrow, S. (1994). A skeptical perspective on the adequacy conception. *Educational Policy* 8(4): 414-24.

Porter, M. E. (1990). The competitive advantage of nations. *Harvard Business Review* 68(2): 73-89.

Portner, J. (1999). Science board calls on educators to reach consensus on content. *Education Week* 18(26): 7.

Poterba, J. M. (1998). Demographic change, intergenerational linkages, and public education. *American Economic Review* 88(2): 315-320.

Rasmussen, E. (1989). *Games and Information: An Introduction to Game Theory.* Cambridge, Massachusetts: Basil Blackwell.

Rawls, J. (1971). *A Theory of Justice.* Cambridge, Massachusetts: Belknap Press of Harvard University Press.

Raywid, M. A. (1985). Family choice arrangements in public schools: a review of the literature. *Review of Educational Research* 55(4): 435-67.

Reich, R. B. (1992). *The Work of Nations: Preparing Ourselves for 21st-Century Capitalism.* New York: Vintage Books.

Reischauer, R. D. and R. W. Hartman (1973). *Reforming School Finance.* Washington, DC: Brookings.

Reschovsky, A. (1994). Fiscal equalization and school finance. *National Tax Journal* 47(1): 185-197.

Reschovsky, A. and J. Imazeki (2001). Achieving educational adequacy through school finance reform. *Journal of Education Finance* 26(4): 373-96.

Resnick, L. B. (1993). Standards, assessment, and educational quality. *Stanford Law and Policy Review* 4(Winter): 53-9.

Roethlisberger, F. J. and W. J. Dickson (1939). *Management and the Worker.* Cambridge, Massachusetts: Harvard University Press.

Romer, T. and H. Rosenthal (1978). Political resource allocation, controlled agendas, and the status quo. *Public Choice* 33(4): 27-43.

Romer, T. and H. Rosenthal (1979). The elusive median voter. *Journal of Public Economics* 12(2): 143-70.

Romer, T. and H. Rosenthal (1982). Median voters or budget maximizers: Evidence from school expenditure functions. *Economic Inquiry* 20(4): 556-78.

Rossmiller, R. A. (1990). Federal funds: a shifting balance? In. J. K. Underwood and D. A. Verstegen, editors. *The Impacts of Litigation and Legislation on Public School Finance: Adequacy, Equity, and Excellence.* New York: Ballinger, 3-25.

Rothstein, P. (1992). The demand for education with 'power equalizing' aid. *Journal of Public Economics* 49(2): 135-162.

Rouse, C. E. (1998). Private school vouchers and student achievement: an evaluation of the Milwaukee parental choice program. *Quarterly Journal of Economics* 113(2): 553-602.

Rubenstein, R., A. E. Schwartz, and L. Stiefel (1999). Conceptual and empirical issues in the measurement of school efficiency. *Proceedings of the 91st Annual Conference on Taxation.* Washington, DC: National Tax Association, 267-74.

Rubinfeld, D. L. (1979). Judicial approaches to local public-sector equity: an economic analysis. In P. Mieszkowski and M. Straszheim, editors. *Current Issues in Urban Economics.* Baltimore, Maryland: Johns Hopkins University Press, 542-76.

Rubinfeld, D. L. and P. Shapiro (1989). Micro-estimation of the demand for schooling: Evidence from Michigan and Massachusetts. *Regional Science and Urban Economics* 19(3): 381-398.

Rutherford, M. (2000). Understanding institutional economics: 1918-1929. *Journal of the History of Economic Thought* 22(3): 277-308.

Salmon, R. G. and M. D. Alexander (1990). State legislative responses. In. J. K. Underwood and D. A. Verstegen, editors. *The Impacts of Litigation and Legislation on Public School Finance: Adequacy, Equity, and Excellence.* New York: Ballinger, 249-71.

Santayana, G. (1920). *The Life of Reason: or the Phases of Human Progress, Volume I: Introduction and Reason in Common Sense.* New York: Charles Schribner's Sons, p. 284.

Schwallie, D. P. (1987). A theory of intergovernmental grants and their effect on aggregate grantor-recipient spending. *Public Finance Quarterly* 15(3): 322-38.

Schwallie, D. P. (1989a). *The Impact of Intergovernmental Grants on the Aggregate Public Sector.* New York: Greenwood.

Schwallie, D. P. (1989b). Measuring the effects of federal grants-in-aid on total public sector size. *Public Finance Quarterly* 17(2): 185-203.

Sebold, F. D. and W. Dato (1981). School funding and student achievement: an empirical analysis. *Public Finance Quarterly* 9(1): 91-105.

Sheehan, J. (1973). *The Economics of Education.* London: Allen and Unwin.

Shepsle, K. A. and M. S. Bonchek (1997). *Analyzing Politics: Rationality, Behavior, and Institutions.* New York: Norton.

Silva, F. and J. Sonstelie (1995). Did *Serrano* cause a decline in school spending. *National Tax Journal* 48(2): 199-215.

Slack, E. (1980). Local fiscal response to intergovernmental transfers. *Review of Economics and Statistics* 62(3): 364-70.

Smith, M. S., B. W. Scoll, and J. Link (1996). Research-based school reform: the Clinton administration's agenda. In E. A. Hanushek and D. W. Jorgenson, editors. *Improving America's Schools: The Role of Incentives.* Washington, DC: National Academy Press, 9-27.

Sparkman, W. E. (1990). School finance challenges in state courts. In J. K. Underwood and D. A. Verstegen, editors. *The Impacts of Litigation and Legislation on Public School Finance: Adequacy, Equity, and Excellence.* New York: Harper and Row.

Spencer, L. M. and R. M. Stonehill (1999). *Profiles of the Regional Educational Laboratories.* Washington, DC: US Department of Education. Internet (http://www.ed.gov/pubs/RegionalEdLabs/title.html), July 20, 2004.

Strayer, G. D. and R. M. Haig (1923). *The Financing of Education in the State of New York.* New York: Macmillan.

Summers, A. A. and A. W. Johnson (1996). The effects of school-based management plans. In E. A. Hanushek and D. W. Jorgenson, editors. *Improving America's Schools: The Role of Incentives.* Washington, DC: National Academy Press, 75-96.

Summers, A. A., and B. L. Wolfe (1977). Do schools make a difference? *American Economic Review* 67(4): 639-52.

Toma, E. F. (1996). Public funding and private schooling across countries. *Journal of Law and Economics* 39(1): 121-48.

Turnbull, G. K. (1992). Fiscal illusion, uncertainty, and the flypaper effect. *Journal of Public Economics* 48(2): 207-223.

Underwood, J. K. (1994). School finance litigation: legal theories, judicial activism, and social neglect. *Journal of Education Finance* 20(2): 143-62.

US Council of Economic Advisors (1993). Table B-56.--Consumer price indexes for major expenditure classes, 1950-92 (all items, CPI-U). *Economic Report of the President.* Washington, DC: US Government Printing Office.

US Department of Commerce, Bureau of Economic Analysis (2003). *National Income and Product Accounts Tables.* Internet (http://www.bea.gov/bea/dn/nipaweb/index.asp), June 25, 2003.

US Department of Commerce, Bureau of Economic Analysis (2004). *About BEA.* Internet (http://www.bea.gov/bea/role.htm), July 7, 2004.

US Department of Commerce, Census Bureau (1974). *Statistical Abstract of the United States, 1973.* Washington, DC: US Government Printing Office.

US Department of Commerce, Census Bureau (1982a). *1980 Census of Housing, Characteristics of Housing Units, General Housing Characteristics*, Connecticut. Washington, DC: US Government Printing Office.

US Department of Commerce, Census Bureau (1982b). *Summary Tape 1A, US Census of Population and Housing.* Printout. Hartford, CT: Connecticut Census Data Center, Connecticut Office of Policy and Management.

US Department of Commerce, Census Bureau (1983). *Summary Tape 3A, US Census of Population and Housing.* Printout. Hartford, CT: Connecticut Census Data Center, Connecticut Office of Policy and Management.

US Department of Commerce, Census Bureau (1996). *Statistical Abstract of the United States, 1995.* Internet (http://www.census.gov/prod/www/statistical-abstract-us.html), July 1, 2003.

US Department of Commerce, Census Bureau (2003). *Statistical Abstract of the United States, 2002.* Internet (http://www.census.gov/prod/www/statistical-abstract-02.html), July 1, 2003.

US Department of Education (2004). *No Child Left Behind: Executive Summary.* Internet (http://www.ed.gov/print/nclb/overview/intro/execsumm.html), March 26, 2004.

US Department of Education, Institute of Education Sciences (2003a). *Identifying and Implementing Educational Practices Supported by Rigorous Evidence: A User Friendly Guide.* Internet (http://www.ed.gov/rschstat/research/pubs/rigorousevid/rigorousevid.pdf), March 31, 2004.

US Department of Education, Institute of Education Sciences (2003b). *Institute of Education Sciences Findings from Interviews with Education Policymakers.* Internet (http://www.ed.gov/rschstat/research/pubs/findingsreport.pdf), March 30, 2004.

US Department of Education, National Center for Education Statistics (2003). *Digest of Education Statistics, 2002*, NCES 2003-060. Washington, DC: US Government Printing Office.

US Department of Education, National Commission on Excellence in Education (1983). *A Nation at Risk: The Imperative for Educational Reform.* Washington, DC: US Government Printing Office.

US Department of Labor, Bureau of Labor Statistics (2003). *Labor Force Statistics from the Current Population Survey: Access to historical data for the "A" tables of the Employment Situation News Release.* Internet (http://www.bls.gov/cps/cpsatabs.htm), July 3, 2003.

US 107th Congress (2002a). *Public Law 107-110: No Child Left Behind Act of 2001.* Internet (http://www.ed.gov/policy/elsec/leg/esea02/107-110.pdf), March 26, 2004.

US 107th Congress (2002b). *Public Law 107-279: Education Sciences Reform Act of 2002.* Internet (http://www.ed.gov/policy/rschstat/leg/PL107-279.pdf), March 30, 2004.

Ward, J. G. (1990). Implementation and monitoring of judicial mandates: an interpretative analysis. In. J. K. Underwood and D. A. Verstegen, editors. *The Impacts of Litigation and*

Legislation on Public School Finance: Adequacy, Equity, and Excellence. New York: Ballinger, 225-48.

Wassmer, R. W. and R. C. Fisher (1996). An evaluation of the recent move to centralize the finance of public schools in Michigan. *Public Budgeting and Finance* 16(3): 90-112.

Wassmer, R. W. and R. C. Fisher (2002). Interstate variation in the use of fees to fund K-12 public education. *Economics of Education Review* 21(1): 87-100.

Webb, L. D. (1990). New revenues for education at the state level. In J. K. Underwood, editor. *The Impacts of Litigation and Legislation on Public School Finance: Adequacy, Equity, and Excellence.* New York: Ballinger, 27-58.

Weiher, G. R. (1988). Why redistribution doesn't work: state educational reform policy and governmental decentralization in Texas. *American Politics Quarterly* 16(2): 193-210.

Wildasin, D. E. (1989). Demand estimation for public goods: distortionary taxation and other sources of bias. *Regional Science and Urban Economics* 19(3): 353-79.

Wilkerson, J. H. (1979). *From Brown to Bakke: The Supreme Court and School Integration, 1954-1978.* New York: Oxford University Press.

Williams, J. (2004). *Thurgood Marshall's "The Sword and the Robe" Speech.* Internet (http://www.thurgoodmarshall.com/speeches/sword_article.htm), July 7, 2004.

Williams, R. F. (1990). State constitutional limits on legislative procedure: legislative compliance and judicial enforcement. In R. F. Williams, editor. *State Constitutional Law: Cases and Materials (with 1990-91 Supplement).* Washington, DC: Advisory Commission on Intergovernmental Relations, 213-17.

Winer, S. L. (1983). Some evidence on the effect of the separation of spending and taxing decisions. *Journal of Political Economy* 91(1): 126-40.

Wirt, F. M. and M. W. Kirst (1997). *The Political Dynamics of American Education.* Berkley, California: McCutchan Publishing Company.

Wise, A. (1968). *Rich Schools, Poor Schools: The Promise of Equal Educational Opportunity.* Chicago: University of Chicago Press.

Wiseman, J. (1959). The economics of education. *Scottish Journal of Political Economy.* 6(February): 48-58.

Wiseman, J. (1989). The political economy of government revenues. In A. Chiancone and K. Messere, editors. *Changes in Revenue Structure: Proceedings of the 42nd Congress of the International Institute of Public Finance.* Detroit, Michigan: Wayne State Press, 9-20.

Witte, J. F. (2000). *The Market Approach to Education: An Analysis of America's First Voucher Program.* Princeton, New Jersey: Princeton University Press.

Wong, K. K. and F. X. Shen (2002). Politics of state-led reform in education: market competition and electoral dynamics. *Educational Policy* 16(1): 161-192.

Wood, R. C. (1990). New revenues for education at the local level. In J. K. Underwood, editor. *The Impacts of Litigation and Legislation on Public School Finance: Adequacy, Equity, and Excellence.* New York: Ballinger, 59-74.

Wright, G. (1974). The political economy of New Deal spending: An econometric analysis. *Review of Economics and Statistics* 56(1): 30-38.

Wyckoff, J. H. (1992). The intrastate equality of public primary and secondary education resources in the U.S., 1980-1987. *Economics of Education Review* 11(1): 19-30.

Zajac, E. E. (1995). *Political Economy of Fairness.* Cambridge, MA: MIT Press.

Zampelli, E. M. (1986). Resource fungibility, the flypaper effect, and the expenditure impact of grants-in-aid. *Review of Economics and Statistics* 68(1): 33-40.

Index

Printed in the United States
49050LVS00001B/7-24